For Asako . . .

and Janet, of course.

Pohnpei, An Island Argosy . . .

REVISED EDITION

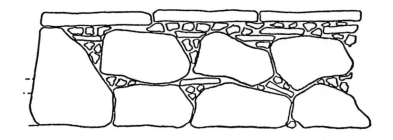

by
Gene Ashby

The Community College of Micronesia

RAINY DAY PRESS

Pohnpei, F.S.M.   **Eugene, Oregon**

First Printing, 1983
Second Printing, 1984
Revised Edition, 1987
Fourth Printing, 1989
Fifth Printing, 1990

Library of Congress Catalog Card Number: 88-90529

International Standard Book Number: 0-931742-14-5

Published by Rainy Day Press

P.O. Box 574   1147 E. 26th Ave.
Kolonia, Pohnpei   Eugene, Oregon
96941   97403

Printed in U.S.A.

ACKNOWLEDGEMENTS

This book was researched, written, revised and edited entirely on Pohnpei. Hundreds of residents of the island deserve a special "kalahngan" for answering thousands of pesty questions that allowed the *Argosy* to be written.

Ms. Iris Falcam, Head Librarian at the Community College of Micronesia, generously provided her time to proofread the manuscript. Her assistance was quite literally invaluable. Father Francis X. Hezel, Director of the Micronesia Seminar in Truk, helped considerably by reviewing the history section and offering suggestions. The Hon. Resio S. Moses, Governor of the State of Pohnpei, also assisted with his knowlege of history and political science—and reminded the author that breadfruit trees grow higher than fifty feet.

Mr. Jimmy Hiyane, formerly Head of the Agriculture Department, Pohnpei District, assisted greatly with his late evening comments on the flora and fauna of the island. Jim Belyea, a Pohnpeian's speaker of Pohnpeian, corrected the author's numerous language errors.

In the previous edition, one Fr. Bachelot was mentioned as having been on Pohnpei in 1837. Actually, he died eight days before reaching the island and was buried in Madolenihmw. This was pointed out in correspondence by both Professor Saul H. Riesenberg of the Smithsonian Institution and Fr. Hugh F. Costigan, Emeritus Director of the Pohnpei Agriculture and Trade School, distinguished critics indeed. Thanks are also extended to other readers who helped clarify points and who offered suggestions for the revised edition. Their input is appreciated as much as the kind and courteous way in which their suggestions were offered.

Gina Marie, age six years, and Asako, Janet, and Lestly, all Micronesian Ashbys, have taught the author more about Pohnpei than has six years of library research.

And finally, sincere thanks to Hon. Bailey Olter, former Vice President of the Federated States of Micronesia, scholar, critic, and friend-extraordinaire, who helped guide the *Argosy* from its inception.

TABLE OF CONTENTS

ILLUSTRATIONS

MAPS AND CHARTS

A GUIDE TO
POHNPEIAN PRONUNCIATION

Pohnpeian Consonant	As in the Pohnpeian Word	Approximate English Equivalent
p	*p*ohn	s*p*in
pw	*pw*ihl	------
d	*d*eke	s*t*ick
k	*k*in	s*k*in
s	*s*oh	miss *you*
t	*t*ih	------
m	*m*ehn	*m*an
mw	*mw*ahu	------
n	*n*ah*n*	*n*o
ng	*ng*ahp	singi*ng*
l	*l*ih	*l*ean
r	*r*ong	------

Pohnpeian Vowel	As in the Pohnpeian Word	Approximate English Equivalent
a	*a*mwer	p*o*t
/e/	*e*sil	b*ai*t
/E/	d*e*	b*e*t
i	n*i*	b*ea*t
o	r*o*ng	b*ou*ght
u	*u*d*u*k	b*oo*t

xiii

CAPSULE DESCRIPTIONS OF POHNPEI

Ponape or Pohnpei?

The name of the island is taken from two local words, *pohn* and *pehi*, meaning "upon the stone altar," and refers to a legend about how the island was created. The story tells of the first migrants who sailed from the east and arrived at a small piece of land jutting from the sea. To it they added land forms, reefs, and vegetation. They also built a stone altar, *pehi*, on which they could worship their gods. The early Spaniards referred to Pohnpei as Quirosa, and the island was called Ascension during the Early Contact Period. The German administration used Ponape, and the Japanese, Ponape To. The new state constitution enacted in 1984 changed the spelling and pronunciation back to the traditional *Pohnpei*.

The island is part of the *Senyavin* group that consists of Pohnpei and its satellite atolls of Ant and Pakin. The group was named by the Russian captain Fedor Lutke after his vessel the "Senyavin" in 1828 (see *History*, p.37).

Pohnpei is in the *Caroline* Islands archipelago, a group of islands extending seventeen hundred miles on a wavy line from the Palaus in the west to Kosrae in the east. A Spaniard, Diego de Rocha, located the islands in 1526. They were originally named the New Philippines, but later called the Carolines after Charles II of Spain. The archipelago extends over an area of 1,300,000 square miles and contains about 936 islands, islets and atolls. The land area is 461 square miles.

Micronesia is more of a geographical than a cultural designation. (The area contains at least eight different cultural and linguistic groups.) The name comes from two Greek words: *mikros*, meaning small, and *nesos*, meaning islands. To many visitors, Micronesia consists of only the Caroline, Marshalls and Mariana island groups, the former U.S. Trust Territory of the Pacific Islands and Guam. The Gilbert Islands and Nauru, however, are also included in greater Micronesia.

Discovery

It is impossible to "discover" a land that thousands of people know to exist because they are living there. However, a Spaniard, Alvaro de Saavedra enroute from the Moluccas to Mexico aboard the vessel *Florida* in 1529, might have been the first European to make Pohnpei known to the outside world. Credit for "discovery" is usually given to Pedro Fernandez de Quiros, a Portuguese navigator sailing for Spain, however. On the *San Jeronimo* during a passage from Santa Cruz to Manila in 1595, he located an island that was almost certainly Pohnpei. The first foreign settlement, by the Spanish administration, did not take place until 1886 (see *History*, pp. 53-59).

Location

Pohnpei is located 414 nautical miles north of the equator in the Eastern Caroline Islands of the Western Pacific Ocean. The island is roughly in the center of a slanting line running between Manila, 2,600 statute miles to the southwest and Honolulu, 3,088 statute miles northeast. Its latitude is 6° 54' north and its longitude is 158° 14' east. The island is 1,380 nautical miles west of the International Date Line. (To convert nautical miles to statute miles, add one-eighth, or twelve and a half percent to the nautical total.)

Land Area and Physical Features

Pohnpei's shape is an indented, jagged circle about thirteen miles in diameter and seventy miles in circumference. With its lagoon islands, the land area covers some 130 square miles. Off of the island proper is a pentagonically shaped outer barrier reef averaging two miles from shore, and nearly surrounding Pohnpei. It encloses a seventy square mile lagoon. About six thousand acres of mangrove forest encircle the island on the inner fringe reef, eliminating sandy beaches entirely. The mangrove is most heavily forested on the southern sections of the island. Strand vegetation covers the coastal lowlands that surround most of Pohnpei to an altitude of about five hundred feet. This area is the most populated on the island (see *Flora of Pohnpei*, pp.109-111).

The mountains of Pohnpei are the highest in the Federated States and are located in the center of the island on a crooked line extending northwest to southeast. The highest is Mt. Ngihneni (the tooth of the spirit) at 2,595 feet. Forty-two streams or large tributaries provide constant surface runoff from the wet, mountainous interior (see *Natural Features*, pp. 99-100).

The land area of the eight permanently inhabited outer islands of Pohnpei State is small, and the islands cannot possibly support their entire populations. The combined land area of Mokil, Pingelap, Sapwuahfik, Nukuoro, Kapingamarangi, Ant, Oroluk and Pakin is only 3.18 square miles. All are atolls with lagoons of varying sizes (see *Pohnpei State Outlying Islands*, pp.221-246).

The best map available of Pohnpei is a fifty inch projection with a scale of 1:25,000 produced on two sheets by the United States Department of the Interior, Geological Survey.

Climate and Tides

The climate of Pohnpei is tropical maritime, characterized by excessive rainfall, and high temperature and humidity. An average of nearly 195 inches of measured rain falls annually in Kolonia town, and an estimated four hundred inches of rain falls yearly in the mountainous interior. Temperature is uniform with mean lows in the low to mid seventies and mean highs in the mid to upper eighties. The average daily range is 12.2 degrees. The humidity on the island is eighty to ninety percent, with March and April being the least humid months (see *Natural Features*, pp. 102-105).

Unlike much of Micronesia, the risk of typhoons on Pohnpei is minimal. The island is close to the spawning grounds of many tropical disturbances that grow into typhoons, but the major tracks are to the north and west of the island. The last severe typhoon struck Pohnpei in 1905 (see *History*, p. 63).

Tides on Pohnpei over the past few years have varied from the lowest low tide of 0'.3" to the highest high of 5'0". The largest variation in tides occurs in November, December, and January.

Time Zone

The time on Pohnpei is Greenwich Mean Time (GMT) plus eleven hours. The island is across the International Date Line from time zones in the United States. When it is noon on Pohnpei, it is three p.m. Pacific Standard Time the previous day in Honolulu, and five p.m. yesterday in San Francisco and Los Angeles. If traveling in the opposite direction, Truk, Yap, and Guam and Saipan are in a time zone one hour earlier. Palau is in a time zone two hours earlier.

Kwajalein Atoll in the Marshall Islands, a stop on the flight enroute to Pohnpei, uses time east of the International Date Line, although the island is located to the west of the 180th meridian. Flying from Honolulu to Majuro in the Marshall Islands on Tuesday, one crosses the date line and arrives there on Wednesday. After refueling, one flies further west to Kwajalein and arrives there the previous day on Tuesday. After a brief stop, one flies on to Pohnpei, arriving on Wednesday—the fourth day in the three hours since crossing the International Date Line.

There are twelve to thirteen hours of daylight on Pohnpei each day throughout the year. The island has never used daylight savings time.

Population

Three quarters of the population of Pohnpei are under age twenty-five, and half of the people are under age fifteen. (According to the *Book of Lists*, Micronesia has the highest percentage of population under fifteen of any area of the world.) In the most recent census of 1985, the population of the island was found to be 26,343, and the population of Pohnpei State was 28,879, including expatriates and other non-citizens.

The estimated population decreased considerably in the mid 1800's because of diseases introduced by traders, beachcombers, and whalers. Population figures from various sources are as follows:

1820 - 15,000	1939 - 5,905
1855 - 5,000	1945 - 5,662
1891 - 1,705	1958 - 9,339
1905 - 3,500	1967 - 12,824
1914 - 4,401	1973 - 17,330
1935 - 5,501	1980 - 20,381

1985 - 26,343
1990 - 32,000 (state)

There are about 21,000 Pohnpeians on the island. Other large groups include a substantial number from Pohnpei's outer islands, second and third generation Mortlockese whose ancestors were originally brought to Pohnpei after a devastating typhoon struck their islands in 1907, groups from other F.S.M. states, particularly Kosrae, a small Palauan community, and expatriate contract workers. At the present rate of increase, the population of Pohnpei will more than double within the next twenty years.

Of a total population of about 32,000 in the state, some 95% are Pohnpeian citizens. The remaining 5%, or 1,500 people, includes citizens of other states as well as those from other countries.

De facto population figures, those actually living in an area, and legal residents, those who consider themselves residents of the area although they may not be living there, of course, differ from each other. For Pohnpei Island, the figures were as follows in 1985:

	De facto Population	Residents
U	2,603	2,797
Madolenihmw	4,339	4,833
Nett	4,038	3,415
Kitti	3,997	5,152
Sokehs	5,060	4,862
Kolonia	6,306	3,152

The de facto sum is higher than the resident total because some of the de facto people counted are residents of areas outside of Pohnpei. For the outer islands of the state, 8.6% of Pohnpei's population are actually living there, while 14% claim to be residents.

Kingdoms, Royalty, Clans and Families

According to Pohnpeian legend, during the Pre-History Period a warrior named Isokelekel came from the east with

333 men and overthrew a group of tyrannical chieftains, the Saudeleurs. He was installed as the first Nahnmwarki, or paramount chief, in the kingdom of Madolenihmw. His son became a chief of nearly as high rank, the Nahnken. Subsequently, four other kingdoms evolved: U, Kitti, Nett and Sokehs. In 1947, these kingdoms became municipalities of Pohnpei by a directive of the U.S. Trust Territory high commissioner.

Each municipality is administered by an elected executive and an elected municipal council. However, traditional leadership is in the hands of two chiefs, the Nahnmwarki and Nahnken of each municipality. Below each of these chiefs is a ranked series of titleholders, the highest eleven or so of whom are the most prominent. There are as many as two hundred titleholders on the municipal or kingdom level, however. The top titles are acquired through birth, but lesser ones are often earned through various forms of service. For each male title there is a female equivalent. About 95% of the adult Pohnpeian population holds section or municipal titles of varying importance.

Each native Pohnpeian is born into two kinship units in addition to a traditional "kingdom," the extended family and the clan. The extended family consists of several generations held together through the patrilineal line, and its main functions are economic. There are usually separate and clearly defined rights and duties for each member of this unit. The larger kinship unit, the clan, consists of a number of extended families who consider themselves descendants of a common female ancestor. (See *Traditional Culture*, pp. 179-185.)

Languages

About three quarters of the people on Pohnpei are native speakers of the Pohnpeian language. Other sizable language groups are Polynesians from Kapingamarangi in Kolonia, and several thousand second and third generation Mortlockese residing mainly in Sokehs municipality. Outer islanders from

Pingelap, Mokil, and Sapwuahfik in Pohnpei State speak dialects that are easily understandable to Pohnpeians, but the languages of the state's two other permanently inhabited atolls, Nukuoro and Kapingamarangi, are quite unintelligible to Pohnpeians. English is used in the schools as a medium of instruction from low primary grades through the community college level, and is the official language of the state. (See *Traditional Culture*, pp. 193-196.)

Religions

Continuous Protestant missionary activity has taken place on Pohnpei since 1852, and continuous Catholic missionary work since 1886. At present, the population of the island is divided about equally between these two Christian religions. Historically, the southern municipalities have been mostly Protestant while the northern areas have been mainly Catholic.

Most religious activity takes place in or near the population center of Kolonia, and the following churches are active: Assembly of God, Baha'i National, Calvary Baptist, Church of Jesus Christ of Latter Day Saints, Jehovah's Witnesses, Roman Catholic, Seventh Day Adventists, and the United Church of Christ.

Education

Public and private education are offered on Pohnpei. Elementary school consists of grades one through eight, and secondary school provides grades nine through twelve. Two years of higher education are offered at a community college in Kolonia.

Attendance at government elementary schools is free and compulsory, but entrance into the government secondary school is determined by examination results. (About one third of those completing elementary school are admitted to high school.) There are forty-two government schools with 440 teachers, nearly all Micronesian, in Pohnpei State. The three private elementary and secondary schools are church-affiliated and charge minimal tuition.

Higher education on the island is provided by the Community College of Micronesia, which offers five different two-year programs to about two hundred resident students. The only four-year institution in Micronesia is the University of Guam (see *Education*, pp. 173-177).

Government

Pohnpeians are governed on the municipal, state, and national levels by elected representatives and executives.

On the municipal level, the state is divided into six political entities—the five municipalities (former kingdoms) of Madolenihmw, U, Kitti, Nett, Sokehs, and the town of Kolonia—each with its own constitution. The government of each municipality consists of an elected executive and a council.

The Pohnpei State government consists of a governor, a lieutenant governor, a twenty-three member legislature, and a judiciary. The two executives are elected by popular vote throughout the state and must receive a majority, otherwise a runoff election is held. The legislators are elected from constituencies based on population, and must simply receive more votes than their nearest opponent for election. Executives and legislators serve four year terms. The three judges are appointed by the governor with the consent of the legislature and serve four-year renewable terms.

The former U.S. Trust Territory of the Pacific Islands districts of Yap, Truk, Kosrae, and Pohnpei joined together to form the Federated States of Micronesia on May 10, 1979. The government of the federation is a representative democracy consisting of executive, legislative and judicial branches, and patterned after that of the United States (see *Government*, pp. 161-168).

Infrastructure

Land, sea and air transportation facilities are still developing on Pohnpei. They were in their finest condition during the Japanese administration, but were almost totally destroyed during World War II (see *History*, pp. 82-84).

In 1983, eighty percent of the roads in Kolonia town were paved. In 1986, a circular fifty-four mile rough-and-ready road, a dream since the German administration, was completed, but not paved (see *Sights and Sites*, pp. 282).

Power for the island is supplied mainly from a renovated plant with six generators located three miles from Kolonia at Nam Pohn Mal. About six megawatts of output are necessary to supply power to the island.

Air transportation to Pohnpei is supplied by Air Micronesia and Pacific Missionary Aviation. Air Mike operates international flights east and west on alternate days of the week. P.M.A. flies to Kosrae State daily except Sundays, and once or twice each week to Pingelap. P.M.A. aircraft are also available for charters. The airport is located at the end of a causeway one mile north of Kolonia on Takatik Island. Architectural and engineering plans were completed for a new air terminal in 1986, and $1.2 million has been appropriated for the facility (see *Sights and Sites*, pp. 274-276).

The only passenger vessel regularly operating out of Pohnpei is the Canadian S.S. *Thorfinn*, which provides adventure cruises between Pohnpei and Truk states and their

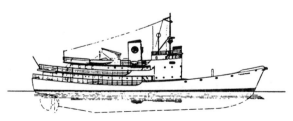

S.S. Thorfinn

outliers from December to May. A number of shipping lines provide service to the island. The largest are the Philippine Micronesia and Orient Line from the U.S. west coast, Kyowa Line from Japan, and Saipan Shipping and Tiger Lines from Saipan. The commercial dock on Takatik Island provides deep water berthing for two medium-sized cargo ships. The area was dredged to a low tide depth of thirty-three feet in 1982.

Communications

Communication facilities available on Pohnpei are local telephones, international telecommunications for telegrams and overseas calls, AM and FM radio broadcasting, ham radios, and the F.S.M. postal service.

The Pohnpei telephone directory has 574 listings, of which 157 are state or F.S.M. numbers. Monthly rates for private subscribers are a minimal—a residential party line costs $8.00 per month. There are no pay phones and a call from a local business establishment is free. The local phone system operates mainly in the Kolonia area.

Telegrams and telephone calls to off-island locations can be made at the Pohnpei State Communications Center at Nan Pohn Mal and also from the telecommunications center in Kolonia. A telephone call to the United States costs $9.00 for the first three minutes and $3.00 for each additional minute.

Local AM radio broadcasting is financed by the state government. Station WSZD broadcasts mainly in Pohnpeian and English from six a.m. until midnight daily. A privately operated FM radio station, KPON, broadcasts intermittently and features popular music. Although satellite facilities at the telecommunications station on Pohnpei are quite capable of receiving television broadcasts from the U.S., there is no station broadcasting programs directly from the U.S.

Several ham radio operators have stations on the island. All are expatriates and so the number varies from year to year with contract obligations.

The F.S.M. postal service was established on July 12, 1984. Although a department of the F.S.M. government, Pohnpei retains its U.S. postal zip code (96941). The island is located in U.S. postal zone #8, and American domestic rates apply for postal service. U.S. postage stamps, however, are not accepted.

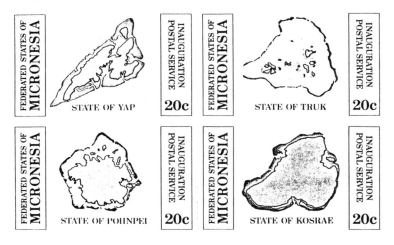

Municipalities of Pohnpei State

The five kingdoms of the island of Pohnpei—Madolenihmw, U, Kitti, Nett, and Sokehs—were designated as municipalities by the High Commissioner, Trust Territory of the Pacific Islands, on May 28, 1947. (The town of Kolonia became a separate political unit from Nett in 1965.)

The municipal governments each consist of an elected executive and a council of elected members. In the census of 1985, the actual populations of the municipalities on Pohnpei were as follows: U, 2,603; Nett, 4,038; Madolenihmw, 4,339; Kitti, 3,997; Sokehs, 5,060; and Kolonia, 6,306.

All municipalities except Kolonia have access to the highlands and the lagoon. Also included in each municipality outside of Kolonia are alluvial and basaltic lagoon islands and a portion of the surrounding barrier reef. Each outer island

13

of Pohnpei State is either a municipality in itself or is a part of a municipality. Pakin is a part of Sokehs, Ant is a part of Kitti, and Oroluk is a part of Kapingamarangi municipalities. Sapwuahfik, Pingelap, Mokil, Nukuoro, and Kapingamarangi are individual municipalities within the state government (see *Government*, pp. 162-163).

The land area in square miles of the mainland municipalities is as follows: Madolenihmw, 40.12; Kitti, 35.86; Nett, 27.09; Sokehs, 18.19; U, 7.16; and Kolonia, 0.58.

Traditional Pohnpei Island Municipalities

Pohnpei State Outer Islands

Until 1977, the island of Kosrae (then called Kusaie) and Pohnpei were part of Pohnpei District of the U.S. Trust Territory of the Pacific Islands. At the beginning of that year, Pohnpei with its eight outer islands, separated administratively. In 1979, Pohnpei and Kosrae became individual states of the Federated States of Micronesia.

Pohnpei State now includes seven permanently inhabited atolls in addition to the main island. Those inhabited with populations as of 1985 are Sapwuahfik (formerly Ngatik), 566; Nukuoro, 395; Kapingamarangi, 507; Mokil, 268; Pingelap, 738; and Oroluk, 2. Ant Atoll, five miles southwest of Pohnpei, is inhabited most of the year by Pohnpeians. (See *Outer Islands* map, and pp. 221-246.)

Pingelap has an aircraft landing strip 1,200 feet long for light planes which became operational in 1982. There are two scheduled flights to the atoll weekly. Mokil had its first landing and takeoff on March 14, 1986, during an emergency medical evacuation when construction on the facility was only half completed. There are plans for runways on Sapwuahfik, Kapingamarangi, and Nukuoro.

None of the outer islands has facilities for docking large, deep-draft vessels. The islands, except for Oroluk, are visited regularly by the MS *Micro-Glory*, a shallow-draft field-trip vessel of five-thousand tons, owned by the Pohnpei State government. The ship has twin 450 h.p. diesel engines and cruises at ten knots, usually at night. The vessel has eight cabins with two bunks each and can accommodate 125 deck passengers. Her crew of twenty-six is made up of very friendly outer islanders. The *Micro-Glory* offers the nautical bargain of the Pacific: a week-long deck passage trip to Sapwuahfik, Nukuoro, Kapingamarangi, and then a return passage north to Ant for $23.00.

Federated States of Micronesia

May 10, 1979 was the Fourth of July for this newly created loose federation of four states. The F.S.M. consists of the former U.S. Trust Territory of the Pacific Islands districts of Pohnpei, Kosrae, Truk, and Yap.

The F.S.M. is a representative democracy consisting of executive, legislative and judicial branches. The president and the vice president are elected by their colleagues in the senate. This legislature consists of fourteen members: six from Truk, four from Pohnpei, and two each from Yap and Kosrae. The Supreme Court consists of a chief justice and one associate justice.

The estimated population of the F.S.M. was 100,000 in 1990, distributed as follows: Truk, 51%; Pohnpei, 31%; Yap, 12%; and Kosrae, 06%. The F.S.M. covers an ocean area of some two million square miles, but only 270.8 square miles are dry land. Pohnpei State is nearly as large as all other states combined with 133.4 square miles, followed by Truk with 49.2, Yap with 45.9 and Kosrae with 42.3 square miles.

Since 1979, the capital offices were located in Kolonia. Construction on a new capital site began in 1986. The new capital was a $14 million project. (See *Government*, pp. 164-168.)

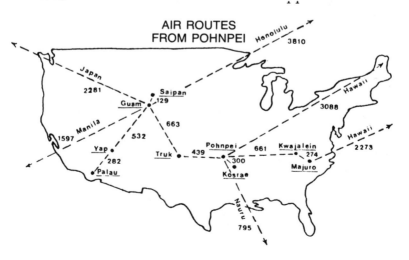

AIR ROUTES
FROM POHNPEI

Visitors' Information

Pohnpei State operates a tourist information office that provides a number of services to visitors. It is located on the main street in the center of Kolonia between the F.S.M. Post Office and a World War II vintage tank vehicle. (P.O. Box 66, Kolonia, 96941.)

The Pohnpei Tourist Commission has two bookcases with information about Pohnpei and Micronesia, and a comfortable, air-conditioned reading room. The center also provides visitors with information about places of interest and will coordinate tours and excursions. Performances at the Micronesia Cultural Center can be arranged through their office.

Tourist Commission Logo

There are eight hotels in the Kolonia area of varying quality and cleanliness, and about two hundred hotel rooms available. One hotel with twenty rooms, the popular *Village*, is located five miles west of the town.

There are thirteen restaurants in Kolonia, including those operated by the hotels. Twenty businesses operate car rental services. A telephone call is free in the town area and all hotels, restaurants, and most businesses have one available. "Don't leave home without it," but it might not do you much good on Pohnpei. At this writing (1990) only six businesses accept credit cards, the Village Hotel, Palm Terrace Hotel, and Air Micronesia.

Kolonia Town

1. Post Office
2. Peace Corps Office
3. Namiki Restaurant
4. Joy Restaurant
5. Police Station
6. Air Micronesia
7. Banks of Guam and Hawaii
8. Pohnpei Hotel
9. Palm Terrace Bar and Hotel
10. Cliff Rainbow Hotel
11. South Park Hotel
12. Seventh Day Adventists
13. Hifumi Inn
14. Joe Henry's Restaurant
15. Pohnpei State Legislature
16. Weather Station
17. P.C.R. Restaurant
18. Ocean View Bar
19. Kapingi Gift Shop
20. Micronesia Legal Service
21. K.C.C.A. Department Store
22. Ambros' Department Store
23. Bernards Department Store
24. Leo's Store
25. F.S.M. Immigration
26. Ace Commercial Center
27. Pohnpei State Hospital
28. Little Micronesia Bar
29. Catholic Church
30. Protestant Church
31. Jerry's Store, Car Rental
32. P.A.M.I. Gas Station
33. Panuelo's Gas Station
34. Martin's Store
35. Pacific Missionary Aviation
36. Pohnpei Tourist Office

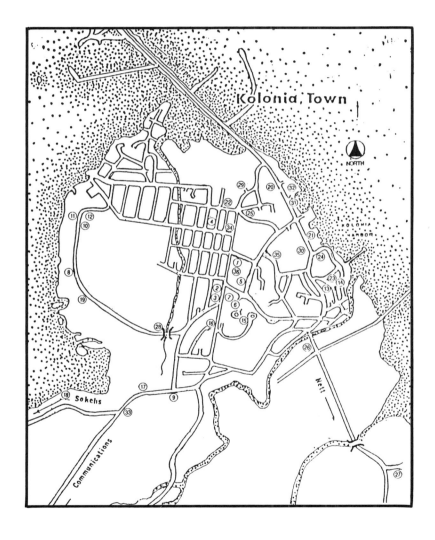

Kolonia Town

NORTH

KOLONIA HARBOR

Sokehs

Communications

Nett

POHNPEI — AN HISTORICAL SKETCH

Introduction

The sources for the following historical data on Pohnpei are European and American. Although Pohnpeians have a rich oral history, written Pohnpeian was not developed until the arrival of the missionaries in the middle of the last century. A list of sources consulted appears in an appendix. By far the best history of the island written by a Pohnpeian is *The Book of Luelen*, authored by Luelen Bernart (1866-1946), and translated by John L. Fischer, Saul H. Riesenberg, and Marjorie G. Whiting. With increased interest in the Western Pacific, and a recent profusion of studies by doctoral students, more material of general interest has been written about Pohnpei in the past twenty years than in the previous two hundred.

Variations in spellings of place names occur frequently on Pohnpei. Those used in the following pages are place name spellings most common on the island. For spellings approved by the U.S. Board of Geographical Names, see *Guide to Place Names in the Trust Territory of the Pacific Islands*, compiled by E.H. Bryan, Jr. (Honolulu, 1971). The Board, however, seems to opt for brevity. Thus we have the locally spelled

Madolenihmw as "Metalanim," *Sokehs* as "Jokaj," and **U** municipality spelled with the fewest letters of any place on Pohnpei (or perhaps anywhere else), as "U" (Pohnpei's only mention in the *Guinness Book of Records*).

A Chronology of Events on Pohnpei

1500 BC   The earliest occupation of Micronesia has been radiocarbon dated on Saipan and Tinian in the Mariana Islands.

1000   Linguists estimate that people entered the area that is now the Eastern Caroline Islands by way of Kiribati and the Marshalls and spread to Kosrae and Pohnpei.

200   Excavations below the tidal level on Pohnpei indicate occupation of the area around Nan Madol.

840 AD   Dwelling and subsistence sites and temporary shelters existed in the valley of Awak in the U section of Pohnpei.

1200   Nan Madol is known to have been occupied as evidenced by tests conducted on carbon in charcoal.

1521   Portuguese Ferdinand Magellan, in the service of Spain, was attempting the first circumnavigation of the earth when he reached Guam in the Mariana Islands of Micronesia.

1526   The Caroline archipelago was located by Spaniard Diego de Rocha. The islands were originally named the New Philippines.

1529   On his second attempt to cross the Pacific from west to east, Alvaro de Saavedra, aboard the Spanish vessel *Florida*, came upon an island at seven degrees north latitude that was probably Pohnpei.

1595   A Portuguese navigator sailing for Spain, Pedro Fernandez de Quiros, aboard the vessel *San Jeronimo*, sighted an island "of twenty-five leagues circumference and well-populated." He did not land and very nearly went aground. The island was almost certainly Pohnpei.

1686   A Spaniard, Francisco Lazcano, was the first to give the name "Caroline" to the archipelago. However, the islands were called "Neuvas Filipina" as late as 1707.

1787   Captain Thomas Read, aboard the trading vessel *Alliance* out of Philadelphia bound for China, was the first American to sight Pohnpei and Ant. He did not land, and named the islands Morris and Alliance.

1828   The Russian ship *Senyavin*, Captain Fedor Lütke, on a scientific expedition around the world, was prevented from landing on Pohnpei by some forty hostile canoes. Besides Pohnpei, Lütke sighted Pakin and Ant atolls.

1830   James F. O'Connell, the celebrated "Tattooed Irishman," was residing on Pohnpei. His adventures were published in a volume entitled *A Residence of Eleven Years in New Holland and the Caroline Islands.*

1830-40 Nearly all vessels touching Pohnpei at this time were British ships arriving by way of Australia, often with impressed, convict or ex-convict crews.

1837   The cutter *Lambton* out of New South Wales with a crew of renegade whites, and towing canoes with fully armed Pohnpeians, attacked the outer island of Ngatik. There they killed the entire male population of the island in reprisal for a purported attack on *Lambton* crewmen the previous year.

1840   American whaling began in earnest in the Pacific and its heyday lasted for the next thirty years. Frequent desertions by seamen kept a thriving community of castaways and beachcombers on Pohnpei.

1852   The first permanent Protestant mission on Pohnpei was established. Continuous missionary activity is dated on the island from their arrival in September.

1854   A smallpox epidemic, spread by crewmen of the American whaleship *Delta*, decimated the population of Pohnpei. More than half of the people died from the disease.

1865   Four American whaleships, the *Edward Carey* of San
        Francisco, the *Harvest* of Honolulu, the *Hector* from
        New Bedford, and the *Pearl* from New London,
        were burned and sunk in Madolenihmw Harbor
        by crewmen from the Confederate raider
        Shenandoah.

1870   A United States-Pohnpei treaty was signed aboard
        the U.S.S. *Jamestown* by the vessel's captain, Cmdr.
        N.J. Truxtun and the principal local chiefs. The har-
        bor and Kolonia were then named "Jamestown"
        by the local foreign residents.

1877   The infamous rogue (or rascal) Bully Hayes was
        done-in by his cook, Dutch Pete, aboard the
        schooner *Lotus* in waters between Pohnpei and
        Kosrae.

1885   The warship S.M.S. *Albatross* raised the German
        flag over Pohnpei. A treaty was then concluded
        with the five main chiefs in which they sur-
        rendered their sovereignty to Germany. (Pope Leo
        XIII, however, decided in favor of Spain in the
        dispute over ownership of Pohnpei.)

1886   The Spanish flag was raised on Pohnpei, July 27,
        marking the beginning of foreign government occu-
        pation of the island that was to last for a hundred
        years.

1887   The colony of Santiago de l' Ascension (Kolonia) was founded on Pohnpei in April. The first Spanish governor, Captain Don Isidro Posadillo, arrived, but was soon slain in a Pohnpeian uprising against forced labor.

1890   A second uprising against Spanish rule took place, sparked by Spanish attempts to build a Catholic mission adjacent to the Protestant mission in Oa, Madolenihmw. On November 2nd, all American Protestant missionaries on Pohnpei were expelled from the island by the Spanish governor.

1898   Religious warfare between Catholic and Protestant Pohnpeians subsided with the Spanish evacuation of the island.

1899   The Caroline, Marshall and Mariana Islands (except Guam) were purchased by Germany from Spain for 17,500,000 marks. The German Period officially began with the flag raising on October 12th.

1905   A severe typhoon struck Pohnpei and the outer islands of Mokil and Pingelap on April 20th. More than 250 people were killed or seriously injured.

1910-11   The last armed Pohnpeian uprising against foreign rule, the "Sokehs Rebellion," took place. In its aftermath, seventeen Pohnpeians were executed and 426 were sent into exile in Yap and Palau.

1912   Permanent land reform that insured private Pohnpeian ownership of individual plots of land was initiated by German District Administrator Heinrick Kersting.

1914   Six Japanese warships steamed into Kolonia Harbor and annexed Pohnpei in a bloodless takeover on October 7th. The third foreign flag in three decades was raised over the island.

1920   Japan was given a League of Nations Mandate to administer Micronesia. Among conditions stipulated were that Japan allow missionary activity to take place and that the islands not be fortified.

1933   Japan announced her intentions to withdraw from the League of Nations because of criticism by the League of her incursions in Manchuria. (Japan actually withdrew in 1935.)

1936   Japan closed Pohnpei to all but Japanese shipping. Economic development ceased and mandatory land sales for military facilities were initiated.

1937   Japan began her "China War" on July 7th. Military activity on Pohnpei increased.

1939-41   More construction for military purposes took place in these years than in the previous twenty-five.

1941   World War II in the Pacific began on December 7th (December 8th on Pohnpei). At the time, Japanese, Koreans and Okinawans outnumbered Micronesians on Pohnpei by two and a half to one in a total population of 19,500.

1944   Military facilities were neutralized on Pohnpei by B24 *Liberator* bomber raids and strikes from aircraft carrier planes, February 15 to 26. About 120 tons of high explosive bombs and 6,000 incendiary bombs were dropped.

1945   The Pacific war ended on August 15th, after 32,359 American casualties in Micronesia. Pohnpei was surrendered by the Japanese army commander, Lt. Gen. Masao Watanabe, aboard the destroyer *U.S.S. Hyman* on September 11th.

1947   A Trusteeship Agreement between the United States and the United Nations Security Council was approved on April 2nd. Admiral Louis E. Denfeld was appointed the first U.S. high commissioner to the Trust Territory of the Pacific Islands.

1951	The United States Department of the Interior assumed responsibility for administering Micronesia from the Navy Department. Former U.S. Senator Elbert D. Thomas was appointed high commissioner with headquarters in Guam.
1952	The first session of the Ponape Island Congress, forerunner of the Pohnpei State Legislature, convened.
1963	The Ponape District Legislature, a unicameral body with representatives from all islands in Pohnpei District, was established.
1964	The Congress of Micronesia was created on September 28th with elected legislators from Trust Territory districts of Palau, the Marianas, Yap, Truk, and the Marshall Islands as well as Pohnpei. (Kosrae was part of Pohnpei District at that time.)
1966	The first U.S. Peace Corps Volunteers arrived on Pohnpei after training in Key West and Miami, Florida, and numbered as many as 120 on the island in their early years.
1970	The first American Civic Action Team (fourteen U.S. Navy Seabees) began work on construction projects. The Future Political Status Negotiations began with the United States. The Community College of Micronesia was established on Pohnpei.
1972	Typhoon Lola hit Pohnpei on May 31 with winds of 70 m.p.h. Damage to property was estimated at $1 million.
1977	The College of Micronesia with campuses in Palau, Saipan and Pohnpei was established.

1978   The Constitution of the Federated States of Micronesia was drafted, signed, and ratified.

1979   Pohnpei joined in a union with Yap, Truk, and Kosrae to form the Federated States of Micronesia. Pohnpei was designated as the capital. The Honorable Leo A. Falcam became the first elected governor of Pohnpei State.

1982   A Compact of Free Association between the Federated States of Micronesia and the United States was drafted, and ratified by the F.S.M. Congress the following year.

1983   The Honorable Resio S. Moses was elected as the second governor of Pohnpei State. Senator Bailey Olter of Pohnpei State was elected vice president of the F.S.M.

1984   The Constitution of the State of Pohnpei was ratified. Lt. Gov. Strik Yoma died in office while visiting Hawaii.

1985   The Compact of Free Association was brought before the U.S. Congress. The Honorable Johnny David was elected Lt. Governor of Pohnpei State.

1986   Centennial of Spanish (and Roman Catholic) arrival. The Compact of Free Association was approved by the U.N. Trusteeship Council. Another Typhoon Lola skirted Pohnpei.

1987   The Honorable Resio S. Moses was re-elected to a second term as Pohnpei State Governor.

1990   A second F.S.M. Constitutional Convention was held. The new F.S.M. capital at Palikir on Pohnpei was completed.

three took place before the arrival of the Europeans, and were initiated by events that caused significant changes in Pohnpeian society. The fourth period dates from the arrival

An Historical Note. . .

Pohnpeians divide history into four time periods. The first three took place before the arrival of the Europeans, and were initiated by events that caused significant changes in Pohnpeian society. The fourth period dates from the arrival of non-Micronesians to the island.

The founding and settling of Pohnpei according to myth and legend took place during the first historical period. At that time a uniform culture developed and a common language evolved. During the second period a dynasty of island chieftains, the Saudeleurs, ruled and Pohnpei was divided into three kingdoms of about equal size. Nan Madol is said to have been built during this period. A warrior named Isokelekel who came from the east and conquered the Saudeleurs ushered in the third historical period. He established himself at Madolenihmw. Subsequently, the five present divisions of Pohnpei took place: Madolenihmw, Kitti, U, Nett, and Sokehs. The arrival of non-Micronesians initiated the fourth period, which is still in progress.

Western scholars, however, usually divide Pohnpeian history into six segments, based primarily on who controlled the islands politically at the time: Pre-History Period (to 1830); Early Contact Period (1830-1886); Spanish Period (1886-1899); German Period (1899-1914); Japanese Period (1914-1945); and the American Period (1945-1986).

Pre-History
(to 1830)

The Beginnings
First European Voyages to Pohnpei, 1595
First Recorded American Voyage to Pohnpei, 1787
Lütke and the *Senyavin*, 1828

Boathouse, Pohnpei

The earliest documented occupation of the islands of Micronesia has been radiocarbon dated at 1500 B.C. in Saipan and Tinian of the Mariana Islands. In general, archaeological evidence suggests that Pohnpei occupation had a westward derivation from the Philippines or perhaps even Indonesia. However, linguists suggest that Pohnpei was populated by migrations northwestward through the Gilbert and Marshall Islands around 1000 B.C.

Oral history of Pohnpei is spotty, except over the past century and a half. Even in comparatively recent times, catastrophes such as a smallpox epidemic in 1854 have caused gaps to appear in the oral history by wiping out entire clans and many Pohnpeians who were familiar with stories of the past. In the three thousand years of occupation of Pohnpei, a system of writing was only begun 130 years ago.

Archaeological studies of Pohnpei have increased considerably over the past decade. Until about ten years ago, most took place at the ancient ruins of Nan Madol. The most publicized early studies were those of F.W. Christian in the 1890's and Paul Hambruch in 1910. Although these mysterious and romantic artificial islets continue to be fascinating to doctoral student and tourist alike, especially in the summer months, other areas of the island have recently yielded interesting archaeological data. This is particularly true of the Awak section of U municipality in northern Pohnpei. There, remains of ancient structures have been located in sand beneath layers of Japanese concrete pavement, and clay and basalt rock. The sand contained artifact fragments, charcoal, and cooking sites, and the remains of house foundations. However, serious archaeology is just beginning on the island, and only steep slopes, mangrove swamps, and deep reef areas are expected to yield no archaeological sites at all.

Much that is known in archaeological terms about the early development of the island comes from investigations in the valley of Awak mentioned above. There, three basic kinds of sites have been identified dating back to A.D. 840: dwelling sites; subsistence sites; and temporary shelter areas.

The dwelling sites located are solitary foundations or small groups of foundations spread in the lowlands in non-swampy areas. They begin mostly at about two or three hundred yards inland. Foundations near the shore seem to have been for boat houses. Dwelling sites were located up to elevations of six hundred feet, but where slopes steepened to more than 30%, few dwelling sites were located. The notable exception to the scattered dwelling pattern that appears even today is the structures of Nan Madol.

Subsistence sites such as agricultural plots seem to be located around dwellings, much as they are on Pohnpei today. Terraces on slopes, walls across water run-off channels, and trenches that lead from streams for irrigation were detected in the area. Fish weirs as expected appear on shallow reefs just offshore in the lagoon.

The most common temporary sites located and identified are caves. In remote areas of the island they seem to have been used as rest stops or camps.

The meat of scientific diggings is in the valley of Awak, but the glamour and the mystery of antiquity remains at the ruins of Nan Madol. There, the shreds uncovered by archaeology mingle with the oral history of the people of Pohnpei.

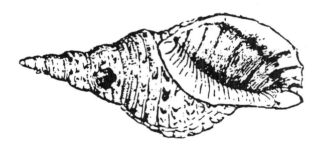

Only twenty-nine years after Columbus first crossed the Atlantic and eight years after Balboa sighted the Pacific, Ferdinand Magellan, a Portuguese navigator sailing for Spain, reached Guam in 1521. (He sailed completely through Micronesia without finding a single inhabited island). Eight years later, Alvaro de Saavedra, crossing the Pacific from west to east aboard the *Florida*, came upon an island at six or seven degrees north latitude that was fifteen miles long and contained high mountains, probably Pohnpei. He remained in the area for two days without attempting a landing. A Portuguese navigator sailing for Spain, Pedro Fernandez de Quiros, aboard the *San Jeronimo* in 1595 is given credit for "discovering" Pohnpei. (His voyage is detailed in *Rascals in Paradise* by James A. Michener and A. Grove Day, "Don Isabel, the Lady Explorer.") He sighted an island some eighty-five miles in circumference which was well populated, at approximately six degrees north latitude. He did not land, but the island was almost certainly Pohnpei. It was later named "Quirosa," one of numerous names recorded for Pohnpei during the next several centuries.

Pedro Fernandez de Quiros

Spaniard Francisco Lazcano gave the name Caroline Islands in honor of Charles II of Spain to the archipelago in 1686. As late as 1707 the islands were still being called the New Philippines, "Neuvas Filipina." After the voyage of Quiros, nearly two hundred years were to pass with no recorded ships sighting Pohnpei, although intermittent contact with the outside world was undoubtedly kept. No records about Pohnpei exist before the 16th Century. Men were strong, but vessels were fragile, and longitude locations were unreliable. The islands offered only a few trade items valuable enough to risk extended voyages in uncharted waters, and the deep-sea whaling industry was in its infancy.

The United States was also in her infancy in 1787 when Captain Thomas Read became the first American on record to visit Pohnpei, aboard the *Alliance* out of Philadelphia bound for China. He named Pohnpei and Ant "Morris" and "Alliance." (Another American vessel named *Alliance* visited Pohnpei 103 years later. Her captain demanded and received 17,000 gold dollars from the Spanish administration as compensation for the expulsion of American missionaries.) As late as 1828, Pohnpei was still being "discovered." Russian Captain Fedor Lütke on a scientific expedition around the world aboard the ship *Senyavin* thought he was the first to chart Pohnpei, Ant and Pakin, the last of the Caroline Islands to be found. (It is rather strange that these scientists had never heard of the voyage of Quiros and that the highest of the Carolines was thought to have been the last to be seen.) He estimated the population at two thousand, without landing. Hostile canoes caused Lütke's chronicler to name the area around Kolonia the "Harbor of Bad Reception." Lutke called the island "Pouynipeti" and sailed off to Ant. He found the atoll to be uninhabited, and very nearly went aground. The three islands—Pohnpei, Ant and Pakin—were named the Senyavin Islands, a name still used on maps, navigational charts, and crossword puzzles today.

The year 1830 is a rather arbitrary time in which to slide from one historical period to another. By then, however, visits from sailing vessels were becoming more frequent, and a number of shipwrecked sailors and deserters had lived for a time on Pohnpei. These beachcombers had to be taken under the protection of local leaders, and most chiefs had one or more in their service. They occasionally acted as pilots, but more importantly as interpreters and intermediaries in trade between their benefactors and visiting ships. In exchange for their service they received food, houses, wives, and all the comforts of an island paradise with "no irksome governments to restrain their exuberance. . .and no missionaries to spoil their fun."

First Recorded Outside Contact
Pohnpei and Outer Islands

Island(s)	Year	Vessel	Nation	Captain
Pohnpei, Ant, Pakin	1529	*Florida*	Spain	Alvaro de Saavedra
Sapwuahfik	1773	*Nuestra Senora de la Consolacion*	Spain	Felipe Tompson
Pingelap	1793	*Sugar Cane*	Great Britain	Musgrave
Nukuoro	1801	*Lydia*	United States	Moses Barnard
Kapingamarangi	1809	*Tonquin of New York*	United States	Edmund Fanning
Mokil	1815	*Marquis of Wellington*	Great Britain	G. Betham
Oroluk	1824	*Rambler*	United States	William North

(Source: *Foreign Ships in Micronesia*, Francis X. Hezel, S.J.)

38

Early Contact Period (1830-1886)

The Tattooed Irishman, 1830
Early Whaler Influences, 1840
Smallpox, 1854
First Permanent Missionaries, 1852
Pohnpei and the American Civil War, 1865
Bully Hayes, 1869
Johann Stanislaus Kubary, 1879
Demise of the Whalers, 1880

One of the increasing number of seamen who by choice or chance resided on Pohnpei was James F. O'Connell, the celebrated "Tattooed Irishman," who was on the island for five years around 1830. O'Connell claimed to have been shipwrecked in a vessel appropriately named the *John Bull* in 1827, and that he arrived on Pohnpei in an open boat from Pleasant Island, eight hundred miles distant, after only four days at sea.

In 1836 O'Connell published a highly imaginative account of his visit to Pohnpei titled *A Residence of Eleven Years in New Holland and the Caroline Islands*. In his book, O'Connell says he was captured by Pohnpeians who wanted to have him for dinner (literally). To save himself and his companion, he leapt to his feet and danced a lively jig to the tune of "Garry Owen," a song about drinking, gambling and high living in times past. Surviving this crisis, he says he was forceably tattooed by a young Pohnpeian maiden. According to O'Connell, "I bore it like a martyr." He was then adopted by a high chief, married the chief's daughter who had tattooed him, and became a chief himself. In his narrative O'Connell goes on to describe physical and cultural aspects of Pohnpei in some detail.

In November, 1833, the Tattooed Irishman left Pohnpei on the brig *Spy*. After numerous misadventures he arrived in the United States where he exhibited his tattoos, and danced in halls and circuses, billed as the "Celebrated Tattooed Sailorman."

Perhaps James O'Connell is still calling the tune because he is remembered, for better or worse, far more than a number of prominent individuals of his time. In 1859, five years after O'Connell's death, the Rev. L.H. Gulick wrote, "So much of the irreconcilably and egregiously incorrect is mingled with O'Connell's narrative...that very little of what he says can be trusted." The noted Pacific scholar, Saul Riesenberg, said a little more bluntly, "Some of O'Connell's information is so patently and flagrantly wrong that one wonders whether we are dealing with a pathological liar," and further questions if O'Connell had some kind of visual disability. But anthropologists Paul Hambruch early in this century, and John L.

Fischer later, agreed that O'Connell offered some valuable information.

Reprobate or adventurer? Liar or dreamer? Certainly James O'Connell exaggerated, but who among us would not exaggerate about Pohnpei at such an exciting time?

James F. O'Connell (circa 1835)

Trading voyages stimulated change on Pohnpei during the first half of the nineteenth century. Many were motivated by the wealth of the Orient and used Pohnpei as both a source of trade items and a pleasant place to reprovision. Ironware and cloth were exchanged for beche-de-mer (sea cucumber), turtle shells and shark fins valued in China. These items were in turn traded in Canton for teas, silks and valuable woods. The beche-de-mer was particularly coveted as a main ingredient in Chinese gourmet soups. Pohnpei in the 1840s also had a reputation as the best island in the Pacific to acquire turtle shell. About five hundred pounds per year were collected with a market value of $2,500. Most local items were paid for with sticks of tobacco (three pounds of tobacco worth one dollar was paid for each pound of turtle shell worth five dollars). As ironware, cloth, and tobacco became common, other items were demanded for trade, particularly firearms. In 1850 it was estimated that 1,500 muskets were available on Pohnpei, one for each two or three males on the island.

The most significant influences of the Early Contact Period were the visiting ships, particularly whalers, in the first half of the period, and missionary activity in the second. From 1830 to 1840, nearly all vessels touching at Pohnpei were British ships coming to the island by way of Australia. American whaling began in earnest around Pohnpei in the late 1840's and its heyday lasted for about the next twenty years. The excesses of the sailors visiting the eastern Carolines stimulated missionary interest and involvement, and the two periods overlapped for about ten years or so beginning around the mid-1850's.

Initial foreign intrusion ran along lines quite familiar on other islands of Oceania. The *Falcon* incident is a good example. While leaving Pohnpei after repairs in 1836, the British vessel *Falcon* was wrecked on a reef. Attempting to prevent looting by natives, Captain Hingston and four crewmen were killed. Crews of three other ships at anchor came to the assistance of the *Falcon* sailors—but for a price of all stores, supplies and cargo salvaged from the vessel. Crewmen of the *Lambton*, *Unity* and *Avon* numbered about seventy and they recruited more than four-hundred Pohnpeians to oppose the looters and their supporters. The chief, Nahnawa, was captured, given a hurried trial by the three captains, and hung from the cross-jack yard of the *Lambton*.

Captain C.H. Hart of the *Lambton* then participated in one of the most tragic footnotes in Pohnpei's early history, which involved a senseless massacre on Sapwuahfik atoll, an outlier ninety miles to the southwest of the island. Early in 1836, after leaving Pohnpei, the *Lambton* had visited Sapwuahfik in search of tortoise shells. While ashore, two crew members were attacked by natives, but escaped to the *Lambton* unharmed. The incident should have ended there. However, in July of the following year, Captain Hart and the *Lambton* returned with a gang of renegade whites and fifteen Pohnpeians. They attacked the island and killed every man and boy there except for one who had been overlooked. The booty from this outrage? Twenty pounds of hawksbill turtle shell. Despite British Admiralty investigations, no participants were ever punished for their crimes.

The New England area of the United States had an inordinate influence on the island. Many of the American whalers arrived from home ports in New Bedford, New London, Nantucket, and Fairhaven, and the parent organization of the first Protestant missionaries to reside on Pohnpei was located in Boston. The whaling vessels were a source of some wealth to Pohnpei, although most money from transactions with the ships went into the hands of chiefs and their beachcomber retainers. In addition to a $20.00 standard pilot fee, wood was sold for $2.00 per load, yams and taro for $2.00 per barrel and fruit for a similar price. Young ladies sold their favors and young men sold their services. (The men were paid from $2.00 to $8.00 for each deserter apprehended and returned to his vessel—and there were many.) The average spent by each ship on a visit to Pohnpei was $200.00. Some Pohnpeians of the day received rather harsh reviews from sea captains, however. Capt. Thomas N. Russell of the whaleship *Lancaster*, January, 1860: "The natives are great thieves. They steal anything they can lay their hands on and even the running rigging from their pins." Capt. Samuel James of the missionary packet *Morning Star*, January, 1864: "The natives are

Morning Star

43

a graceless set of scamps. They did not steal the main mast or anchors for the simple reason that they could not carry them off." Capt. Zenas E. Bourne of the whaling bark *Avola,* June, 1872: "We have male and female on board—females as boarders and males as bummers." To some salty sea captains, Pohnpei of the last century was a worthy successor to the Ladrones (Marianas) of Ferdinand Magellan, to the Isles of Thieves (Palau) of Sir Francis Drake and to the petty thievery of the Hawaiians of Captain James Cook.

Pohnpei extracted a price from many visiting vessels. Desertions by crew members, frustration from contrary winds, and damage from uncharted reefs were common. Frequently the sailors of "iron men in wooden ships" fame preferred the uncertainty of living on Pohnpei to the rigors of chasing sperm whales. According to Fr. Francis X. Hezel in *Foreign Ships in Micronesia, 1521-1885,* the American ship *Eliza* in 1837 spent ninety days at Pohnpei because of contrary winds. In that time sixteen of her original crew deserted. From the whaleship *Offley* from London, 1841, "so many men deserted the ship on Pohnpei that it had not enough hands to get underweigh," and the whaler *Fortune* of Plymouth, in 1843, departed with only four men before the mast. The Belgian ship *Constance* had a more macabre experience. After being grounded on Oroluk Atoll, 180 miles from Pohnpei in July, 1858, her crew took to open boats and attempted to sail to the Philippines. Instead, they landed in New Guinea in late September after being forced to kill and eat two of their members. The whaleship *Sharon* out of Fairhaven had a different sort of harrowing experience after leaving Ascension (Pohnpei). From the *Boston Courier,* June 27, 1843:

SHIP SHARON OF FAIRHAVEN

Some account of the mutiny on board this vessel, in which Captain Norris the master, was killed, is given in the New Bedford Mercury, in the following extract of a letter from the mate of the ship Hope of New Bedford. The Sharon had lost eleven of her men at Ocean and Ascension Islands, and had taken some natives on board in place of them; but did not prove good men, and Captain Norris intended to go to Port Jackson for others. Some days after, (no date given) whales were raised, when the boats were lowered in pursuit, leaving Captain Norris, a boy, and three natives on board to keep ship. A whale was struck and killed, and the boat had gone in pursuit of others, when the signal of the ship was discovered to be set at half mast. The boat immediately made for the ship, and on approaching her learned from the boy, who was aloft, that the natives had murdered the captain. Attempts were made by the boat's crew to board the ship, but they were repelled by the natives who had armed themselves with cutting spades. The ship in the meantime had been got before the wind, and the boats had great difficulty in keeping up with her. The boy, who still continued aloft, was ordered by the mate to cut away the haulyards of the top sails, jib, &c., and to cut away the top sails clear of the yards, which he did by passing from one mast to the other on the stays; and in the evening, the boats came up to the ship, when the second mate, giving the crew instructions to board the ship when they heard the report of a musket, got overboard and swam to her, and climbing up the rudder succeeded in getting into the cabin through the window. He then loaded some muskets, and was arming himself, when one of the natives came down, armed with a cutlass. A severe contest ensued, and the native getting the worst ran upon the deck, when another came down whom the second mate shot dead. At the report of the musket, the boat's crew rushed on board, and found one of the natives armed with a cutlass and knife, who, making resistance was shot. The other concealed himself and was not found until the next day, when he was put in irons, carried into Sydney, where the Sharon arrived in December the last.

Whaleship *Sharon* of Fairhaven. From a painting in the Peabody Museum of Salem.

The most tragic consequence of foreign contact was disease brought to Pohnpei, and there are many documented cases of sick seamen being left ashore and replaced by castaways, beachcombers and Pohnpeians. At the beginning of the period in 1830, Pohnpei's population was estimated to be fifteen thousand. By the time of the Spanish occupation in 1886, barely two thousand people were alive. The smallpox epidemic of 1854 was the most decimating. In March of that year the American whaler *Delta* landed six men who were infected with smallpox. Stories vary, but it is known that clothing of the infected sailors passed into Pohnpeian hands, and the disease soon spread throughout the island, killing about half of the population. The *Margaret Scott* of New Bedford lost nine men, and the *Miantonomi*, also of New Bedford, had several crew members sick from smallpox after leaving Pohnpei. The *Miantonomi* was wrecked on a reef when re-entering the harbor, and was then plundered by runaway sailors during the night. The few missionaries on the island at the time were also in a precarious position when giving medical treatment to Pohnpeians. From the diary of Rev. Albert A. Sturges: "Today I have given the chief a vaccination . . . If he does well, then everything will turn out alright. If he dies, then the people will probably kill us." Happily for all concerned, the chief did well.

Albert A. Sturges mentioned above, and Luther Gulick were the first two Protestant missionaries to reside on Pohnpei, and continuous missionary activity is dated from their arrival in September, 1852. They were sponsored by the Board of Hawaiian Evangelical Association, a daughter society of the American Board of Commissioners for Foreign Missions, with headquarters in Boston. They were not the first missionaries on Pohnpei, however. As early as 1837, a French priest of the Picpus Fathers, Désiré Maigret, arrived on Pohnpei aboard the vessel *Notre Dame du Paix*. After completing the sad task of burying his traveling companion, Fr. Alexis Bachelot who had died at sea eight days earlier, Fr. Maigret resided on the island of Na of Pohnpei for about six months. While there, two Mangaravan crewmen married Pohnpeian women. When time came to depart, the families of the women objected to the wives leaving, especially since both were pregnant. The traditional leader of the area, the Nahnmwarki, solved the problem by sending two young and strong Pohnpeian lads to replace the Mangaravans as crewmen aboard the *Notre Dame du Paix*. The two immigrant settlers founded families in a section of Sapwalap on Pohnpei. To this day, nearly 150 years later, the families are known as "mehn Daidi" (those of Tahiti). And what of the wandering Pohnpeians? Following their exodus they settled in Tahiti where they raised families whose descendants are alive and well on the island today. Father Maigret, who started it all, was later to become Roman Catholic Bishop of Hawaii.

In 1855 the Honolulu Board sent Rev. Edward T. Doane, his wife, and his Hawaiian helper Kamakahi to Pohnpei. Early missionary effort was not immediately successful and there were only three Christian baptisms of Pohnpeians by 1860. The missionaries were constantly undermined by the fifty or so white castaways residing on the island, and believers were persecuted by non-believers.

The resident population of Pohnpei temporarily increased by 120 foreigners in April, 1865, when Pohnpei (at the time called Ascension Island) became a footnote in the American Civil War. At anchor in Madolenihmw Harbor were the whaleships *Edward Carey* of San Francisco, *Harvest* of Honolulu, *Hector* of New Bedford, and *Pearl* of New London. (The *Pearl* reportedly brought measles to the island, resulting in the death of many Pohnpeians.) The Confederate raider *Shenandoah* arrived on April Fool's Day, 1865, put ashore the crews of the four ships and burned and sank the vessels. The skipper of the *Shenandoah*, Lt. Cmdr. James I. Waddel, claimed to have left the crews with large quantities of provisions and their personal effects. However, Rev. Sturges said that the men were destitute. The *Shenandoah* then sailed north on April 13th, with thirteen new crew members, some Pohnpeians, and certainly the first and only Pohnpeians to join the Confederate Navy. Subsequently, the *Shenandoah* continued raiding the Yankee whaling fleet. She captured and burned the whaler *Abigail* in the Sea of Okhotsk in May, and burned the vessels *Euphrates, William Thompson,* and *Jireh Swift* on June 20th in the Arctic Ocean—ten weeks after the Confederate surrender at Appomattox. Five months were to pass before the bark *Kamehameha* took the castaways on Pohnpei off to Honolulu, at the price of $50.00 per head. However, Captain John P. Eldridge, master of the *Harvest*, and ten seamen chose not to be rescued.

Shenandoah

A short five years after the American Civil War, a United States naval cruiser, the *U.S.S. Jamestown*, called at Pohnpei on June 16, 1870. The Captain, Cmdr. N.J. Truxtun, managed to assemble all of the principle chiefs aboard his vessel and influenced them to sign a treaty with the United States by offering them gifts they couldn't refuse. Among the provisions of the treaty were the guaranteed freedom for missionaries to preach, protection for traders and shipwrecked sailors, and a fine of $50.00 for enticing seamen to desert, or concealing them ashore. Cmdr. Truxtun then named the present town of Kolonia "Jamestown" and sailed happily off into history.

USS Jamestown

Among the rogues or rascals who called Pohnpei their favorite island at this time was the infamous Bully Hayes, although he is better known for his skullduggery on Strong's Island (Kosrae). Hayes visited Pohnpei on a number of occasions between 1869 and 1877. On one voyage, he sailed into Pohnpei's Ronkiti Harbor with a cargo of a dozen thirty-pound cases, tightly and properly sealed, and marked "Tobacco." He traded the empty cases to a local chief for a bull and three pregnant cows, and then quickly sailed off to further mischief. It was between Pohnpei and Kosrae on board the schooner *Lotus* on March 31, 1877, that Bully was finally done-in. According to the most accepted version of the story, he was killed by his hot-tempered cook, Dutch Pete (who was actually a Norwegian). Pete was reported to have smashed Bully with a heavy metal bar as Bully emerged from a companionway, and then rolled his 240 pound frame over-board. In another version of the story, Dutch Pete knocked Bully overboard, and then watched and laughed as he was eaten by sharks. At any rate, no legal authorities saw fit to prosecute Dutch Pete for the killing.

Bully Hayes

The work of the best known scientist of the early-contact years transcended the period into the Spanish occupation of Pohnpei. Johann Stanislaus Kubary was born in Warsaw in 1846 of a German mother and a Hungarian father. He was raised, however, by his Polish stepfather. Political problems resulting from Kubary's agitating for Polish independence forced him to leave his native land and spend more than half of his life in Oceania.

Kubary selected as his permanent base a large tract of land on Pohnpei which is presently owned by the Etscheit family. There he purchased land and established botanical gardens. Supported by the Godeffroy Trading Company of Hamburg, Pohnpei's first ethnographer collected artifacts throughout Micronesia and wrote scientific descriptions about them in German. He married Anna Yalliott, the daughter of an American Methodist missionary and a Pohnpeian mother, who bore him two daughters. (Kubary's wife died on Pohnpei in 1937, and one daughter grew up in Singapore's Convent of the Holy Infant Jesus where she took her vows as Sister Hombeline. She died in 1961.)

From 1870 to 1879, Kubary continued scientific work for his benefactors. Unfortunately, a large number of his specimens were lost when a hundred cases of artifacts were sunk with the ship *Alfred* off of a reef on Jaluit in the Marshall Islands in 1874. A final fatal blow to Kubary's efforts fell when his sponsors went bankrupt as a result of the Franco-Prussian War.

Throughout the 1880's and the early 1890's, ill luck and ill health plagued Kubary. During those years, he wandered throughout the Pacific and Europe, working as a trader and looking for financial support for his research. He returned to Pohnpei in 1896 only to see the botanical gardens he had previously developed destroyed by Spanish bombardment during a Pohnpeian uprising.

Kubary died at age fifty that same year, perhaps from assassination, possibly from ill health, but most likely from suicide. His original grave site was excavated, but no body was found. It is thought that his remains were moved from the original site by his friends. The present location of Kubary's grave is unknown.

A Kubary memorial plaque was sent by admirers and friends in Europe to Pohnpei during the early years of the German administration. The pedestal remains, but the plaque has been temporarily removed. It sits outside of the Catholic Mission in the shade of a large tree and the Spanish Wall. The brass plaque displays a scholarly appearing professor-type individual, Victorian completely. His photograph before his death, however, shows a strongly built man, nearly bald, with wonderfully penetrating (or perhaps terribly haunting) eyes.

Missionary activity continued to increase on Pohnpei throughout the decade of the 1870's, but not as rapidly as on neighboring islands. This was partly because of traditional rivalry among tribes on Pohnpei. Often one group would oppose new beliefs simply because a rival group accepted them. By 1870, however, the Protestant church was so well established that it could send missionaries to the outer island of Mokil, and in 1873, to Pingelap where they established the Congregational churches that are dominant on these islands today.

As missionary activity increased, the influence of the whaling fleet declined. Alternate sources of fuel were developed to replace whale oil. Only seven whaleships were reported to have visited Pohnpei in 1880, whereas forty-two were reported twenty-five years earlier.

Spanish Period
(1886-1899)

The Spanish Period on Pohnpei was very nearly the German Period. By 1885, eighty percent of the trade in the Caroline Islands was in German hands. Government supported companies had trading stations in Yap and Kosrae as well as Pohnpei. On October 13, 1885, the warship S.M.S. *Albatross* arrived and the German flag was raised on the island. A treaty between the five kingdoms and Germany was concluded in which the Pohnpeian chiefs surrendered their sovereignty to the Kaiser.

The dispute between Germany and Spain for possession of the Mariana and Caroline Islands was submitted to Pope Leo XIII for arbitration. The Pope decided in favor of Spain, based on the Papal determination of 1494, and Spanish claims of discovery of the Caroline Islands in 1686. Germany, however, was granted freedom of trade in the area. Great Britain was given the same right by Spain in January, 1886.

Two Spanish warships called to claim Pohnpei and raise their flag on July 27, 1886. The following April Captain Don Isidro Posadillo was sent as governor, accompanied by other colonial officials, fifty Filipino soldiers, and six Capuchin missionaries. The colony of Santiago de l' Ascension was founded in an area called Mesenieng by Pohnpeians, the location of the present-day Kolonia. And so began the Spanish Period, or more appropriately, the Spanish-Pohnpeian Conflict Period, that was to continue for the next twelve years.

In retrospect, conflict was inevitable. The Spanish, like the Americans sixty years later, arrived with no fixed colonial policy, except to keep the area from another nation's possession. In an era of colonialism, little thought was given to the established social and political structure, or to the Pohnpeian culture. Also, the Catholic Spanish arrived on an island where the Protestant religion was well established.

Acquiring land for the colony of Santiago caused an immediate conflict. The Rev. Edward T. Doane, mentioned earlier, the most prominent Protestant leader on Pohnpei, claimed that the land desired by the Spanish was his property. He produced a paper dated July 26, 1880, which was signed by a local leader, the Lepen Nett, to substantiate his claim. The governor disavowed the claim, however, arrested Doane, and deported him to Manila for a hearing.

The first armed conflict resulted from a Spanish forced labor policy, not uncommon in colonies at the time. On June 16, 1887, Pohnpeian workers refused to report for labor on the fort being constructed in Santiago by the government. Twenty-seven soldiers were sent to Sokehs to force workers to comply with the labor requirement. The soldiers fired, and the Pohnpeians retaliated. When the smoke cleared, an officer and sixteen other soldiers had been killed. The ten survivors fled to the colony. Negotiations for peace failed, and on the Fourth of July, the governor and a number of officers tried to escape to a vessel, the *Maria de Molina*, lying offshore. They were killed, and the colony was thoroughly blockaded.

Relief for the Spanish arrived in September and October, 1887. First, the *San Quintin* returned with Rev. Doane and provisions aboard. His land claim had been upheld, influenced by the American Consul in the Philippines. By October 29, three warships had arrived: the *Dezo* and the *Manila* in addition to the *San Quintin*. A new governor, Don Luis Cardarso, had also arrived with two hundred soldiers and two artillery batteries.

The new governor seemed to have made an honest effort to establish peace. He threatened no reprisals, and offered full pardons if the people of Nett and Sokehs would convert to Catholicism. He also stipulated that looted valuables should be returned, weapons turned in, and the men responsible for killing the governor surrendered. Some accommodation was reached on all conditions. However, a chief was believed to have been the actual killer of the governor. Consequently, two men of lesser traditional status volunteered themselves to be punished in his place. The two men were subsequently tried, convicted, and hanged by the Spanish in Manila.

Several years of cold war followed the arrival of the new governor. During this time, the Nahnmwarki of Kitti allowed the Spanish to build a Catholic church at Wone. Also, *Fort Alphonse XIII* was completed in Kolonia. Both Catholic and

Protestant missions were located outside of its limits. To protect the colony, a wall was built, the remains of which are very evident today. At that time, however, a ditch facing Sokehs fronted the wall and a large field of fire was cleared for protection.

The uneasy peace was again shattered in 1890 when the Spanish attempted to increase their influence. The governor planned a road from the Catholic mission in Kitti through Wone, Madolenihmw, U and Nett to Kolonia. The Spanish attempted to build a mission station at Oa in Madolenihmw, directly in front of the Protestant mission station. On June 25th a group of Pohnpeians attacked the Catholic project and killed some thirty-five soldiers in the ensuing battle. More would have been killed had it not been for Henry Nanpei, the most prominent Pohnpeian of his time. Nanpei rescued a number of Catholic workers and two priests and took them to the Protestant girls' school in Oa. Other survivors escaped to Kolonia and then returned to attack on a steam launch, only to be repulsed.

The Spanish troops proved to be quite ineffectual against Pohnpeians. At Sapwalapw, where Pohnpeians built defenses in the hills, the Spanish sent naval units whose range of guns only reached their own infantry ashore. In an assault on Kitamw in Madolenihmw, five hundred Spanish infantry attacked concealed Pohnpeians. After the battle, 118 Spanish soldiers were dead and eighty-five wounded.

Governor Cardarso blamed the latest outbreak of violence on the influence of Protestant missionaries, rather than on attempts by his administration to extend their control. Most of the Protestant missionaries on Pohnpei at the time were Americans. As one of his last acts before being relieved of his duties, the governor ordered all American missionaries expelled from the island on November 2, 1890. The Americans left for Mokil and Kosrae on the U.S.S. *Alliance*, which had been sent to investigate complaints of Spanish treatment of Americans.

A series of governors followed Cardarso, as Catholicism made increasing inroads throughout the decade of the 1890's.

With the most prominent Protestant clergymen expelled, conversion to the new religion met less opposition. Also, Catholics were more tolerant of drinking sakau and smoking than Protestant pastors, and this appealed to a number of Pohnpeians. Nett, Sokehs, and particularly the Awak section of U were becoming centers of support for Catholicism, while the southern kingdoms remained firmly Protestant.

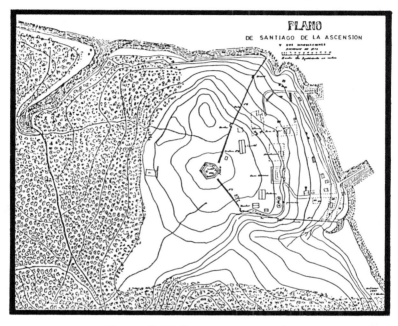

Spanish Kolonia (circa, 1890)

The hostilities of 1898-1899 were purportedly for religious reasons. However, local rivalries and politics were certainly influential in causing the bloodshed. As in previous uprisings, a single event or incident sparked the conflict.

A chief from Catholic Awak was acquitted of murdering a Protestant from the island of Mwand. At the time, a religious zealot, William of Mwand, was an influential Protestant pastor and teacher. Not only did William cry for revenge, but he incited his followers to drive out the Catholics once and for all.

In March, 1898, a force of men from Mwand and Madole-nihmw assembled to attack Awak, primarily to destroy the Catholic mission there. Initially the men of Awak remained on the defensive when attacked, but later fought a three-hour sea battle in the lagoon, forcing the attackers to withdraw. The reaction of the Spanish administration was to send the cruiser *Quiros* to restore order, and to immediately arrest Henry Nanpei whom they believed had incited the rebellion. Nanpei pleaded guilty to the charges and said he would not encourage rebellion in the future, and then was, ironically, released from custody.

On April 16th, a week before the beginning of the Spanish-American War, nine hundred men from Mwand, U, Kitti, and Madolenihmw assembled to again attack Awak. The following day some five hundred men from Nett and Sokehs reinforced the beleaguered force on Awak, along with the warship *Quiros*. On April 20th, the Awak forces attacked and drove back the enemy.

The governor again arrested the influential Nanpei after several chiefs who supported the administration signed a declaration accusing him of being the "sole mischief-maker" involved in the conflict. By then, however, Santiago de Cuba, where the Spanish fleet was sunk by Americans, determined the fate of Santiago, Pohnpei. The governor chose to hide his warships from potential American attack, and so the *Quiros* and the recently arrived *Villalobos* were removed from the exposed area of Awak.

Tensions reached their height at the beginning of 1899. The ammunition of the pro-Spanish forces was being depleted while that of the attackers was being replenished by ships calling at Pohnpei. Finally, on February 8th, the *Villalobos* came out of hiding and hostilities subsided. In the peace negotiations that followed, Henry Nanpei was once again released from confinement, with his prestige considerably enhanced.

On the 31st of May, 1899, the *Espana* arrived on the island flying the American flag and bringing the interim governor, Don Ricardo de Castro. She also brought with her an end to the Spanish period on Pohnpei.

Despite violence and conflict, the Spanish left very little impression on the minds of Pohnpeians. Aside from sponsoring Catholicism, the Spanish had no policy or program, and did not attempt to interfere in local affairs. Their armed forces, mainly from the Philippines, were held in contempt by Pohnpeian warriors, and Spanish influence was limited to the town of Santiago (Kolonia). Historians regard the Spanish Period as the last era of actual Pohnpeian traditional rule in which native institutions were allowed to continue untouched and unchanged.

German Period
(1899-1914)

German Acquisition of Micronesia, 1899
German Policy on Pohnpei
Typhoon, 1905
Prelude to the Sokehs Rebellion, 1909
Sokehs Rebellion and Aftermath, 1910-11
Land Reform, 1912
End of German Rule on Pohnpei, 1914

Spain's Micronesian possessions were liquidated by treaty following the Spanish-American War. The United States annexed Guam, and Germany purchased the remainder of the Marianas, the Marshalls, and the Caroline Islands for 17,500 German marks (about $4,250,000 at the time). Thus, the second foreign flag in less than fourteen years was raised on Pohnpei on October 12, 1899. For a few million dollars, Germany had gained political and economic control over a vast area of the Western Pacific, larger than that of the continental United States. Administrative stations were then established at Saipan, Palau, Yap, Truk, and Jaluit as well as Pohnpei.

Germany's primary interests in her island possessions were to develop sources of raw materials and as markets for German goods. Initially, Pohnpeian institutions were left to themselves unless they obstructed German policy of social and economic reform. American missionaries expelled by the Spanish were encouraged to return, and the administration attempted to treat Protestants and Catholics with an even hand.

For economic reform to succeed, a number of social changes were instituted by the District Administrator, Dr. Albert Hahl. The chiefs of the five kingdoms were brought together and encouraged to cease local warfare, to which they agreed. They were also asked to influence their people to surrender all arms and ammunition, but this request had mixed results. The administration closed the brothels that were allowed to flourish under the Spanish, and stipulated that no alcoholic beverages be sold or traded to Pohnpeians. As a show of confidence and friendship, the Germans tore down many of the fortifications constructed by the Spanish and eliminated the armed guards at the entrance of the administrative compound.

The first nine years of the new century was a period of relative tranquility when compared with the previous decade. The Catholic-Protestant conflict simmered, however. Under District Administrator Viktor Berg, who replaced Dr. Hahl in 1901, a directive was issued stating that German be the only foreign language taught in the schools. This, of course, was an advantage for the German Catholic Capuchin missionaries and a disadvantage for the American Protestants. Also, Catholic moves to expand in U and Madolenihmw were resented by Protestants in those areas.

Attempts by Berg to disarm the Pohnpeians had little success. The owners of firearms realized that the value of their Remingtons and Winchesters was far more than the forty dollar purchase price of the rifles. An act of God, or rather nature, helped the administration acquire Pohnpeian weapons, however. On April 20, 1905, the most devastating typhoon in human memory smashed Pohnpei, and the outer islands of Mokil and Pingelap. All breadfruit and banana plants were destroyed, and public and private losses were estimated at $135,000. There was an alarming scarcity of foodstuffs, and the economic potential of Pohnpei was set back years by the disaster. About 250 people died or were seriously injured and nearly all livestock were killed. To encourage the surrender of weapons and cartridges, the administration offered to exchange government food stores that had survived the typhoon for weapons and ammunition. District Administrator Berg offered thirty-five marks per weapon, or rice and tinned meat of higher value. Initially, only old rifles and those in poor condition were offered for exchange. As the food shortage became more acute, however, rifles in prime condition were exchanged. By July of 1906, nearly four thousand cartridges and 545 rifles were in government hands, about one weapon for every three males on the island. As was discovered in the Sokehs Rebellion at the end of the decade, all of the rifles and cartridges in private hands were not exchanged.

Besides accumulating weapons, another result of the typhoon was a redistribution of the outer island population by moving a number of Mokilese and Pingelapese to Pohnpei for resettlement. At the time, the population of Pohnpei was estimated to be around 3,300.

Viktor Berg died on Pohnpei, and his death is still remembered by very old Pohnpeians. On April 29, 1907, the district administrator visited the sacred ruins of Nan Madol to dig for the bones of ancient rulers. Although he had been warned not to, Berg exhumed a number of large bones from the burial site. The next day he was dead. The government said Berg died of heat exhaustion; the Pohnpeians say it was retribution by the spirits.

A stiffening of German policy came with the arrival of a new district administrator, George Fritz, in April, 1908. Fritz came to Pohnpei after nine years service in the then-pacified Mariana Islands. Among the new governor's directives were

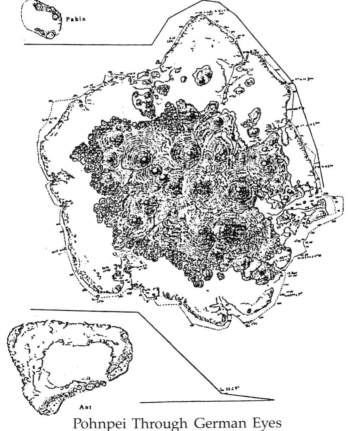

Pohnpei Through German Eyes
1910

to end tribute payments to chiefs in order to encourage commercial agriculture, and a requirement that all able-bodied men between the ages of sixteen and forty-five contribute fifteen days of labor on public projects each year. Also, planting of coconut trees was to be planned and regulated to ensure abundant copra production.

Mounting tension occurred during the administration of Fritz, and he often had to revert to threats or a show of force to avoid Pohnpeian violence. Quite suddenly, Fritz was transferred to Yap. In October, 1909, Gustav Boeder arrived as the new district administrator, and the prelude to the Sokehs Rebellion.

Boeder had served in German East Africa, and was no stranger to violence in protectorates, having experienced a rebellion in Tanganyika. The new district administrator had little regard for Pohnpeians. He was authoritarian, demanding, and impatient, qualities that certainly would not endear him to Pohnpeians, or to anyone else.

The Sokehs Rebellion was the last armed uprising by Pohnpeians against foreign rule. John L. Fischer notes in *The Eastern Carolines*, "It is hard to assess the degree to which the various Pohnpeian leaders were motivated by resentment of foreign rule, opposition to the road building program, the sectarian religious struggle, and indigenous political feuds stemming from olden times." Even traditional beliefs had their influence. The most sacred location at historic Nan Madol is **Pahn Kadira**, which has corners symbolizing various districts of Pohnpei. If any corner fell or crumbled, it meant that the particular area that it symbolized would be destroyed. In 1910, the corner representing Sokehs, Pwapwalik, crumbled, and so Sokehs had to die. Like uprisings in previous years, the violence was sparked by a single event.

On April 6, 1910, the district administrator ordered work to begin on a five-meter wide road around Sokehs, which he claimed had been "willingly advanced by the people who were drafted for compulsory work." The road on Sokehs was to join a more ambitious project, a road completely around Pohnpei. There was much dissatisfaction about the forced labor, however, and as early as four months before the actual uprising, an attack against the government had been planned. This plan became known to the administration and was never carried out.

Under Boeder, corporal punishment was introduced for disobedience, lying, and "unashamed conduct toward whites," among other offenses. The first beating was administered to Eliu Santos of Kitti in September. Also, more restricting rules for confined prisoners were instituted, including shaving a prisoner's head, a grave insult in Pohnpeian custom. Shortly before the rebellion, this sentence was carried out for the first time on a man accused of lying. Feelings intensified when a man from Sokehs, Lehdeleng, was punished with a beating, unjustly according to the Pohnpeians. Lehdeleng had allegedly been insubordinate to a German labor overseer named Hollborn, and was given ten strokes with a wire-lined rubber hose, well laid on by a Melanesian soldier. The shock waves from the beating were felt throughout Sokehs. According to Peter T. Hempenstall in *Pacific Islands Under German Rule*, Boeder was brutal, insensitive, inconsistent in behavior, and felt beatings were legitimate punishment. The district administrator "had treated Lehdeleng like an animal in a culture where dignity and strength, courage and patience were the touchstones of manhood." And area pride was strong. The people of Sokehs considered themselves foremost among Pohnpeians. They were the first to rise against the Spanish in 1887 and felt superior to interlopers of any language. Their island isolation was guarded jealously and reforms of the Spanish and German administrations were resisted in order to retain their independence.

After the departure of the only large vessel in the harbor, the steamer *Germania*, no ship was due to arrive on Pohnpei for the next seven weeks. On October 18th the labor force on Sokehs, led by a popular chief, Soumatau, stopped work and the district administrator was informed. Boeder, refusing a police escort, crossed the channel to Sokehs, arriving around 3:30 p.m. He was accompanied by his secretary,

Brauckmann, two servants, and a five-man boat crew. Hardly had Boeder and Brauckmann left the dock area when they were cut down by rifle fire. The district administrator was shot twice in the stomach, and then killed by Soumatau with a bullet in the head. The secretary was shot three times and then stabbed to death. Two German labor overseers, Hollborn and Haeffner, were also killed when they attempted to escape, as were all others in the boat except one.

When news of the killings reached Kolonia, the senior administrator, Dr. Max Girschner took command. Girschner had lived on Pohnpei for ten years and had personality traits almost opposite of those of his superior, Boeder. He was respected, and appreciated for his medical skill. (Actually, Girschner could easily have been slain while enroute to Sokehs to check on the rebellion.) Troops at his initial disposal consisted of fifty police/soldiers against an estimated 250 insurgents on Sokehs armed with dynamite and fuses and some ninety rifles and pistols.

Dr. Girschner was well aware that he must rely on Pohnpeians for survival of the German colony, so he immediately sent messages to the chiefs of Nett, U, Awak, Madolenihmw, and Kitti with pleas for assistance. For the Germans, the response was gratifying. Nearly five hundred men arrived to support the government. Each man was then armed with a machete, and every fifteenth with a rifle. Until reinforcements arrived, the government hoped to contain the enemy on Sokehs, send out reconnaissance patrols, and tempt the insurgents to exhaust their ammunition, a rather unappealing assignment.

Kolonia was effectively blockaded. The insurgents had freedom of movement on Sokehs Island and on the main island in the less-populated Palikir area. The *Germania* returned as scheduled on November 26th, remained at Pohnpei for two hours, and then sailed to Rabaul for reinforcements. When she returned again on December 5th, the *Germania* brought sixty-eight Melanesian troops. Shortly afterward, the steamer *Siar* arrived on December 13th with seventy black troops, followed by the warships S.M.S. *Cormoran* on

December 20th and S.M.S. *Emden* and S.M.S. *Nurnberg* on January 10th, 1911, with a landing corps.

January 10th was also the day that the channel dividing Sokehs from the main island was closed by government troops. On the 13th of January, strongpoints and known rebel positions on Sokehs were shelled continuously by the three German warships from 7:45 to 9:00 a.m. The nine hundred foot heights of Sokehs Island were assaulted on the relatively weak western slope. The initial attack consisted of a hundred Melanesian troops led by German officers. By 9:00 p.m. the summit was secured with the help of reinforcements.

Government casualties were two Melanesians killed and nine wounded, and three Germans killed and seven wounded, remarkably light in the nearly impassable terrain. The bodies of only two defenders were found, most having slipped through to the mainland at Palikir. Thirty men and eighty-four women and children were found on Sokehs Island.

The assault on Sokehs broke the back of the rebellion, but fighting continued for another month. On January 26th, a rebuilt fort left from the Spanish times at Nan Kiop was assaulted, resulting in heavy government losses. Resistance became disorganized as insurgents scattered in small groups. Lack of food, depleting ammunition, and combat fatigue caused the fighting to end. By February 11th, only thirty men remained at large. On February 13th, Soumatau surrendered, followed by another leader, Chief Samuel, three days later. Finally, on February 23rd, the government was in complete control once again, four months and six days after the death of District Administrator Boeder.

In the aftermath of the rebellion, retribution by the German government was severe. Seventeen men who were accused of taking part in the slaying of Boeder and his party were sentenced to death by a firing squad. Nearly the entire population of Sokehs and Palikir, 426 people, had their lands confiscated and were exiled initially to Yap and then to Palau. All healthy young men—a total of 107—were sent to work in the mines of the Deutsche Sudsee-Phosphat-Aktein-Gesell-

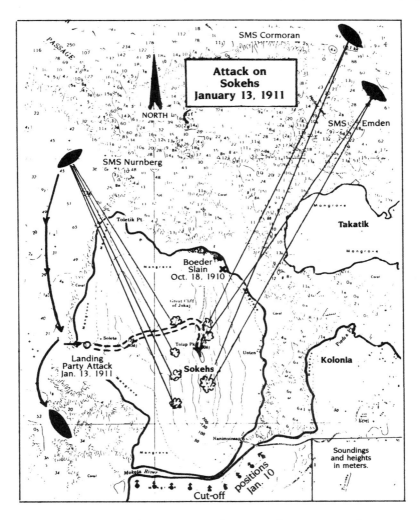

Attack on
Sokehs
January 13, 1911

SMS Cormoran

SMS Emden

SMS Nurnberg

NORTH

PASSAGE

Toletik Pt

Takatik

Boeder
Slain
Oct. 18, 1910

Great Chff
of Jokaj

Tolap Pt

Uoten

Landing
Party Attack
Jan. 13, 1911

Sokehs

Kolonia

Nanimuinen

Soundings
and heights
in meters.

Mokela River

Cut-off

positions
Jan. 10

schaft company. Their wages of ten marks per month were
turned over to an "uprising fund." They were not to return
to their native land until the end of the decade, landless and
destitute.

A new district administrator, Dr. Heinrick Kersting,
replaced the slain Boeder at the height of the Sokehs conflict and directed military operations. He also presided over
the court proceedings which followed the end of hostilities.

Unlike his predecessor, Kersting had no general dislike of Pohnpeians. He managed to avoid taking sides in any Catholic-Protestant controversy and never resorted to threats or violence.

Under Kersting, the land confiscated on Sokehs was redistributed. Land was allocated to families from Mokil, Pingelap, and Ngatik who were victims of the severe typhoon in 1905, and to Mortlockese immigrants who suffered through an equally devastating typhoon in 1907. Three parcels of land were also awarded to Pohnpeians who had significantly assisted the government during the crisis. In all, about 1,250 people were resettled on Sokehs and adjacent Palikir.

Older Pohnpeians interviewed by William R. Bascom in 1946 had warm feelings in retrospect for the Germans and resentment for the pride of the Sokehs people. Dr. Girschner and district administrators Hahl and Kersting were particularly admired. Pohnpeians appreciated German courtesy, neatness in dress and appearance, and versatility in accomplishments — including the road building program that ignited the insurrection.

The most significant and lasting influence of the colonial periods of Spain, German, and even Japan took place between 1912 and 1914. Land reform initiated by Kersting assured private and continuous ownership of land by individual Pohnpeians in all municipalities, and effectively took land control out of the hands of the traditional leaders. German motives for land reform were not entirely altruistic, however. By dividing the land, the government hoped to increase productivity by allowing more farmers to work the land, and also to curtail the power and influence of the traditional leaders. Between 1912 and the end of the German rule in 1914, nearly a thousand (poorly surveyed) parcels of land were distributed to a Pohnpeian population of about four thousand people. The German Land Title Code published in both German and Pohnpeian specified the following:

1. Ownership is permanent and can be lost only by death or exile.

2. Land will not be divided in an inheritance, and will be inherited by the next entitled male relative.
3. Land will not be given away by a will or testament.
4. All male relatives without property can live on and use the land of the deed holder.
5. Sale, giving away, or renting land is not allowed unless approved by the government.
6. The government has the right of eminent domain without remuneration.
7. All land not deeded to individuals belongs to the government.
8. Food and labor must be donated annually to the traditional leaders as partial compensation for the land.
9. Disobedience of legitimate requests by a traditional leader is punishable by five days of forced labor.

To stimulate copra production, ten coconut trees per month were required to be planted on each farmstead, along with other crops thought to be of commercial value by the administration.

Future colonial administrations were to adjust the German Land Title Code—the Japanese allowed inheritance to include females, and foreign nationals to own land, and the Americans allowed inheritance by adopted children and also through a will or testament. The concept of private ownership of land by individuals, however, initiated by the German administration, has evolved into a most cherished concept to all Pohnpeians.

The end of the Spanish Period on Pohnpei arrived with a single Spanish vessel flying the American flag in May, 1899. The end of the German Period on Pohnpei arrived with a squadron of six warships flying the Japanese flag on October 7, 1914.

(A footnote to the period: Most records of the German times are, surprisingly, found at the Australian National University at Canberra. Pohnpei was ultimately administered by the Germans from Rabaul where their records from all of Micronesia were centered. When Japan occupied Micronesia in 1914, Australia occupied Rabaul and shipped

all German records and documents to the Australian university, where they remain today.)

Japanese Period (1914-1945)

Japanese Annexation of Pohnpei, 1914
League of Nations Mandate, 1920
Japanese Development of Pohnpei, 1921-36
Education under the Japanese
Prelude to War, 1936-41
World War II on Pohnpei, 1941-45
Japanese Surrender of Pohnpei, 1945

The rising sun of Japan was the third foreign flag to fly over Pohnpei in three decades, and Japan's tenure on the island was equal to the total of Spain's and Germany's combined. The year 1914, however, was not the first incursion of Japanese on the island. As early as 1890, a branch of the Nanyo Shokai trading company was operating on Pohnpei. All Japanese were expelled by the German government for selling firearms and spirits to Pohnpeians in 1899. Since Japan was allied with Great Britain, France, and the United States in World War I, no substantial fleet in the Pacific would challenge her occupation of Micronesia. Two German warships at Pohnpei, the *Gneisenau* and the *Scharnhorst* had earlier left to seek glory elsewhere, with several Pohnpeian crew members aboard, incidentally.

The original bamboo curtain closed on Micronesia immediately. Deported traders and missionaries reported a buildup of coaling stations and temporary naval facilities, particulary in Truk. Even Japan's allies were excluded as the British steamer *Mawatta* was turned away from the Marshalls as early as 1916. Military administration continued until Japanese civilians took over after the war.

Japan obtained legal control of Micronesia in the Versaille Peace Conference in 1920, two years after Germany's surrender. Among the conditions of the League of Nations Mandate were that Japan must allow missionary activity and must not fortify the islands. Consequently, Japan established and subsidized Congregational Protestant missions on Pohnpei in 1920, and in 1921 allowed Spanish Catholic Jesuits to assume the work of the expelled German Capuchin priests. In 1920, Japan also began a withdrawal of military forces that was completed in 1922. Japan's original motives in taking control of Micronesia were to have an area available for resettlement of a growing population, and supply products needed for her economy. Later, the paramount reasons were to provide a defensive buffer for her home islands, and a springboard for further conquest.

The Japanese administration recognized most German land acquisitions and took more Pohnpeian lands, some by purchase and others by expropriation. Land acquisitions increased in the late 1930's with approaching World War II by purchases and by eminent domain acquisitions for military purposes.

To develop Pohnpei economically, the Japanese concentrated on fishing and agriculture in the years between 1921 and 1937. The largest single industry was processing and exporting dried bonito, the only fish exported in any real quantity to Japan, incidentally. All fishing by non-

Bonito (Skipjack)

Micronesians was licensed and supervised; the Japanese fishing activities neither helped nor hindered local fisherman. The government offered subsidies for purchase of marine engines, boats and equipment to any group of expatriates willing to enter the industry. Consequently, fishing on Pohnpei actually consisted of many small groups whose catches were sold to several larger companies for processing and export. The average yearly catch of tuna off of Pohnpei between 1930 and 1940 was 3,617,000 pounds, and twenty-six million pounds annually in all of the mandated islands of Micronesia.

To stimulate agricultural production, new facilities, built on the site of a former German agricultural station, were constructed in 1926. This area was called the Tropical Industries Research Institute, Ponape Branch. (The building that housed the institute is one of the three in Kolonia to survive the bombing and naval gunfire of World War II.) The institute was staffed with trained experts, many from imperial universities, and contained departments of livestock and forestry as well as agriculture.

Starch production, originally from arrowroot and sweet potatoes, was Japan's second largest industry on Pohnpei. By the late 1930's, tapioca had replaced the sweet potato fields and about 1,300 acres were under cultivation. In 1938, the starch acreage was converted to sugar production.

Copra, not as abundant on Pohnpei as on the atolls of the Marshall Islands, was an important export crop which brought growers about 660,000 yen annually. Some three thousand tons of copra were exported each year before World War II.

The Japanese made Pohnpei almost entirely self-supporting in produce. Among the crops developed were pumpkins, squash, pineapples, papaya, sugar cane, watermelon, onions, cucumbers, beans, rice, egg plant, and coffee. Foods introduced were tomatoes, green peppers, okra, spinach, cabbage, lettuce, parsley, water cress, turnips, radishes, carrots, peas, peanuts, and soy beans. The government subsidized truck gardens as an incentive, and many were grown in the Palikir area.

The South Seas Trading Company—Nanyo Boeki Kaisha —dominated the export of copra until the beginning of World War II, and also had an interest in the import trade. Exports included sugar and pineapples, medical plants, wood for geta shoes or rayon, hibiscus bast, dried fish, copra for making candy, coir, mangrove bark and trochus shell. With the coming of the war, local production was converted to supply local Japanese needs. Coconuts provided oil and soap, sugar was used for alcohol, ivory nuts for buttons, bark for paper pulp. Cigarettes were manufactured, cloth was woven, salt produced, and a liquor known as "shochu" was concocted.

Besides the Tropical Industries Research Institute, the Japanese developed, planted, and supervised the growth of coconut trees, sweet potatoes, vegetables, and rice on a 9,900-acre plot of land. In Madolenihmw, a plant to process manioc flour and tapioca was built. A sugar mill completed shortly before the war to process locally-grown cane for export was converted to alcohol production to meet military needs. In 1936, the Nanpil Dam to supply power for Kolonia was completed. Prospecting also took place on the island. For about eight months in 1937-38, the Japanese South Sea Aluminum Mining Company prospected for gold and bauxite and set up a laboratory to test samples. Small quantities of gold were discovered, but the deposits were too small to be commercially viable.

Medical facilities provided by the Japanese were not equaled until the third decade of the American administration on the island. In the ten years between 1927 and 1937, over 14,000 patients were treated at a large Japanese hospital. Expenses were nominal. Two dentists provided gold teeth at $2.50 each.

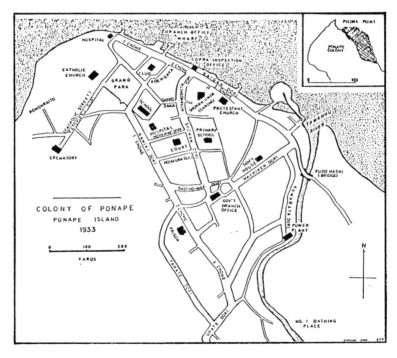

Japanese Kolonia
1933

If you meet Pohnpeians aged fifty to sixty-five, chances are they attended a Japanese elementary school. If they happen to be community leaders, they might even have visited Japan on a government-subsidized tour. Pohnpeian children aged eight years and older were offered the opportunity for three years of study at one of six elementary schools. The school year was forty-eight weeks in length, six days per week, and half of the regular course consisted of learning the Japanese language. The other half emphasized arithmetic, physical education, singing, and manual work or housekeeping. For the brighter students, a two-year supplementary course was offered. Japanese pupils on Pohnpei attended a six-year regular course with two additional supplementary years. In 1935, attendance at a government school became mandatory for all pupils within walking distance of a school, and by 1937, nearly seventy percent of the eligible Pohnpeian children were attending. In the thirty-one years of the Japanese Period, however, only three Pohnpeians received schooling in Japan.

As with previous administrations, events elsewhere influenced activities on Pohnpei. Because of criticism by the League of Nations of her incursion in Manchuria, Japan announced her intention to withdraw from the League as early as 1933. Japan actually withdrew in 1935, but continued to send annual reports on Micronesia until 1938. However, in 1936, she closed Micronesia to all but Japanese shipping, and military needs took precedent on Pohnpei in all activities. Economic development ceased with the beginning of Japan's "China War" on July 7, 1937, unless it was directly related to military purposes. Mandatory land sales for military facilities were initiated, and the first priority on Pohnpei was the building of air and fuel installations. More military construction took place between 1939 and 1941 than in all of the previous years of the Japanese administration. On the eve of World War II, Japanese nationals outnumbered Micronesians on Pohnpei by about two and a half to one. At the time, there were two Belgian families on the island and a Czechoslovakian. By a quirk of political fate, the Belgians were interned as enemy aliens and the Czech was allowed his freedom. Other foreigners were three Spanish Catholic priests, six lay brothers, and twelve nuns. Since Spain was neutral in World War II, the Catholic church group was allowed to continue working in their five parish areas. (The seven Protestant places of worship were in the hands of Micronesians and a Japanese minister.)

World War II in the Pacific began when Japanese carrier-based aircraft attacked and damaged or sunk most of the U.S. Pacific fleet at Pearl Harbor on December 7, 1941. For Pohnpeians, however, either of two dates marked the beginning of the conflict rather than Pearl Harbor Day: July 7, 1937, the beginning of Japan's "China War" causing the military garrison on Pohnpei to be massively increased; and February 10 to 20, 1944 when Kolonia was destroyed by air raids that were to continue until mid-1945. Neutralizing Micronesia in the war took three and a half years and 32,395 American casualties.

Pohnpeians remember the war as a time of hardship, especially the last year and a half. There were shortages of food, and especially clothing, because imports for civilians ceased. Also, there was a decrease in the birth rate when families were separated by conscription for forced labor, and inadequate medical care. Nearly two hundred laborers were sent to other islands. One hundred and seventy were returned from Kosrae in October, 1945. Ten Pohnpeian workers were found in Truk and ten more in Palau. Twenty Pohnpeians were drafted into the Japanese army in July, 1942, to serve in Rabaul. Two returned in September, 1943, twelve were killed, and five were taken prisoner. One of the original number is unaccounted for.

Pohnpei's importance in the war varied with the changing strategic aims of the allies. Originally, the island was high on the hit list of the Joint Chiefs of Staff. At the Quadrant Conference in Quebec in August, 1943, a tentative plan called for offensive thrusts from the Gilbert Islands, through the Marshalls and Kosrae to Pohnpei. The offensive would then continue through the central Carolines, including Truk, to the Mariana Islands and Palau. The assault on Pohnpei was scheduled for May 1, 1944.

Several factors contributed to a decision to bypass Pohnpei. From campaigns in the Gilberts and the Marshalls it was learned that fast carrier forces could seal off enemy islands if landbased aircraft could be neutralized. In February, 1944, the Joint Chiefs of Staff agreed to let Pohnpei be bypassed because the island had too much rainfall for a major air base and was not worth the price of a large scale amphibious landing.

Pohnpei's physical characteristics made the island a natural defensive position, but also provided limited offensive potential. Rain, mangrove swamps, sharp, shallow coral reefs and mountainous terrain made the island a U.S. Marine infantryman's nightmare. However, the same features prevented construction of large airfields and facilities for deep-water anchorages for naval vessels. The eight thousand defenders, digging and constructing fortifications daily for the three and a half years of the war, not to mention the forced Micronesian laborers, constructed defenses that by any standards were formidable.

Defensive weapons on Pohnpei were not excessive in number, but were strategically placed to inflict maximum destruction on an attacking force. There were eight six-inch British Armstrong Whitworth rifles in naval mounts cleverly concealed. Of these, four covered Madolenihmw Harbor from atop a hill, two were on a two thousand foot hill covering U, one was high on Langar covering approaches to Kolonia, and one was located some nine hundred feet up on Sokehs Island. Also on Sokehs were twin 127 mm. naval mounts. There were ten 80 mm. high and low angle guns, six of which protected Kolonia and four placed to cover Madolenihmw Harbor. All of these batteries were separate and concealed in fortifications made of reinforced concrete. Four to ten mines were placed at every harbor entrance except Kolonia.

The mystery of how massive basalt stones were moved by human effort in constructing Nan Madol can be solved when considering how large weapons were moved by

Pohnpeian labor. Extremely heavy artillery pieces were carried long distances on shallow-water craft between dangerous reefs. They were then moved through thick jungle up steep hills to positions carved in the ridges. A year of work by a daily average of sixteen men was required to install twin mounts on Sokehs. The six-inch British Armstrong Whitworth rifles took seven months to place using twenty-four men daily. A gun on Langar took nine months to install, and another atop a hill 1,970 feet in U took fifty-five men almost eight months to position.

A number of defensive structures built during the war can still be seen today. Numerous blockhouses, shelters, and gun emplacements remain, and several skeletons of destroyed aircraft hangars can still be located. The most evident destruction is the missing Catholic church, where only a bell tower remains. The church, built by German Capuchin fathers from 1909 to 1914, was dismantled and used for construction materials and fortifications. To provide equal desecration, the Congregational church was used for a barracks and warehouse. Two hundred feet of its concrete floor were removed to build an air-raid shelter elsewhere. (It is interesting that the Catholic bell tower and the Protestant church were two of only three large structures that remained standing in Kolonia at the end of the war.)

Two airstrips for fighter planes were located on the island, one at Nan Pohn Mal and the other at Palikir. The Nan Pohn Mal field with a hangar was built before the war and was too small to accommodate all but the slowest of planes. The Palikir strip was built in just sixteen days during the war by one hundred Japanese naval construction workers and 820 Pohnpeians. Only one takeoff and landing was ever made from the airstrip. After its completion, American bombs with delayed action fuses made operations impossible.

Pohnpei's only real offensive facility was on historic Langar in Pohnpei Harbor. There, a small but complete seaplane base was used until neutralized in late February, 1944, by allied bombers. It contained a hangar with a repair shop, a seaplane ramp and a plane parking space. The installation had large underground fuel storage tanks of 3,300-ton capacity, and also six water tanks of one thousand gallons each. On February 12, 1944, six four-engine flying boats from Saipan staged through the Langar facility enroute to a high-level bombing raid on Roi Namur at Kawjalein Atoll. Very heavy damage was inflicted, and the raid caused more American dead and wounded from a bombing attack on a land target than any action since Pearl Harbor.

The war exploded onto Pohnpei in mid-February, 1944. Allied forces were scheduled to assault Eniwetok in the Marshall Islands, and the Japanese raid on Roi Namur showed that Pohnpei could be a link in an offensive chain that reached to intended Allied objectives. Pohnpei was 382 miles from Truk, 583 air miles from Kwajalein and only 363 from Eniwetok.

Two days before the amphibious landing on Eniwetok, forty-two B-24 *Liberator* bombers of the VII Air Force based on Tarawa, struck Pohnpei on February 15th, then bombers struck again on February 17th and again on February 20th. Two more attacks with incendiary bombs occurred on February 22nd and 26th. These aircraft, flying nine hundred miles each way, dropped 118 tons of high explosive and six thousand incendiary bombs. The areas hardest hit were Langar, Kolonia, and the airstrips at Nan Pohn Mal and Palikir. Pohnpeian casualties were notably light throughout the action because of the Japanese propensity for secrecy which kept most Micronesians away from military installations. In less than two weeks Pohnpei was effectively taken out of the war. All three air facilities were destroyed and the town of Kolonia was nearly leveled. (Shortly before the bombings, a large quantity of ammunition had arrived on Pohnpei. For temporary concealment the explosives were stored under Japanese residences in Kolonia, and under tarpaulins on an athletic field opposite the present location of the Community College of Micronesia. Ammunition was still being dug up from the field in 1988).

Air raids continued on Pohnpei throughout 1944. On March 28th, U.S. Marine fighter aircraft escorting bombers encountered twelve Japanese planes. They shot down eight and destroyed another on the ground. Other missions taking place over Pohnpei throughout the year encountered no enemy planes.

American submarine action accounted for the sinking of the freighter *Okitsu Maru* and its destroyer escort *Suzukaze* sixty miles north of Pohnpei on January 25, 1944 with the loss of 144 lives. More critical to Japan's defense, however, was the loss of construction equipment vital for aircraft runway building and maintenance. With the *Okitsu Maru* went down fifty trucks, ten tractors, five bulldozers, five large generators, ten steamrollers, and six hundred tons of cement.

Pohnpei received its most punishing attack on May Day, 1944. Six battleships with escorts were stationed off of the northern coast of the island. The battleships were the U.S.S. *Iowa*, U.S.S. *Massachusetts*, U.S.S. *New Jersey*, U.S.S. *Alabama*, U.S.S. *North Carolina*, and the U.S.S. *South Carolina*. They shelled Langar, Kolonia, Palikir, and Nan Pohn Mal for seventy minutes, and then departed, having received no damage from Japanese fire.

As American action moved closer to the Japanese homeland in late 1944 and early 1945, Pohnpei fell into the backwaters of the war. After the intense air attacks of February, American raids followed set schedules for periods ranging from several days to several weeks. Fishermen were able to adjust activities to American raids and went to sea immediately after the planes left Pohnpei. There was actually a period of only a month or two when deep-sea fishing had to be completely abandoned because American planes were in the air continuously.

Of some 250 air strikes on Pohnpei during the war, only one American plane actually crashed on the island in condition for the remains of the dead aviators to be removed. The aircraft was shot down on February 6, 1945, a B-25 bomber of VMB 613, an army plane attached to a U.S. Marine squadron. The bomber carried a crew of six and crashed near the aircraft runway in the Palikir section of the island. (The tail of the plane and a possible Japanese memorial mark the site today.) The remains of the dead Americans had a remarkable sojourn enroute to their final resting place on American soil. The bodies were first buried at the crash site, later disinterred, and buried again in Kolonia where the state legislature stands today. After the war, if the standard procedure was followed, the remains were sent to Ulithi to be concentrated with other dead from actions in the Caroline Islands. From Ulithi in August, 1946, they were sent to Guam to be reinterred at Agat Cemetery, and later disinterred again and sent to Saipan for storage. Then, according to the Department of the Army Memorial Affairs Division, Final Disposition of World War II Dead, a last journey to their final burial in Punchbowl Cemetery in Hawaii.

World War II ended with the surrender of Japan to the Allies on August 15, 1945. However, the official surrender of Pohnpei did not take place until nearly a month later. When the Japanese commander was first contacted on September 6th, he was prepared to surrender. A request was made that the garrison not be held captive for the sake of honor, and that food be provided to the outer islands. It was also noted that there were four repaired docks that were usable and a runway for fighter aircraft that was serviceable. Cases of spinal meningitis were reported.

For the fourth time in less than a century, Pohnpei was surrendered to a foreign power because of events that happened elsewhere. In 1885 it was because of a decision of Pope Leo XIII in Rome; in 1899 it was because of the defeat of the Spanish fleet at Cuba; in 1918 it was because of the loss of a European war by Germany; and in 1945 it was because of two atomic bombs dropped on Japan by American B-29 bombers.

American Period
(1945-Present)

Lt. Gen. Masao Watanabe officially surrendered Pohnpei aboard the destroyer U.S.S. *Hyman* on September 11, 1945. Six days later American officers arrived to set up a government headquarters. The surrendered island contained a military garrison of 5,805 army troops and 2,005 navy ratings, along with 5,679 Japanese/Okinawan civilians. At the end of the war there were 5,864 Micronesians on Pohnpei.

For the amount of bombing sustained, the number of fatalities during the war was relatively small. Japanese military deaths totalled 316, only a third of which resulted from American bombing. This figure, however, does not include 144 lives lost when the *Okitsu Maru* sunk off of Pohnpei while attempting to bring irreplaceable equipment for air facilities. Among Japanese civilians, about one hundred were killed from bombings and four hundred died from other causes. Of Micronesians, 187 died during the war, only eighteen of which were directly attributed to bombing. According to a report by Navy Captain Albert A. Momm, Commander of U.S. Forces on Pohnpei, dated 19 September, 1945, "The town (of Kolonia) had been totally destroyed by bombs and fire from Allied aircraft; the only original buildings standing were the weather station, Protestant church, and forward section of the Catholic church...the few roads are little more than rocky, mucky trails, deeply pitted in many places and little attempt was made to keep them repaired." One road led a mile and a half south of Kolonia into Nett and another five miles to Sokehs. There was a two mile road to Madolenihmw. The four mile road into U had been built during German times. All roads were deliberately neglected to minimize the effectiveness of a mechanized American invader, according to Momm. For Pohnpei's roads to disintegrate in the wet, tropical environment, however, *deliberate* neglect was really unnecessary.

Japanese soldiers and sailors were classified as Disarmed Military Personnel (DMP), but were not confined before repatriation. The most severe shortage was of clothing. Much of the food consumed by the Japanese community was supplied from their own gardens because the American forces were ill-prepared to feed 13,489 former enemy civilian and military personnel. Repatriation was begun almost immediately using Japanese vessels. Pohnpeian wives and children of Japanese and Okinawans were given a choice of staying on Pohnpei or leaving. Most chose to remain rather than face a very uncertain future in postwar Japan or Okinawa. By December, 1945, all repatriation was completed on Japanese bottoms and U.S. liberty ships. No Japanese military or civilians from Pohnpei were tried in the Pacific war trials held on Guam from 1946 to 1949, incidentally.

Another exodus, on a more happy note, was taking place at the same time. During the war the outer islands had been stripped of able-bodied young people for labor on Pohnpei. In November, 1945, 243 Pingelapese and 147 Mokilese were returned to their homes, to be followed a short time later by seventy-seven natives of Kapingamarangi.

Initial American military regulations published in English, Japanese, and Pohnpeian, emphasized human rights, and gave Pohnpeians freedom that they had never been allowed under Spanish, German, or Japanese administration. The eleven commandments according to the Commander of U.S. Forces on Pohnpei are summarized below:

1. Standard time shall be GMT minus twelve hours.
2. Civilians cannot be questioned, molested, or detained without cause.
3. Rights of civilians shall be strictly observed, and no punishment will be allowed without due process.
4. Authority of the police to administer summary judgment and punishment is suspended.
5. Property rights of all shall be strictly observed, and property shall not be taken without compensation.
6. Sale of property between Pohnpeians and Japanese is prohibited.
7. All work of Pohnpeians shall be on a voluntary basis and compulsory labor is strictly prohibited.
8. Collection of any taxes whatsoever shall be suspended.
9. Teaching of materials inimical to the interests of the Allied nations is prohibited.

10. Japanese military shall exercise no control over civilians.

11. All civilian and military records shall be preserved.

Liberation, however, did not bring prosperity to the island, and the next two years were a time of severe shortages in commodities and trained administrators. According to William R. Bascom writing in 1946:

> After the end of the war, the standard of living on Ponape was so far below prewar conditions for the poorest as well as the wealthiest Ponapeans, that there is no point in making a comparison. Not the most chauvinistic could claim that American occupation meant an improvement of conditions under the Japanese before the war.

No copra was produced and consequently there was little income. The average per capita income for all Pohnpeians at the beginning of 1946 was forty-five cents per month, or a cent and a half a day. A can of stew cost more than a day's wages and a carton of cigarettes, two and a half days. The American occupation was in its tenth month before the arrival of a supply of clothing. Progress in rehabilitation of Micronesians came to a standstill in mid-1946 because of a lack of effective military administrators and a very low priority on shipping to Pohnpei. In July, 1946, there was only a single military government officer on Pohnpei, and fifty-eight officers and 119 enlisted men to administer the nearly one hundred inhabited islands of the former Japanese mandate. It was not until the U.S. School of Naval Administration began to produce enough graduates in September, 1946, that conditions began to improve. Of ninety-nine graduating officers that month, fifteen were sent to Pohnpei.

Unlike previous foreign administrations, American efforts in Micronesia were directed toward the creation of democratic institutions and the establishment of schools. A change to missile weaponry decreased the strategic need for island bases. A Trusteeship Agreement between the United States and the United Nations Security Council was approved on April 2, 1947, and became effective on July 18th. It allowed the U.S. to administer the former mandated islands and to establish military bases. President Harry S. Truman delegated interim responsibility for civil administration of the islands to the Secretary of the Navy. Admiral Louis E. Denfeld was appointed the first high commissioner with headquarters 3,000 miles away from Micronesia in Hawaii. Forty years later this Agreement had become the longest lasting U.N. Trusteeship Agreement in history.

Administration of Pohnpei was transferred from the U.S. Department of the Navy to the Department of the Interior in July, 1951, although the Navy controlled the Northern Mariana Islands until as late as 1962. A former U.S. Senator, Elbert D. Thomas, was appointed the first civilian high commissioner of the Trust Territory of the Pacific Islands, with headquarters in Saipan.

The municipalities of Pohnpei first became legal entities in a directive of May 28, 1947 by which 116 were created throughout the Trust Territory. These municipal governments were more or less independent of the Trust Territory government, and were influenced on Pohnpei by traditional leaders. The chief executive of a municipal government is elected. A judge is appointed to each municipality by the Governor of Pohnpei, upon recommendation of the people of each municipality.

In 1952, Pohnpei received a charter and the first session of the Ponape Island Congress met. This body was replaced in May, 1963 by the Ponape District Legislature, a unicameral body with representatives from all islands in the Pohnpei district. Its precincts were defined largely along existing traditional political boundaries. It consisted of twenty members, elected to four-year terms and its legislative power covered all matters concerning the people of Pohnpei. In 1979, the

Ponape District Legislature became the Ponape State Legislature.

The first Congress of Micronesia was created on September 28, 1964. In January of the following year, two senators and two representatives were elected to this new body from Pohnpei district. The first regular session of the congress met on Saipan, July 12, 1965. (The year 1965 was also the first time Pohnpei's population reached 15,000 since that number was estimated 130 years earlier.)

Economic development slumped throughout the American administration and political development has been almost too prevalent. At present, Pohnpeians are influenced by their municipal governments, the legislature of the State of Pohnpei, the Congress of the Federated States of Micronesia, and the United States government through the Compact of Free Association.

Beginning in the late 1960's, the United States rediscovered Micronesia and increased programs, projects, appropriations and political change. The first U.S. Peace Corps Volunteers arrived on Pohnpei in 1966, and numbered as many as 120 in Pohnpei district during their early years. In 1970, the first American Civic Action Team of fourteen U.S. Navy Seabees arrived to work on construction projects. In the same year, the Future Political Status Negotiations began that were to last for more than a decade and a half. An offer was initially made by the U.S. government to give commonwealth status, and U.S. citizenship to Micronesians, and to continue funding Micronesia indefinitely. (The offer was rejected by the Congress of Micronesia.) The Community College of Micronesia was established in 1970 from roots of the Micronesian Teacher Education Center. The two-year college has since become a fully accredited member of the Western Association of Schools and Colleges. It has a resident enrollment of approximately two hundred students, and an extension enrollment of some 1,000. Quite suddenly, lavish attention was being paid to Micronesia after twenty years of relative neglect, indecision and indifference.

What should prove to be the most important historical

event of the American Period on Pohnpei took place when the island joined the Federated States of Micronesia. The union of Pohnpei, Kosrae, Truk, and Yap became official on May 10, 1979, when the new national flag, four white stars circled on a light blue field, was raised at the capital on Pohnpei. The following day the Congress of the F.S.M. met and elected Senator Tosiwo Nakayama of Truk as the first president and Senator Petrus Tun of Yap as the first vice president. Senior statesman Senator Bethwel Henry of Pohnpei State was elected the first speaker of the new senate. The Honorable Leo A. Falcam became the first elected governor of the new state of Pohnpei.

The United Nations Trusteeship with the United States as administering authority of Micronesia has been the longest lasting U.N. trusteeship in the history of the organization. After the Congress of Micronesia refused an offer by the U.S. of commonwealth status in 1970, negotiations began to determine the future political status of the territory. A Compact of Free Association was finally signed between the Federated States of Micronesia and the United States in 1983, but was not implemented until 1986.

On May 1, 1983, the Honorable Resio S. Moses was sworn in as the second governor of the State of Pohnpei, and the Honorable Strik Yoma was sworn in as the reelected lieutenant governor. On May 11th Senator Bailey Olter of Pohnpei State became the Vice President of the Federated States of Micronesia.

Also in 1983, delegates from all municipalities of the state were elected to form a constitutional convention. Pohnpei constitutional government took effect on November 8, 1984. The constitution changed the name of Ponape to "Pohnpei," and allows a great deal of control by individual municipalities. In 1985 and 1986, each of the eleven municipalities of the state drafted its own constitution.

As a constituent member-state of the F.S.M., Pohnpei entered a new historical era in 1986 with the approval in the United Nations of the Compact of Free Association. After sixteen years of negotiation, and approval by the F.S.M. state legislatures, the Congress of the F.S.M., the Senate and the House of Representatives of the United States, and American President Ronald Reagan, the Compact ended four decades of American stewardship. It was approved by the United Nations Trusteeship Council on May 29, 1986 by a vote of three to one with the Soviet Union objecting. A resolution of that body directed the United States to grant semi-independence to the F.S.M. not later than September 30, 1986.

Even positive inevitabilities are seldom celebrated when they finally occur. They are more often greeted with exhaustion than with festivities. Since April 2, 1947 when the Trusteeship Agreement between the U.S. and the U.N. Security Council became effective, it has been inevitable that a new political status would evolve for the Micronesian entities. On November 3, 1986, nearly forty years after the beginning of the Trusteeship Agreement, the period of patient persistence ended. Full self-government began in the F.S.M. with the implementation of the Compact of Free Association with the U.S.

And the pulse of history is quickening in the Venice of the Pacific...

NATURAL FEATURES

Introduction

The beauty of physical Pohnpei is legendary. James F. O'Connell writing in 1836 called Pohnpei's Nan Madol the Venice of the Pacific because of its island-studded lagoon and numerous channels. Just as characteristic of the island are Pohnpei's two thousand foot mountains, its plunging waterfalls and its steep cliffs, the most famous being Sokehs Rock *(Peipalap)*, the Diamond Head of Micronesia. Co-pilot Paul Boyles on a record breaking around-the-world flight in February, 1983, referred to Pohnpei as "a paradise island...just like the home of King Kong."

Pohnpei is a weathered volcanic, or "high" island, the largest and the most developed of the nine islands that comprise Pohnpei State. Its two close neighbors in the Senyavin group, Ant and Pakin, are atolls, often referred to as "low" islands.

In the micro world of the Federated States of Micronesia, Pohnpei is a land of physical superlatives. The island has the biggest land area, the tallest mountains, the deepest valleys, and the most uninhabited land of any place in the F.S.M. It also has the longest road and the largest population.

Topography

Pohnpei Island is a deeply indented, jagged circle, some thirteen miles in diameter, seventy miles in circumference, and about 130 square miles in land area, about twice the size of Washington, D.C. (If mangrove swamps and lagoon and reef islets are included, the total is 138 square miles.) Pohnpeians divide the island into land categories according to use: mangrove swamp and trees *(naniak)* used for building materials and firewood; freshwater swamp *(lehpwel)* mainly used for taro cultivation; private cultivated farmsteads *(sahpw)* used for traditional subsistence crops; areas of stones and loose boulders *(paip)* not particularly desirable land, but used for small crops such as bananas and pineapples; and uncultivated forest *(nanwel)* mainly mountainous government land.

The main features of topography on the island are the outer barrier reef, the intertidal lagoon, the fringe reef and mangrove forest, the lowland area of strand vegetation and lower mountain slopes, and the highlands and rainforest.

Both the barrier reef seen beyond the island and the fringe reef attached to the shoreline are composed mainly of calcium carbonate (coral) and are a tropical, shallow water phenomenon. Coral polyps can only survive in water 70°F or warmer, and are found between the tropics of Cancer and Capricon. Pohnpei's 80°F water temperature is ideal for growth of these microscopic animals. The food of the coral polyp, algae, requires sunlight to live, and the rays are only strong enough to penetrate to a depth of about 200 feet. Consequently, new and live coral formations are not found in deeper water off of the island. Immediately beyond Pohnpei's barrier reef, the ocean floor abruptly drops to a depth of more than 3,000 feet, but the lagoon is shallow enough for coral to thrive in most areas.

The barrier reef is pentagonally shaped and surrounds the 68.89 square mile lagoon (44,089 acres), except at the southwest side of the island. There, the barrier reef is joined to the fringe reef of the main island and so no lagoon exists.

There are twenty passages of varying sizes and depths through the reef, the largest being off of Sokehs, Langar, and Madolenihmw harbors. These passages allow for the circulation of the water in the lagoon caused by the twice daily incoming and outgoing tides.

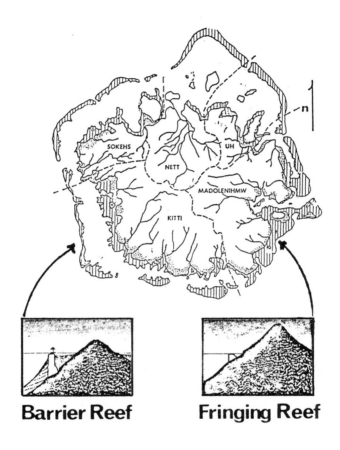

Barrier Reef   **Fringing Reef**

More than thirty islets, mostly on the southern half, dot the outer barrier reef. All are privately owned but few are inhabited continuously. For centuries they have served as hideaways, and rest stops and way-stations for Pohnpeian fishermen. More recently, several have been used as recreation areas. For a few dollars per night, visitors are supplied with a thatch structure and barbecue facilities. All have small beaches and are air-conditioned with year around cooling breezes. Since rainfall is significantly lighter on the islets than on the main island, they have developed into desirable retreats for both residents and visitors. Laiap, Nahnningi, Nahpali, and Kehpara are four of the most popular.

Historically, Pohnpei's lagoon has been an obstacle course for sailing vessels. It is a marine basin encircled by the barrier reef, which averages about two miles in distance from the main island. In the lagoon, mainly in the north and the east, are twenty-three basaltic islets, many permanently inhabited. There are also a number of alluvial islets, the most prominent being Takatik, the location of the commercial dock and the air terminal (see *Sights and Sites,* p. 274). The lagoon varies in depth from sea level to about 300 feet. Coral heads and reefs are sprinkled throughout the lagoon making it quite hazardous for navigation unless one is familiar with the channels.

Nearly 6,000 acres of mangrove forest are found on the alluvial and basaltic islets in the lagoon and on the irregular fringe reef surrounding Pohnpei proper. These forests protect the shoreline from erosion caused by the tidal currents, normal wave action, and storm waves that are not dissipated by the outer barrier reef. The forests also trap silt and sediments running off of eroding land caused by rainfall. They serve as a habitat for young and larval stages of marine life, six species of birds and two types of bats. The roots and lower trunks of trees are normally covered by salty or brackish water. The trees, however, are a readily available source of firewood as well as material for use in construction and carving handicrafts. Although picturesque South Sea island beaches are absent because of the mangrove forest, the trees serve an invaluable function in maintaining Pohnpei's shoreline. Fourteen percent of the island consists of mangrove forest.

Most cultivation on Pohnpei is done in the area of lowland strand vegetation, in valleys, and on the lower slopes of mountains. Over the years the low, shallow agricultural shelf surrounding the island has been altered by burning, watershed runoff, and subsistence farming. Edible products are grown in the foothills as well as lumber and materials for local medicine and handicrafts.

Eighteen different kinds of soil have been identified on Pohnpei, based on the variation of five characteristics: climate, plant and animal activity; relief; parent material; and geological time. The soils vary widely in potential for major uses, and only about thirty percent of the land is used for subsistence farming (and 0.7 percent for urban complexes). Pohnpei, however, contains some of the most weathered soil found in tropical areas anywhere, and poor soil fertility is a key reason why commercial agriculture is limited. Without lime and fertilizers, most soil is leached and low in phosphorus, potassium, calcium and magnesium. Soil in the coastal areas is generally mustard-brown and reddish-brown in color. Small areas of black soil with a powdery consistency can be found, especially near Kolonia. Soil in the mountains is dark brown to black and rich in organic matter. In level areas it may be a few feet deep, but only a few inches on the mountain slopes. An average farm size is ten to fifteen acres and dwellings and family agricultural plots are concentrated in the north and northeast section of the island and on mountain slopes.

Uninterrupted dense jungle covers most of the highland interior above the 1,000 foot altitude in rugged topography with almost continuous cloud cover and rainfall. The mountains are the highest found in the F.S.M. and are located in the center of the island extending northwest to southeast. The Everest of Pohnpei is Mt. Ngihneni (the tooth of the spirit) at 2,595 feet, but there are at least nine other peaks above 2,000 feet in altitude. Nahna Laud (big mountain) is popularly thought to be the highest, however. These rugged central mountains form a system of ridges separated by deep valleys, and are accessible only by little-known foot trails.

The mixed forest area of the interior mountains provides no economic plants and consists mainly of herbaceous vegetation unsuitable for construction. It includes most plants native to the island. Mosses, ferns, liverworts and other epiphytes are constantly damp from mist and rain in the uplands. The steep, wind-swept terrain does not allow the growth of any but gnarled and dwarfed trees, bare branched, with tuffed tops. The dense, moss-covered vegetation and the accumulated spongy humus does soak and hold rainwater that continually falls, contributing significantly to Pohnpei's watershed. The steep, mountainous areas make up sixty percent of the island (and rolling hills another twenty percent). In the rugged interior, air lies thick and hefty over thin, leached soil on steep slopes. It is, however, a natural, untouched wildlife habitat and the origin of Pohnpei's forty or so streams and tributaries and two larger rivers. In Madolenihmw, the river Pilen nan Riohk rises near Nahna Laud, changes its name four times and flows into Dewen Sapwalap, an inlet of Madolenihmw Harbor. The Pilen Kiepw rises in the highlands above the Nett Valley and becomes the well-known Nanpil River before flowing north into Kolonia's harbor.

The Nanpil River feeds the reservoirs and storage tanks for Kolonia and has been found to have very high quality water. Samples were analyzed by the U.S. Geological Survey Central Laboratory in Denver, Colorado. They were found to be of excellent quality, uniformly soft, and low in dissolved solids. "The concentration of all chemicals analyzed are well within the maximum permissible level recommended for domestic use by the World Health Organization." Visitors and newly arrived contract workers frequently boil their water, but it hardly seems to be necessary if taken from reservoirs supplying the Kolonia area. When a possibility of water contamination exists, as happened after a brush by Typhoon Lola in 1986, people are warned by way of the local radio broadcast.

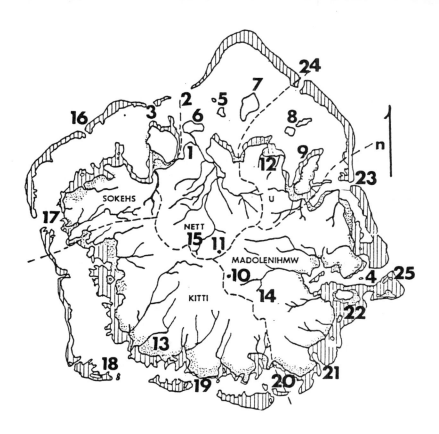

1. Kolonia town
2. Langar (Kolonia Passage)
3. Sokehs Passage
4. Madolenihmw Harbor
   and Passage
5. Langar Island
6. Takatik Island
7. Parem Island
8. Mwahnd Islands
9. Dehpehle Island
10. Mt. Ngihneni
11. Mt. Nahna Laud
12. Awak
13. Ronkiti
14. Pilen nan Riohk River
15. Pilen Kiepw River
16. Palikir Passage
17. Tauak Passage
18. Kehpara Island
19. Laiap (Rainbow) Island
20. Mutok Harbor
21. Lohd Harbor
22. Nahnningi (Joy) Island
23. Aru Passage
24. Mant Passage
25. Nahpali (Fantasy) Island

Climate

Said a weathered old beachcomber wag to the author, "Pohnpei was nearly washed away in the dry season." According to a longtime resident, "Last year the dry season I think was on a Tuesday."

The tropical maritime climate of Pohnpei is predictable, consistent, and extreme. The only real seasons are the short wet season in January and February, and the long wetter season throughout the rest of the year. Monthly mean temperatures are fairly constant at about eighty degrees Fahrenheit.

Measurable rain falls an average of 300 days each year on the island. However, the amount of rainfall tabulated varies considerably, depending on where the rainfall data is accumulated and the particular year. It is estimated that at the highest elevations in the mountains, 400 inches of rain falls annually, making the interior of Ponhpei one of the wettest places on earth. (The wettest spot is on Mt. Waialeale, Kauai, Hawaii, with 460 inches.) These tropical mountain downpours provide a watershed that supplies a number of year-around rivers and streams. The east side of the island, the direction from which most storms arrive, has more rainfall than the west. In any year, precipitation may vary twenty percent from the previous year. Data on rainfall collected in Kolonia indicates an average of nearly 195 inches annually. The heaviest rainfall recorded in a seven-hour period was 4.44 inches in 1966.

Average Precipitation
Kolonia, Pohnpei
(Thirty-five Year Period)

January	11.41"	July	17.73"
February	11.21"	August	16.72"
March	14.30"	September	16.39"
April	18.74"	October	15.94"
May	20.42"	November	16.62"
June	17.24"	December	15.70"

Total: 194.42 Annually

As a comparison to other areas, the average annual rainfall for Honolulu is 23.10 inches annually, for San Francisco, 19.53 inches, and for wet Seattle, 38.80 inches. Droughts do occur on Pohnpei, however. The total rainfall for January, February and March, 1983, was 5.13 inches whereas the average total should have been nearly 37 inches in Kolonia. The lowest monthly rainfall recorded since records have been kept in 1900 was 1.05 inches in February, 1977; the highest was during the Japanese Period in April, 1942, 39.12 inches. Despite rainfall with which the biblical Noah might be familiar, raingear is never seen on the island and many fewer umbrellas than one would expect to see are in evidence.

Temperature is uniform throughout the year with less than one degree separating the averages of the warmest and the coolest months. Mean highs are in the mid to upper eighties and lows are in the low to mid seventies. The average daily range is 12.5 degrees. The highest temperature recorded within the last thirty-eight years was in September, 1950 at 96 degrees F, or 35.6 degrees C. The lowest for the same period was in December, 1977, a frosty (for Pohnpei) 66 degrees F, or 18.9 degrees C.

Average Monthly Temperatures
(Fahrenheit degrees)

Month	Mean	Maximum	Minimum
January	80.7	86.0	75.3
February	80.8	86.0	75.6
March	80.8	86.4	75.2
April	80.7	86.8	74.8
May	80.7	86.8	74.5
June	80.4	87.0	73.8
July	80.0	87.1	72.9
August	80.1	87.6	72.6
September	80.1	87.6	72.6
October	80.1	87.6	72.6
November	80.4	87.4	73.4
December	80.7	86.6	74.8

Unlike most of Micronesia, the risk of typhoons on Pohnpei is minimal. The island is close to the spawning grounds of many disturbances that grow into typhoons, but the major tracks are to the north and west of the island. An average of twenty-five typhoons do take place in the Caroline Islands annually, however, and are most common in September. The last time that a very severe typhoon struck Pohnpei was in 1905 (see *History*, p. 63). Two moderate blows in the past fourteen years have caused damage to the island, and both were named Typhoon Lola. Gusts up to sixty m.p.h. were recorded on May 31, 1972, and on May 18, 1986. There were fortunately no major casualties during either storm.

November to June is the period of the northeasterly trade winds. In July winds tend to be lighter and more variable. From August to November they are moist and somewhat southerly. Most tropical disturbances occur at this time. The months of the lightest winds are June and July. Data on wind direction and speed at both surface level and in the upper air are recorded at the Pohnpei Weather Station, a facility of the U.S. National Weather Service in cooperation with the government of the F.S.M. in Kolonia. Under normal conditions, wind velocity on Pohnpei is a gentle breeze averaging six to eight knots per hour.

Beaufort Wind Scale

Force Number	State of Air	Velocity in Knots
0	Dead Calm	0 - 1
1	Light Airs	1 - 3
2	Slight Breeze	4 - 6
3	Gentle Breeze	7 - 10
4	Moderate Breeze	11 - 16
5	Fresh Breeze	17 - 21
6	Strong Breeze	22 - 27
7	Moderate Gale	28 - 33
8	Fresh Gale	34 - 40

9	Strong Gale	41 - 47
10	Whole Gale	48 - 55
11	Storm	56 - 65
12	Hurricane, Typhoon	65 and above

The clouds seen too often over Pohnpei are predominantly cumulus. Meteorological data indicates that Pohnpei receives only thirty-seven to fifty percent of available sunlight annually. Over a twenty-four year period registered in Kolonia, cloud cover averaged the following number of days each year:

Clear	3
Partly Cloudy	63
Mostly Cloudy	299

The humidity on Pohnpei is high, about eighty to ninety percent. The least humid months on the island are March and April.

A building is situated off the main street in Kolonia across from the office of the College of Micronesia. It is colored light brown and white, sits on manicured grounds, and has minaret like the one at St. Basil's in Red Square in Moscow. But there the resemblance to Russia ends. It is the Pohnpei Weather Station.

Atoll

A series of islets, all extremely low, and strung together upon a coral reef in the way small green beads might be strung upon a gold necklace cord.
James Michener and A. Grove Day
Rascals in Paradise

The State of Pohnpei also includes eight small atolls, seven of which are permanently inhabited and one which is inhabited intermittently. Except for Oroluk, only one-fifth of a square mile in area, Pohnpei's atolls are each about one-half square mile in land area. All of the atolls are represented in the Pohnpei State Legislature (See *Pohnpei State Outlying Islands*, pp. 221-46). Although tiny, the outer islands of the state are hardly inconsequential. In 1986 the elected Speaker of the F.S.M. Senate and the Vice President of the Federation were both from Mokil Atoll—population 268.

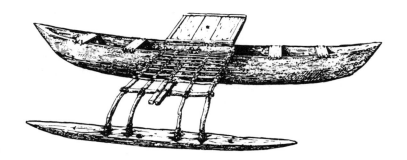

Canoe, Mokil Atoll

Nautical Miles from Pohnpei

Ant Atoll - 8 SW
Pakin Atoll - 18 WNW
Oroluk Atoll - 164 WNW
Sapwuahfik Atoll - 75 SW
Nukuoro Atoll - 251 SW
Kapingamarangi Atoll - 415 SW
Mokil Atoll - 88 E
Pingelap Atoll - 163 ESE
Minto Reef - 265 WNW

Pohnpei State

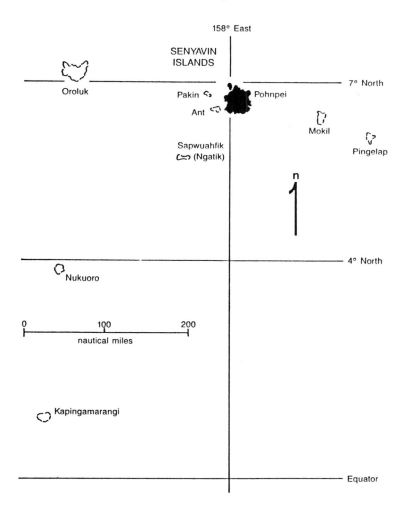

To convert nautical (sea) miles to statute (land) miles, add one eighth to the nautical scale, or twelve and a half percent.

FLORA OF POHNPEI

Introduction

More than six hundred species of higher plants are found on Pohnpei, and simply to list them would require a number of pages. This section will be limited to the plants that enter significantly into the Pohnpeian diet, and to vegetation that has other widespread local use. The best study of vegetation on Pohnpei is *The Flora of Ponape* by Sidney F. Glassman, published by the Bishop Museum in Honolulu and last reprinted in 1971. Another good source is *Ponape Island Land Use Guide, A Comprehensive Study Based on Natural Elements*, published by the Office of Planning and Statistics, Trust Territory of the Pacific Islands in 1979.

The vegetation of Pohnpei is separated into three main divisions: mangrove forest at the shoreline; strand vegetation in the lowlands; and rain-forest in the uplands.

The mangrove forest on Pohnpei covers some 5,900 acres of coast and tideland and nearly encircles the entire main island, except where trees have been cut away for passages. It also extends to areas a mile upstream in rivers where mangrove trees over a hundred feet tall are found. The forest is practically free of undercover plants because of poor penetration of sunlight through dense foliage and daily tidal flooding. Mangrove wood is strong and insect-resistant and frequently used for building material.

The lowlands surrounding the island from sea level to about eight hundred feet in altitude have been altered over the years by the cultivation of familiar subsistence and cash crops. Human activities, though, have resulted in a decrease in numbers of many native plants, and are a threat to the existence of others. Commercial agriculture is limited in the lowlands by a number of factors: few large land holdings; shortage of willing labor because of government competition on wages; a lack of widespread local demand for truck crops; difficult logistical problems; generally poor soil fertility; and restrictions on available capital.

The mountainous interior contains over fifty thousand acres of forest. Frequent clouds and winds on mountain tops have stunted trees to seven to ten feet in height. The rainforest is dense and rich, the most extensive native forests in Micronesia, and is covered with a blanket of soft, green moss. These pristine forests are nearly untouched by cultivation and shield flora seldom seen except by botanists.

A number of trees in the coastal swamps and uplands have potential for timber production. These include red sandalwood *(kaikes)*, campnosperma *(dong)*, blue marble *(satak)*, and parinarium *(ais)*. Other trees found in small quantities are barringtonia *(winmar)*, eucalyptus, rhizophora *(aakelel)*, sonneratia *(koatoa)*, Honduras mahogany, teak, and xylacarpus *(pwulok)*. The last mentioned is the prime wood used by Kapingamarangan carvers and is found mostly in Madolenihmw. Its Pohnpeian name is nearly always used, possibly because its English name is unpronounceable. (There are no Pohnpeian words for eucalyptus, mahogany and teak woods.)

Forty-two local plants enter into the Pohnpeian diet. Some 430 varieties of these plants were recorded during the Japanese administration, of which half are varieties of yams and breadfruit. Consequently, the basic item in the Pohnpeian diet is a starchy fruit or vegetable, usually accompanied by a protein dish of meat, fowl or seafood. Starch and protein are usually cooked separately and served as different dishes. Fruit, and occasionally green vegetables, may supplement the diet, but are seldom served with the main dishes. Sugarcane and fruits in season, particularly mangoes, are eaten as between-meal snacks, especially by children.

Breadfruit, yams, taro, coconuts, tapioca, bananas and mangoes are the most popular local foods grown on Pohnpei. They do not require extensive land-cleaning, machine cultivation, or commercial fertilizers. Sweet potatoes, quite popular during the Japanese Period, are making a comeback and becoming increasingly popular. The most prominent food in the diet, rice, is imported, mainly from Australia.

AGRICULTURE
SOILS VALUES

MOST
SUITABLE

Pohnpei Island
Most Suitable Agriculture Areas

111

Plants Used for Food

Starch Plants

Breadfruit	*mahi*
Yams	*kehp*
Taro	*mwahng*
Cassava	*kehp tuhke*
Sweet potatoes	*pedehde*
Rice	*rais*

Fruit Plants

Coconuts	*nih*
Bananas	*uht*
Mangoes	*kehngid*
Papayas	*memiap*
Citrus	*peren*
Limes	*karer*
Mountain apples	*apel*
Avocados	*apakahdo*

Starch Plants

Although Captain Bligh of the HMS *Bounty* made bread-fruit (*mahi*) known to millions of readers and movie-goers, few Pohnpeians ever heard of either Bligh or the *Bounty*. They have always been familiar with breadfruit, however, which dates from the Pre-history Period on Pohnpei. (The word "breadfruit," incidentally, was supposedly coined by Captain Cook on a trip to the Pacific, accompanied by William Bligh— bread growing like fruit from trees.)

The names of seventy-eight varieties of breadfruit are recorded, most of them differentiated by their leaves, but several by distinctive characteristics of the fruit or the tree. The fruit is very high in carbohydrates and Vitamin B, and contains more starches and sugars than its distant cousin, the potato. It is also a fair source of Vitamin C and calcium.

Breadfruit trees are found sixty feet high and taller, and need no cultivation when established. They have large luxuriant leaves, one to three feet long, dark green and shiny on top and pale green and rough underneath. Breadfruit trees are planted from a root sucker off a parent tree, two to three feet in height and containing some leaves. The fruit is picked shortly before it ripens by climbing the tree and using a long pole to pluck the fruit from the limbs. A tree will begin bearing fruit about four years after it is planted.

The main breadfruit season is in June, July and August, and a shorter season takes place around the first of the year. Two types are grown, and both are seedless. One has a smooth skin and is round or slightly oval in shape. This type is preferred for its flavor and its earlier maturity. A second type is more pimply and elongated.

The time of maturity of the fruit varies somewhat annually, and depends on several factors: the variety of the fruit; conditions during the particular year grown; and the section of Pohnpei where the tree is growing. By planting both early and late maturing varieties, it is possible to eat fresh breadfruit from May of one year until February of the next. Breadfruit is tastiest just before it is fully ripe, and occasionally is preserved for several months by fermenting it in covered pits lined with banana and wild ginger leaves.

Fresh breadfruit is most often prepared by being baked in a stone oven, the *uhmw*. It may also be boiled or fried, however, and breadfruit chips deep fried and prepared like potato chips are popular snacks. Breadfruit may also be mashed (pounded) similar to preparing mashed potatoes.

Breadfruit

In baking, the fruit is halved or quartered and then wrapped in large leaves. A popular variety of breadfruit, with the proper degree of ripeness, well prepared in the traditional *uhmw*, and served steaming hot with melted butter, is a treat that would make even the ghost of Captain Bligh forget Fletcher Christian.

Yams (*kehp*) on Pohnpei are coveted far beyond their commercial value. They are the main plant food in the prestige economy as well as a starch staple in the Pohnpeian diet. Growing yams by Pohnpeian males is wrapped in sound agricultural practices, but also shrouded in ritual and secrecy. *Yam* in the *Ponapean/English Dictionary* is given the most extensive treatment of any word. There are 104 definitions, eighty-nine of which explain varieties and characteristics of different types of yams.

Paul Bunyan would have thrived on the yams of Pohnpei. Some grow to more than ten feet in length. Clusters of yams grown together can weigh as much as a thousand pounds, and there is a Pohnpeian story of a cluster that required fifty men to lift.

Historically, the only Pohnpeian taboos in planting were associated with yams. For yams to grow well, it was believed that the planter had to abstain from sexual relations for ten days prior to tying his yam vines, and must eat no fish or copra at that time. Food and sex taboos have not been observed in yam growing since before World War II.

As food, yams are preferred to breadfruit, although they are grown in smaller quantities. Between breadfruit seasons, they are the main local starch eaten. Both wild and cultivated varieties are found on the island. Nutritionally, yams are of less value than breadfruit, or most other local starches.

The usual planting season is between December and April, and yams normally grow for a year before fully mature. A hole must be prepared in the shape that the yam is to grow. Loose soil is then refilled in the hole along with a section of the root from another yam, buried a few inches deep. According to Bascom, "The care with which the Pohnpeian farmer grows his prize yams shows both knowledge and skill, and the labor he expends is far greater than would be necessary to produce the same quantity from a larger number of small yams of the same variety." Yams are cultivated in small, scattered plots, each surrounded by a bank of stones. The vines are tied to trees for support and cultivation is so shrouded in secrecy that plots are often tended only before sunrise. The secrecy does not apply to foraging beasts such as pigs, however, and yams must be protected from animals.

Time of maturity varies somewhat, and depends on the variety of yam, the weather during the particular year, and the time of planting. By planting at intervals and selecting early and late maturity yams, a Pohnpeian cultivator can have yams at anytime of the year, although some might be harvested before fully matured.

Like breadfruit, yams can be cooked by baking, boiling, or frying. They are preferred baked in the traditional *uhmw* and are often served with coconut cream. The flavor of a baked yam is not sweet and the taste is rather mild.

Worldwide, some 400 million people use taro *(mwahng)* in their diets throughout humid tropical areas. The seventeen varieties grown on Pohnpei are distinguished by whether they grow in wet or dry areas, or if they are cultivated or grow wild. Taro on Pohnpei is often a substitute food when breadfruit, yams or rice are unavailable.

The taro root is cultivated, usually during the season of high rainfall, in fresh water marshes. The area for planting must first be cleared of sticks, branches and stumps, and then the soil is turned over by hand, very tedious work done mostly by women in swampy land. Taro patches are seeded with shoots from parent plants, about eighteen inches in height. The leaves of hibiscus and other trees available near the swamp are used for fertilizer. After the soil has been prepared, the water is drained from the area to facilitate mulching. From planting to harvest takes one to three years, depending on the variety. An outstanding feature of taro is its leaves, which are as long as five feet in length and may grow to ten or twelve feet in height. They are often seen used as temporary umbrellas during sudden Pohnpei downpours.

Several types of taro are eaten on the island. The preferred taro is fairly small and tender and matures early. A wild variety of taro is also found on Pohnpei, but it has a bitter taste and is seldom eaten. A popular variety is Hawaiian taro, first introduced by the Japanese.

Like breadfruit, taro can be stored for later use after being harvested. The taro root is cut into pieces which are dried in the sun to remove moisture. They are then stored in sacks in a dry place. When needed for food, the taro is soaked in water until tender, boiled, and then often served with coconut cream. Most taro on Pohnpei, however, is eaten freshly harvested.

There are more than two hundred varieties of cassava or tapioca *(kehp tuhke)* known in the world. In Micronesia, it is most popular in Palau, where forty varieties are grown. On Pohnpei, the San Salvador variety introduced from Hawaii in 1958 is the most high yielding and best quality.

Compared to other root staples, cassava is low in nutrient value. It also exhausts soil quickly. However, its leaves are fairly rich in protein and carbohydrates, making them especially suitable for swine food.

The tuber of the plant is durable, and requires little cultivation. It will grow in almost any soil, but grows best in areas with less than one hundred inches of rainfall per year. The two main kinds on Pohnpei are the sweet and bitter varieties. They are propagated from cuttings ten to twelve inches long, preferably during the rainy season. Cassava, however, can be planted the year around. The sweet variety matures in as little as six months. Bitter cassava takes twelve months to mature, but can be left in the ground for several years if necessary.

Cassava can be prepared for eating in a number of ways. Some can simply be boiled and eaten. A more popular method is to serve it in a cake or pudding form *(pihlohlo)*. The tuber is first grated and squeezed to separate the starch from the water. The starch is then combined with the grated cassava and coconut cream, mixed with ripe bananas or with taro, and then baked.

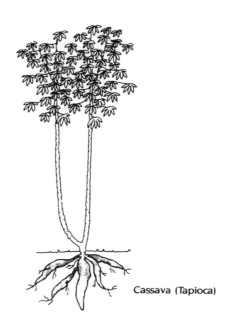

Cassava (Tapioca)

Sweet potatoes *(pedehde)* were cultivated extensively by the Japanese on Pohnpei, but their fields were abandoned with the exodus after World War II. They are a staple crop in Polynesia, from where they are thought to have originally spread to Micronesia. There are three main varieties grown on Pohnpei.

Glassman wrote in 1950 that sweet potatoes were not particularly relished by Pohnpeians. Since then, however, the starch has enjoyed a resurgence of favor on the island. Sweet potatoes have high nutritive value and a large yield per acre. They are easily stored and the tubers and vines are good pig food.

From planting to maturity takes about three and a half months, but the potatoes may be left in the ground for as long as six months. They are planted from cuttings ten to twelve inches long in well drained mounds, usually at the beginning of the rainy season. The three main varieties, Hyakugo, Tokoisho, and Kagoshima, are slightly different in shape varying from nearly round to oval, and are popular

117

in local markets. Although sweet potatoes may be baked, they are nearly always boiled for meals.

It is ironic that in a community of farmers and gardeners the main food in the Pohnpeian diet is imported rice *(rais)*. Although rice was grown on Pohnpei mostly during the Japanese Period, it has actually been known on the island since pre-Spanish times, and was planted in small quantities as early as the German period.

Pohnpeians seem to have a love/hate feeling toward this popular starch. They love to eat it, but hate to cultivate it. There is a possible historic precedent for the latter. According to William Bascom, writing shortly after World War II, "Work in the [rice] paddy fields, with its long hours and hard work, was probably the most disliked and resented of all forms of forced labor required by the Japanese." More than 6 million pounds of rice were imported into Pohnpei in 1985, about ninety percent of it from Australia. This was enough rice to provide about 231 pounds annually for every man, woman, and child on the island.

During the American administration, several attempts to produce rice locally have failed. In 1972, the Congress of Micronesia appropriated $270,000 to clear and prepare 228 acres for rice fields at sites in Nett and Madolenihmw. The areas were expected to yield three hundred tons of polished rice annually, which could be sold for about a third of the cost of imported rice. The project did not succeed because financing was not available through loans for farmers to continue development after the initial appropriation was spent.

Rice has the advantage of being easily stored and prepared. Also, unless rice gets wet or infested with mice, it seldom spoils in the tropics. Pohnpeians prefer rice boiled and spiced with shoyu.

Fruit Plants

Visitors find fruits surprisingly scarce on Pohnpei. All land is privately owned, government owned, or leased, and so all fruit on the land belongs to someone else. Also, a basket of fruit is often a gift to a friend, or relative in the extended family, and so choice fruits other than the plentiful bananas and coconuts seldom reach the Farmer's Market in Kolonia in any quantity. The main fruits available besides coconuts and bananas are mangoes, papaya, pineapples, citrus, mountain apples, and avocados.

No single feature symbolizes life on a tropical island more than swaying coconut palms *(nih)* mentioned in nearly all romantic literature of the Pacific. The resilient tree grows out of a fallen or planted nut, preferably with some liquid inside, and reaches bearing stage after about eight years. For the next sixty years or so, the tree produces about fifty nuts per year. Pohnpei's conditions of year-around warm temperature, abundant moisture and sunlight, and also low coastal altitudes and well-drained soil, are helpful to the growth of the palms.

Seven varieties of coconuts are referred to in Pohnpeian, determined by such characteristics as size, color, and readiness for harvest. In preparation for eating, the coconut meat is usually grated and then served with a variety of local foods. Coconut liquid is also prominent in the diet on Pohnpei. (Drinking coconuts must be picked at an appropriate time rather than gathered when fallen to the ground.) Besides food and liquid, products of a coconut palm have a number of other traditional functions. Husks provide sennit for binding of beams often seen in Pohnpeian traditional homes, and are also used for fuel. The hard shells of the coconuts are ideal for liquid containers and the manufacture of jewelry as well as charcoal. Fronds are commonly used for making brooms, disposable baskets and are woven into thatch, although pandanus or ivory-nut palms are preferred for the latter. Trunks of palms are cut and used in construction to support large structures.

Copra *(mwangas)* produced from coconut meat is the largest cash export crop on Pohnpei, although the main source of income is government employment. For preparation of copra, the mature nut is split in half and the meat cut out. Excess moisture is then removed by some form of drying.

Copra is bagged in 105 pound burlap sacks and sold to a government-authorized merchant before being shipped to Japan. From 1950 to 1980, Pohnpei State produced three to eight million pounds of copra per year. There was a significant drop in the 1970's to an average of 3.3 million pounds. In 1986, copra on Pohnpei sold for $100 per ton or five cents per pound (about three coconuts are required for a pound of copra), a drastic reduction in previous prices. The tiring work of gathering coconuts, husking them, separating the meat from the shells, drying the meat, bagging the copra and delivering it to the state center for sale, however, was not reduced at all.

Oil for cooking and other household uses, as well as anointing *(marekeiso)*, is extracted from coconut meat, processed, and sold locally. Ponape Coconut Products distributes scented baby, body and hair oil, soap and shampoo, under the brand name of *Oil of Ponape*. The company, begun by Ponape Agriculture and Trade School in 1974, now averages profits of $25,000 annually.

Marekeiso

coconut oil
baby · body · hair

(There is no contemporary count of the number of coconut palms on the island. Bascom in 1946 mentioned a too-exact figure of 239,867 trees. He also noted that 40,000 palms were destroyed by the Japanese for fortifications. The promised payment of two yen per tree due to the owners was a casualty of World War II. Glassman in 1951 estimated two to three million palms were on Pohnpei.)

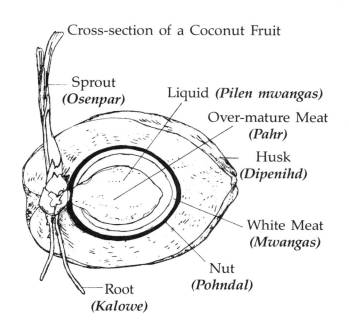

Cross-section of a Coconut Fruit

Sprout
(Osenpar)

Liquid *(Pilen mwangas)*

Over-mature Meat
(Pahr)

Husk
(Dipenihd)

White Meat
(Mwangas)

Nut
(Pohndal)

Root
(Kalowe)

Banana *(uht)* trees are spread over an estimated 1,500 acres on Pohnpei, and forty-one varieties of bananas or plantains are found. They are not considered to be a main food source and do not enter into the prestige economy, although they are quite rich in calories and vitamins. Bananas are often eaten either fresh or cooked after or between meals. The trees are propagated from sprouts of a parent. They are not seasonal and require no cultivation. Bananas ripen in ten to twelve months and are one of the most plentiful and inexpensive fruits available.

Four varieties of mangoes *(kehngid)* are available on the island. The trees are found mostly on the edge of the lowland farmbelt, and are sometimes planted for shade. Mango trees bear seasonally and are not found in the mountains. Some varieties ripen in early summer and others around December. They may be picked green and taken home to ripen, and a desired snack of many pregnant ladies, incidentally, is sliced green mango dipped in shoyu with salt and often vinegar.

The two varieties of papaya *(memiap)* found on Pohnpei are more different in appearance than in taste. One variety is about eight inches in length with a dark green leaf stem. The other is longer, more than a foot in length, and has a reddish leaf stem. Papaya, also called "mummy apple," was first introduced to the island by an American during the Spanish Period. The fruit grows wild and is in season throughout the year.

Citrus *(peren)* on Pohnpei consists of eight species, only four of which have distinctive names. Limes *(karer)* are the variety preferred, and are used mostly to flavor seafood. Local oranges with a green rind are mostly imported from Kosrae.

There are two main varieties of mountain apple *(apel)* on Pohnpei. Both are small, about the size of an American crab apple, and red in color when ripe. Neither is confined to growing in mountains, however. One kind is flower-shaped, is in season twice a year, and has been used for making wine. The more popular variety is round, tart, and usually eaten with salt. Like other fruits, mountain apples are most often eaten after meals or between meals as snacks.

Large avocados *(apakahdo)* in Hawaii cost about a dollar each. On Pohnpei they are used for pig food. The pear-shaped green tropical fruit originated in Mexico and was probably brought to Pohnpei during the Japanese Period. The tree grows from a planted seedling and bears fruit after some six years. There are more than twenty varieties of avocado on the island, but the fruit has never entered significantly into the Pohnpeian diet.

Plants Used for Food Flavoring

Chili peppers	*sele*
Cinnamon	*sinamon*
Wild ginger	*sinter*
Pohnpei peppercorns	*sele*
Sugar cane	*sehu*
Seaweed	*dihpw en nan sed*

The most common flavoring and spices for food on Pohnpei are imported shoyu and Tabasco *(dopasko)* sauces. Locally grown chili peppers *(sele)*, however, are often used in cooking. They are planted on a small scale in gardens, ripen in six to eight months, and are picked when they are red in color. Green, or bell-shaped peppers (also called *sele*) are seen occasionally in the markets.

Cinnamon *(sinamon)* is taken from the inner bark of a tree which grows wild on the island. It is yellowish-brown in color, and is often used in cooking.

Wild ginger *(sinter)* is quite widespread in the strand area lowlands of Pohnpei. It is found with white, yellow, and yellowish red flowers. The root of the plant is used for food flavoring, and roots and leaves are both used in soups. Two other uses: the plant makes an attractive floral decoration, and its Pohnpeian word, *sinter*, is a popular name for pretty female children.

The aromatic black pepper (*sele*, again) of Pohnpei is famous throughout Micronesia and is also sold in gourmet shops in the United States. Wild pepper on the island pre-dates written records, and thrives on Pohnpei's ideal conditions for growth: at least one hundred inches of rainfall per year evenly distributed in a tropical jungle near the equator. There are two species of wild pepper on the island. The commercial variety originated in Sarawak and was introduced to Pohnpei from Fiji in 1960.

The pepper vine produces three years after being planted. Cultivated peppercorns are the dried fruits of the pepper vine, and are processed into both black and white pepper. For black pepper, the berries are picked green in their mature stage and processed by being dipped in scalding water. They become black after drying in the sun. White peppercorns are produced from the ripe red berries, fermented in fresh-water streams until the red coat is removed. They are also dried in the sun. White pepper is milder than the pungent black peppercorns, and is preferred in food where black specks of pepper might detract from the dish.

Other than copra, black pepper is Pohnpei's largest export

crop, and it is the single most important spice crop in international commerce. Pohnpei has the climate, drainage, soil, humus, nursery stock and available land to produce some of the highest yields of pepper in the world. Only four countries—India, Indonesia, Brazil and Sarawak—produce 90% of the world's pepper, and Japan and the United States are natural markets for Pohnpei. However, limitations on production such as financial and technical assistance needed during the three-year establishment exist on the island.

There are about thirty acres of pepper vines under cultivation. In 1977, an American company, Specialty Brands (Spice Islands), was interested in developing 1,500 acres of pepper vines. Their study, however, determined that land, labor and management requirements were too expensive on Pohnpei.

Sugar cane *(sehu)* was grown commercially on a rather large scale by the Japanese. A sugar mill was completed shortly before World War II in Madolenihmw, but was converted to production of alcohol to meet military needs during the war. Sugar cane is now grown by individuals on a small scale. The plant requires little cultivation and is propagated from a section of a parent plant. It is popular among children, and is often served between meals or as a dessert. The cane is chewed and the juice sucked out. The fibers that remain are then discarded. Sugar cane is also significant as an offering in traditional Pohnpeian society.

Seaweed *(dihpw en nan sed)* refuses to be neatly categorized in this chapter. It is not eaten by Pohnpeians, but has been grown on an aquatic farm off of Takaieu Island in Pohnpei's lagoon. The first crop of 829 pounds was harvested in 1985. Exported to Japan, a ship's container load of seaweed sells for $7,000 to $10,000.

Plants Used for Beverages and Stimulants

Kava	*sakau en Pohnpei*
Tuba	*sikaliwi*
Coconut milk	*uhpw*
Coffee	*koahpi*
Tea	*dih*
Betelnuts	*pwuh*
Tobacco	*dapaker*
Marijuana	*maru*

The root of a pepper shrub, *piper methysticum (sakau)*, provides the king of beverages on the island. It is the *kava* of Micronesia, only found on Pohnpei and Kosrae, but widespread in Polynesia. The origin of sakau is wrapped in legend. In one story, also known on some islands of Polynesia, the discovery of sakau is attributed to a rat seen nibbling on a root and acting quite intoxicated. In another legend, more detailed, the original is traced to a Pohnpeian god, Luk. The skin of the heel of a mortal man, Uitannar, was given by Luk to a woman in payment for her kindness. She was told to bury the skin, and a plant would grow in its place. The juice of the plant would make people intoxicated and change their lives. This was done and the sakau plant was later spread throughout Pohnpei.

Sakau is found in two varieties, a "spotted branch" and a "smooth branch." (The former is preferred because it is more potent.) It grows best when planted during the time of the heaviest rains on damp, shady land near fresh water. The plants are rather easy to tend and it is only necessary to clean around them once each month. Sakau is propagated from cuttings, usually off of young branches of an old shrub, and is seldom found growing wild on the island. Like yams, sakau is a great source of pride for a Pohnpeian man. He will try to grow it secretly and conceal the amount planted.

To prepare sakau to drink, the roots of the shrub are pounded on a large, flat stone *(peitehl)*, selected especially for its ringing tone. The stone may be as large as six feet in diameter, and is slightly raised from the ground with coconut husks to increase the volume of sound. The stalks, leaves and dirt are first removed from the plant. The roots are broken off at the stem and placed on the pounding stone. Experienced men then pound the roots vigorously with stones, keeping a cadence or rhythm. Some pulp is laid out on wet hibiscus bast wound around in a specific manner. The juice is then squeezed out as small amounts of water are added, and the sakau is ready to be served in a coconut shell cup.

The *Ponapean/English Dictionary* lists thirty-one different sakau ceremonies, but there are more. Sakau is served at functions during pregnancy and commemorating births, when proposing marriages and following weddings, at funerals, when beginning and ending construction on a feast house, a home, or a canoe, and for departing and returning fishermen and friends. Feasts also take place at the beginning and the end of yam or breadfruit season and often in-between. There is even a feast, *uramai*, to celebrate the first use of a new sakau stone that will be used to celebrate future feasts. A sakau ceremoney is also the greatest inducement when seeking atonement from a traditional leader for an offense. A Nahnmwarki or Nahnken would lose popularity among his people if he scorned an offer of sakau from an offender. Repeated offers might be necessary to mollify the leader before he accepts the apology feast, *tohmw*, however.

The ceremony of serving is wrapped in great formality and is in strict accordance with rank. The leader of a ceremony is usually a man of high title who is well informed in the proper procedure of serving. The sequence may differ from one municipality to another, but the Nahnmwarki is always served first. After drinking, the cup is not passed from one man to another, but returned to the server to be refilled. After all chiefs present have drunk, it is then the turn of the commoners. The sakau makers continue to pound the roots and add water until the liquid becomes thin and weak. New plants are then prepared. At occasions such as funerals, sakau might be pounded continually for a number of days. There is no restriction on women drinking sakau, incidentally.

Half of the roots of an average size plant is enough sakau for one stone, and twenty people can drink the whole evening on the amount of sakau pounded. The immediate effect of the drink is a numbing of the lips and tongue, and a slowing of speech. Some drinkers prefer to sip a beer while taking sakau in order to increase the pace of intoxication. However, a gourmet drinker of sakau, F.W. Christian, writing in 1899 had this to say about mixing sakau with other drinks: "If a white trader insists on mixing good kava with bad gin, he has simply to face the consequences. Beer, whiskey and wine are strictly to be avoided...as incompatible with the true kava frame of mind. If these simple and useful instructions are disregarded, as the writer has no doubt they will be, the innocent kava root cannot be held responsible. Into the hands of doctors I commend it."

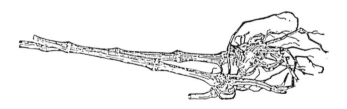

Sakau Root

After several cups of sakau, speech becomes thick although the head remains clear. Eventually, some control of the limbs is lost. As Christian put it, after more than three cups, "one leg struggles south while the other is marching due north." After a night of sakau, some drinkers become famished and eat large quantities of food after returning home. Others prefer a bowl of warm soup or broth which they claim increases their "high." In all cases, though, a pleasant, deep sleep follows a night of sakau drinking.

"Music hath charms to soothe the savage beast," and so does sakau. In fact, there is a Pohnpeian story told about how sakau in olden days was served to upset Nahnmwarkis to calm them down. However, sakau and loud music are forever enemies. Any noise, even loud conversation, is intolerably magnified and very unpleasant to any sakau drinker.

Some foreign administrations have influenced the growth and consumption of sakau. The Spanish exerted no influence over sakau drinking during their short tenure on the island. (Catholic clergymen, incidentally, have always been more tolerant of sakau drinking than their Protestant counterparts.) During the German Period, each land deed holder was required to present a yam and a sakau plant to the chief of the area in which he lived each year. This was intended to partly compensate the chief for relinquishing claim of ownership to the land. During the Japanese Period, growing sakau was restricted because drinking interfered with attendance and proficiency of laborers—Pohnpeian moonshiners must have been abundant at the time. After 1930, an official license was required from the administration to grow the plant. This law, however, was not enforced during World War II. The American administration lifted all restrictions on growing or drinking sakau.

Sakau drinking on the island at present is a form of night time entertainment, and there are about sixty-five sakau bars located throughout the six municipalities of Pohnpei. According to an acute observer of Pohnpeian society, Fr. William McGarry writing in *West from Katau*, "I would take a guess and say that out of any six or seven houses any place in Pohnpei, you will find sakau at one of them with some of the neighbors very likely present." The typical sakau bar is a clean, open-air, dimly lit, undecorated thatch-roof structure, furnished with benches and tables made of local wood. The price of one drink varies only slightly from one bar to another, and a coconut shell cup filled with rich Pohnpeian culture and tradition can be had for a mere quarter of a dollar.

Another intoxicating drink made from the fermented sap of the coconut tree *(sikaliwi)* is often called a coconut toddy or *tuba*. It is much more common on atolls than on Pohnpei proper. The beverage is produced by bending the spathe of a palm to a horizontal position, and tightly binding the spathe before the blossoms open. The tip of the spathe is then slit, allowing sap to drip into a coconut shell or a bottle. It may be served full strength or diluted with water.

Coconut liquid, referred to in different publications as milk, water, or juice, is taken from green drinking coconut *(uhpw)*. It is an important, constantly available, safe water supply, especially on the atolls of Pohnpei State where drought can be a problem. The soft flesh of the drinking nut is jellylike, and often fed to infants.

Coffee (koahpi) was grown by the Japanese, but is no longer cultivated. Some remnants of the coffee bean plants, however, can still be found growing wild in unused fields on the island. In 1985, several coffee trees were grown as an experiment by the State Agriculture Division. Following processing, drying and roasting, the product was rated good to excellent by local coffee drinkers. A research center in Costa Rica has been contacted to determine varieties of coffee best adaptable to Pohnpei's soil and climate.

The only fruit juices available locally are coconut liquid, mentioned above, and occasionally *limeade*. A delicious *tea (madeu)* is made from boiling small pieces of the inner bark of a cinnamon tree that grows wild on the island.

Betelnut (pwuh) is chewed by more non-Pohnpeians (especially Palauans and Yapese) on the island than Pohnpeians. The two varieties of the areca tree from which the nut is picked are usually found in highlands, but grow on Pohnpei from the coastal plain into the mountains. The graceful palm has a very slender trunk and reaches to forty or fifty feet in height.

Chewing betelnut is estimated to be a habit of one-tenth of the world's population, mainly centered in southern Asia and the East Indies. For chewing, the nut is cracked in half and sprinkled with granulated lime to stimulate salivation. The nut is then wrapped in a leaf of betel pepper and is ready to be chewed. To add to its potency the tobacco of a cigarette may be added. The result is a mild narcotic high that lasts perhaps ten minutes. The teeth of James Michener's Bloody Mary have been a terrible advertisement for the rather innocent betelnut. Contrary to popular belief, the teeth of habitual chewers are not permanently darkened.

Tobacco (dapaker) is cultivated and cured on a very small scale on individual farmsteads. The Japanese in the 1930's experimented with tobacco, but never developed it commercially. During World War II when imports ceased, locally grown tobacco was the only source for smoking.

Tobacco is planted from seeds, and takes eight months before it is ready to be cured. As packages of imported cigarettes on Pohnpei creep up to one dollar each in price, local tobacco might well experience a renaissance.

Marijuana (for which there is no native Pohnpeian word) grows on Pohnpei. However, it is a crime to either grow or sell it. It is an imported plant and has only appeared in any quantity in the last ten years. Marijuana is smoked mostly by foreigners, and gourmet users have informed the author that it is not of particularly high quality, probably because of poor soil and excessive rainfall. Marijuana is propagated from seeds of a parent plant. Its dried leaves used for smoking mature in about four to five months.

Plants Used for Building, Weaving and Decorations

Mangrove	*ahk*
Breadfruit	*mahi*
Bamboo	*pehri*
Coconut palm	*nih*

Nipa palm	*parem*
Ivory nut palm	*oahs*
Pandanus	*kipar*
Hibiscus	*keleu*
Reeds	*sihr*
Copper plant	*kurodong*
Jasmine	*sampakihda*
Fragraea seir	*seir en Pohnpei*
Ylang ylang	*seir en wai*
Plumeria	*pwohmaria*
Orchids	*lamwahk*
Bougainvilla	*pwukenwilia*

Preferred building materials on Pohnpei are imported cement, structural rebar, and corrugated metal roofing. Pohnpei's high humidity, excessive rainfall, and termites are not kind to locally-grown building materials. A palm thatch roof, for instance, will last for only three or four years before it must be replaced, whereas a corrugated metal roof lasts ten to fifteen years and can also be used to funnel water into a catchment. The greatest advantage to using locally grown materials for construction is, of course, the cost. A family dwelling, an outdoor kitchen, a storeroom or a canoe house, with mangrove wood supports and beams, walls made from reeds, roofing of thatch from an ivory nut or nipa palm, flooring made from the lumber of breadfruit trees, and sleeping mats of woven pandanus, might cost the builder little more than the price of the food supplied for his helpers.

Pohnpei has nearly sixty thousand acres of forest, and they contain some varieties of hardwoods used in construction. While demolishing a building at the Agriculture Station recently, treated timbers of cedar fifty years old were found to still be in good condition. In the mixed forest area of the interior, however, the vegetation consists mainly of herbaceous plants unsuitable for construction projects. These extensive forests include most plants native to Pohnpei. Mosses, ferns and other epiphytes are constantly damp from rain or mist in the uplands. Sawmills have been more or less in continuous operation since the German Period, and two are presently operating on Pohnpei, one in Nett and the other in Madolenihmw.

The most readily accessible source of wood, and the most inexpensive, is the 5,900 acres of *mangrove* trees *(ahk)* surrounding Pohnpei. Because of mangrove forests, Pohnpei has few sandy beaches. However, these same trees surrounding the island prevent erosion of the shoreline from tides, waves, and currents. Conditions on Pohnpei are ideal for this type of vegetation: a relatively mild climate; saline or brackish water; a substratum of silt deposited from rivers and streams; and a surrounding barrier reef to prevent the surf from striking the shore. The roots and trunks of the mangrove trees are continually or intermittently immersed in water. When the land level begins to rise, mangrove is succeeded by strand or rain-forest vegetation.

There are five species of mangrove trees on Pohnpei, with three distinctive root characteristics. The **Rhizophora** has long roots that arch through the air, the **Bruguiera** has knee-like root projections, and the **Sonneratia** has a spike-like root. The outstanding characteristic of all types is their strength. Mangrove is used in construction and also for making furniture. The wood is extremely heavy, hard, and will not float. If allowed to dry for several weeks after being cut, the wood becomes almost too hard to work with. The Japanese used mangrove for charcoal, but it is used more often for firewood at present. During World War II, mangrove trees were tested as an obstacle to amphibious tractors and tanks. They proved to be an impenetrable barrier to even the most determined attacking force, and certainly influenced the decision to bypass Pohnpei in the war.

Mangrove is the preferred wood of the expert Kapingamarangan carvers on Pohnpei. Branches can be found in all sizes, but more significantly for carving, in any desired shape. The wood seldom splinters, and has a very attractive grain.

Breadfruit (mahi) trees provide good lumber, but they are not a main source of wood because of the value of their fruit.

The wood is excellent for making hulls of large canoes. It is strong and can be easily worked. Breadfruit planks are also used for flooring for homes, although a concrete slab is preferred because of termites.

Bamboo (pehri) was first introduced on Pohnpei in pre-Spanish times, and different varieties were brought by both the Germans and the Japanese. At present it grows wild or is planted in small quantities by individual farmsteads. It was cultivated and used extensively by the Japanese and Okinawans on Pohnpei in their fishing industry before the development of suitable synthetics. At present, bamboo can mostly be seen as supports for forms in construction, and occasionally bound into rafts on the rivers.

Palm trees (nih), cut into sections, are used for posts and heavy duty supports, although other woods are usually preferred. *Fern logs (katar)* are most often used for supports for vines of pepper plants, and also used in growing orchids. The *nipa palm (parem)* and the *ivory nut palm (oahs)*, however, are preferred material for thatch roofing. The life of a thatch roof, incidentally, depends on the angle of the peak and the tightness of the weave—and the fickleness of the winds.

Much weaving is done to provide handicraft for the island's several souvenir and gift shops, and a sizable amount of woven items is exported, mainly to Hawaii.

Pandanus (kipar) is used for both weaving and as a supplementary food source, and is one of the most utilitarian of fibrous plants. Large woven mats, expertly made by the girls and women of the Kapingamarangan community in Pohnpei State, are especially popular. Other items woven from pandanus are containers such as fruit bowls and baskets, decorative serving trays, table placement mats, and even Texas-style ten-gallon hats.

Pandanus has both a male and female variety, but only the latter bears fruit. It grows wild, and can be found throughout Pohnpei. Historically, pandanus was baked and made into a paste or flour. Taken on long sea voyages, it was used as energy food and also a source of emergency rations. As paste, pandanus can be kept for a year or more, so it is always available out of season. To make flour, the fruit is steamed in an oven and then pounded into a paste. It is molded into flat cakes and dried in the sun or over hot stones. When needed, the cakes are broken and pounded into the consistency of flour, which can then be kept for years, if necessary. Pandanus fruit can also be eaten raw and is quite juicy. Cooked and pounded, the fruit looks very much like yellow mashed potatoes.

Hibiscus (keleu) is not cultivated, but its wood, flowers and fiber have significant uses on Pohnpei. Hibiscus is a very light wood and its young branches are used for carrying poles *(arepe)*. The larger sections of the tree are the preferred logs for fastening outrigger sections of local canoes. The inner bark has several important uses. When dried, it is a readily available supply of cordage and is also used as weaving material. Until the Japanese administration, the inner bark of the hibiscus tree was a main source of material for making clothing. It is soft and durable, excellent for making grass skirts. Even today, the native hula skirt of Hawaiian dancing fame, purchased as a souvenir on Waikiki Beach, might well have been made on Pohnpei. The skirts are sold by the piece on the island to three exporters. Following shipment to a wholesaler in Honolulu—one order filled an entire ship's container—the skirts are treated with fire-proofing liquid, colored, and distributed to retailers in Hawaii and the U.S. mainland. Some 18,000 skirts were exported in 1984. To a traditional Pohnpeian, an important use today is as bast for preparing *sakau*. The most common decorative plants are the numerous varieties of hibiscus flowers seen throughout the lowlands and the lower mountain slopes on the island.

Colors autumn has are unexpected in seasonless Pohnpei, except for the *Copper Plant (kurodong)* and its varied deep reds, dark browns, and maroons, a startling contrast to the island's uninterrupted greenery. An imported plant, it is used mainly as hedges around homes for decoration and privacy. The plant grows quickly from branches of a parent plant stuck into the ground, but will not grow wild. It reaches a height of fifteen to twenty feet if not trimmed. Pohnpeians often plant it around new graves as a distinctive marker, a contrast to the enshrouding green jungle.

Reeds *(sihr)* about a half inch in diameter and of varying lengths are used for walls and floors in some homes, much more in the past than at present, however. Their most apparent use today is as a vehicle in a competition game called *pei sihr*, the only game that predates foreign administration of Pohnpei, incidentally. A reed about three feet in length is skimmed along the ground, flies into the air, and lands some distance away. The competitor whose reed is the farthest distance away wins the contest.

> *If on your way*
> *To Pohnpei,*
> *Be sure to wear*
> *Flowers in your hair.*

Garlands made of flowers, *mwaramwars*, are the most popular floral decoration for Pohnpeians, and visitors to the island as well. They are worn by both men and women, particularly on festive occasions, when welcoming friends, and when parting to go on journeys. Mwaramwars may be made with any kind of flower. One of the most popular is strung with white *jasmine* buds *(sampakihda)* that bloom several hours after being picked. Other popular wreaths are made from cream colored *fragrea seir* flowers *(seir en Pohnpei)* that slowly turn to a golden hue as their fragrance increases, and the green, pleasant smelling, grass-like *ylang ylang (seir en wai)*. Leis are also worn on festive occasions, but somewhat less frequently than mwaramwars. The loveliest are made of yellow, white, and pink *plumeria (pwohmaria)*, *orchids (lamwahk)* or hibiscus flowers. Purple, red, orange and white *bougainvilla (pwukenwila)*, along with palm fronds, are often used to decorate homes, halls, and nahs' on special occasions.

Seir en Pohnpei
Mwaramwar

A very interesting book is waiting to be written about the uses of plants in local medicines, and the requirements and rituals surrounding them. Traditional cures using plants, however, are often coveted information which is not given away casually.

Small quantities of a large number of other plants have been grown on Pohnpei over the years, but are not significant in the diet. Included among these are pumpkins, squash, watermelon, onions, cucumbers, beans, egg plant, tomatoes, spinach, cabbage, lettuce, parsley, turnips, peas, soy beans, and okra (see *History*, p. 76). Actually, the tapestry of vegetation covering Pohnpei is a bit of a green deception, and conceals soil rather poor in plant nutrients. For truck crops to prosper on the island, large amounts of fertilizer and pesticides are always required.

FAUNA OF POHNPEI

Introduction

There is no single publication available that concentrates on mammals and reptiles on Pohnpei, or in Micronesia for that matter. The best source of information is *Ponape: A Pacific Economy in Transition* by William R. Bascom, written in 1946. A good list of selected species of animals with scientific terminology appears in *Ponape Island, Land Use Guide,* a study published in 1979 by the Office of Planning and Statistics, T.T.P.I.

Over the years, Pohnpei has been home for visitor and resident mammals, fowl, reptiles, rodents, and other creepers and crawlers. Among the immigrants have been carabao, first brought from the Philippines via the Mariana Islands during the Spanish Period, and pheasants and quail imported from Hong Kong during the German administration. (The sturdy carabao remain, but the pheasants and quail are no longer on the island. Also gone are two other birds, ostriches brought originally by the former patriarch of the Nanpei family, the first Henry Nanpei.) Cattle were introduced in the last century from Hawaii by American missionaries, and goats were also brought to the island at that time. Two buck deer and one doe were imported from Saipan in 1904 by Germans, and were set free. (These were the progenators, incidentally, of deer occasionally seen as close as the outskirts of Kolonia.) Horses have been on Pohnpei during the

German, Japanese, and American administrations, but none are on the island at present. The most important animals to Pohnpeians, pigs, have been on the island since the Early Contact Period.

Mammals and Fowl

Deer	*tie*
Pigs	*pwihk*
Dogs	*kidi*
Cows	*kou*
Carabao	*karapahu*
Goats	*kout*
Sheep	*sihpw*
Chickens	*malek*
Ducks	*tehk*

As mentioned above, deer *(tie)* were first brought to Pohnpei from Saipan during the German administration, and were set free. The three original animals were able to increase to a herd because the interior of Pohnpei was much more penetrable by deer than by humans, and there were only an estimated 3,500 Pohnpeians on the island at the time. (Presently, the population is some 27,000, but the interior is no more penetrable.) Deer are hunted by setting up blinds on deer trails. They are also killed by using dogs to chase them into rivers and streams. There is no hunting season on the island, nor is there a limit on the number of deer that may be killed. A small herd is kept in captivity on a farm in the Palikir section of Sokehs municipality.

Pigs *(pwihk)* mentioned in the earliest written records, are the most prized animals on Pohnpei. They are an economic asset as well as a prestige symbol at traditional feasts. (A birthday, wedding, or funeral gathering, or a *kamadipw* given for a traditional leader, would hardly be complete without the slaughter of one or more pigs.) Except around Kolonia where they are penned in piggeries, most swine roam free. They are fed minimally in the morning by their owners, and then allowed to forage for themselves. Often pigs will cause damage to crops on the farmstead of a neighbor. The owner of the pigs is then liable for damages caused by his animals. At feasts, pigs are most often baked in an *uhmw,* a cone-shaped oven constructed by stacking heated stones on burning wood. At this writing (1986) the price for swine on the hoof on Pohnpei is nearly two dollars per pound. There are an estimated 6,000 pigs on the island whose longevity is directly related to the number of funeral feasts and traditional celebrations that take place at any given time.

Dogs *(kidi)* on Pohnpei are mostly scrub varieties, small in size, often underfed, but hardy. They are valued as watchdogs, and ceremonially as a food at feasts. They are usually fed enough leftovers by their owners to discourage them from wandering too far afield, but must also forage for much of their food. Historically, dogs have been a main source of protein, along with pigs, chicken, and fish. For consumption, they are baked in an *uhmw* in the same manner as pigs. Dogs, and also cats, are often kept as pets, particularly by Pohnpeian children. Vegetarian dogs were found in Polynesia during the Early Contact Period, but there is no record of any on Pohnpei.

Cattle *(kou)* have had mixed reviews by Pohnpeians, although they have been used for meat, milk, and plowing. On small farmsteads, they can cause damage because of limited grazing space and a propensity for eating vines— particularly those of coveted Pohnpeian yams. There had been as many as six hundred head of cattle on Pohnpei at the start of World War II, concentrated mainly in Madolenihmw. They were utilized as draft animals and for controlling weeds in coconut groves (two cows were needed for each hectare containing 120 trees). By 1946, however, the herd had decreased to sixty-eight. Most fell victim to a food shortage by the Japanese during the War.

The carabao *(karapahu)* of Pohnpei are fearful in appearance, and look much like the dangerous African Cape Buffalo. But the resemblance ends with the appearance. The pacified carabao have been recorded off and on for a century in Pohnpei. Japanese figures in 1925 and 1931 show no carabao, but there were twenty-six on the island in 1937, sixty at the beginning of the American administration, and sixty-four in the last animal census in 1977. Carabao have been used mainly for plowing and hauling. The meat of slaughtered animals was eaten by Japanese, but had no appeal to Pohnpeians.

There are about 500 goats *(kout)* on Pohnpei, and they are found throughout the island either tethered or foraging for food. They are raised for their meat. Goats are presented at traditional feasts and are sold mainly to Filipino and Korean workers temporarily on Pohnpei.

The German government attempted to raise sheep *(sihpw)*, and in 1904 had a flock of thirty-seven on Pohnpei. Being a temperate climate animal, it is doubtful that they would thrive on a tropical island near the equator where there is little demand for wool. It is also possible that the severe typhoon of 1905 (see *History,* pp. 63) hurried their departure.

Chickens *(malek)* on Pohnpei date from the Prehistory Period, and are raised for both meat and eggs. Along with fish, chicken is the main source of protein for Pohnpeians, and nearly every homestead outside of Kolonia has at least one rooster and a number of hens. Chickens roam free and must forage for most of their own food. They are usually provided a bit of grated coconut or papaya or small pieces of yams and bananas to entice them to return to the home of their owners. Local chickens are rather scrawny, but hardy, and only produce some seventy eggs per year. There are, however, four poultry farms on Pohnpei, one with about 3,000 layers. These farms produce the fresh, quality eggs sold in most stores on the island. Nearly all of the chickens sold are imported frozen.

The only other fowls raised are ducks *(tehk)*. They are few in number, and do not enter into the prestige economy. Oceanic birds are caught and eaten often, but of course are not raised (see *Birds*, pp. 152-154).

Reptiles, Mollusks, Rodents

Crocodiles	*kieil*
Geckoes	*lamwer*
Lizards	*kieil*
Sea Turtles	*wehi*
Toads	*kairu*
Snakes	*sinek*
Snails	*dendenmwosi*
Rats	*kitik*
Bats	*pwehk*

The most famous reptile of recent vintage was a salt-water crocodile *(kieil)* trapped and killed in 1971. As it happened, the disappearance of pigs from Pwok village in Kitti and strange, unfamiliar tracks prompted a creature-hunt and the construction of a sturdy trap that measured 8 feet by 11 feet by 7 feet. A pig was used as bait. The crocodile was trapped and killed, and measured nearly thirteen feet in length. After being displayed in Kolonia, the reptile, minus its claws that were kept as souvenirs, was given to a group of Palauans and promptly consumed. Relatives of the crocodile are occasionally reported to have been seen around Pohnpei, but no sightings have been confirmed. (There is on record a report that the Polish ethnologist Johann Stanislaus Kubary brought two small alligators to Pohnpei nearly a century ago. For some reason, he let them loose. A noted contemporary observer of Kubary, F. W. Christian, in *The Caroline Islands—Travel in the Sea of Little Lands,* wondered about the ethnologist's sanity. Shortly afterward, Kubary committed suicide.)

The most commonly seen reptile, at the opposite end of the spectrum from the crocodile, is the gecko *(lamwer)*. This small (two to four inch) tropical, nocturnal lizard, light brown in color, can be found in most homes on Pohnpei—nearly always in a perpendicular or upside down position. (Geckoes have expanded toes equipped with adhesive disks, ideal for travel on walls and ceilings.) These small reptiles make a rather loud, crackling noise, but are completely harmless to humans, and are valuable as predators of pesty insects. Besides geckoes, five other varieties of lizards are found on Pohnpei.

Salt-water Crocodile

Monitor lizards *(kieil)* ugly and fearful in appearance, but harmless and shy around humans, are on Pohnpei. They are various shades of green in color and some measure more than three feet in length. The lizards were brought to the island by the Japanese and used as a supplemental food source. Pohnpeians, however, did not eat them. Civilization seems to be this reptile's biggest enemy and encroaching homesteads have driven many of the lizards into the unin-habited interior of the island. However, a colleague of the author made acquaintance with a monitor lizard at the top of a coconut tree he had climbed. It was a most shaking exper-ience — for both.

144

Sea-turtles *(wehi)* are found around Pohnpei, particularly on the off-shore atoll of Ant. The most common is the Pacific green turtle, which is a protected species. (It can be caught for food, but not for profit.) Two other common turtles found in the area, the leatherback and the hawksbill, are among the endangered species. The leatherback turtles weigh up to a ton, and are the only turtles that cannot retract their heads and fins, making them vulnerable to shark attacks. Turtles fully grown can measure more than three feet in diameter. They are highly prized by Pohnpeians for their meat, and the eggs of turtles are considered to be a delicacy. Consequently, sea-turtles always avoid inhabited areas of islands.

Hawksbill Turtle

Toads *(kairu)*, often mistaken for reptiles, are found too often on Pohnpei. Originally brought to the island by the Japanese for insect control, these prolific amphibians have no natural enemies. Fully grown, they are about five inches in length and weigh more than half a pound. They are dark brown to black in color and are often seen pancaked on the roads of Pohnpei. Toads also die in wells, catchments and drains, causing a stench and a possible health hazard.

Toad

There are no terrestrial snakes *(sinek)* on the island, although fresh-water eels in creeks and rivers are often mistaken for them. A salt-water snake, however, is found in Madolenihmw Harbor.

Probably the worst pests on Pohnpei are the giant African snails *(dendenmwosi)* because of their ability to eat almost anything. They were first introduced on the island around 1937 by an Okinawan as a commercial venture and were originally raised in boxes. A number of snails slowly escaped and spread with such profusion that the Japanese administration required all school children in Kolonia to gather a bucketfull each on the way to school and dump them in the lagoon. During World War II the snails were used as a source of protein by the Japanese. However, Pohnpeians would not eat them because the snails fed on animal and human waste. The giant African snails are not really giants at all. They have moist, rubbery skin, black-brown in color, measure four to five inches in length and no more than three inches from the ground to the top of their conical shells. They are active chiefly at night during overcast or wet weather and cause the most damage during rainy months—which is all year around on Pohnpei. They lay eggs under trash, rocks and debris on moist ground. The snails have no natural enemies on Pohnpei and usually live out a complete life cycle of about five months, barring crushing accidents. Mosquitoes breed in their empty shells that fill with water, adding to the snails' nuisance value. For eating, the snails were boiled into a soup to which shoyu, napa, papaya and other ingredients were added by the Japanese.

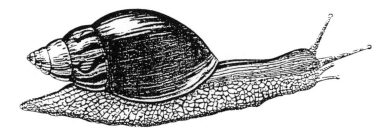

Giant African Snail

Rats and mice *(kitik)* are quite common on Pohnpei and were eaten as late as the early part of the German Period. Rats feed mainly on garbage, drying copra, young coconuts, melons, and insects. The large fruit bats of the genus *Pteropus* are the most widespread of native mammals, unless rats are considered native. They can be seen leaving the caves on Sokehs most evenings. Small insectivorous bats are also found on the island.

Insects

Mosquitoes	*amwise*
Houseflies	*loahng*
Gnats	*mahn en losapw*
Cockroaches	*kol*
Termites	*lohng*
Centipedes	*meninrahn*
Lice	*likarak*
Fleas	*likarak*
Wasps	*loangalap*
Scorpions	*eskorpion*
Beetles	*kisin mahn*

One of the most comprehensive studies on any aspect of Micronesia is the twenty volumes, *Insects of Micronesia,* published by the Bishop Museum in Honolulu.

More than 2,000 species of insects are known on Pohnpei, of which perhaps fifteen percent have been introduced by man. Other means of arrival are through atmospheric movements such as winds of storms, on floating vegetation carried by currents, and by migratory birds. Although numerous, insects on Pohnpei actually comprise only a relatively small number of genera living in unexposed areas. Large day-flying insects are few and large insects in general are much more rare on the island than they would be in a tropical areas of a continent.

Five insects mentioned below are most frequently encountered by visitors to Pohnpei. The most irritating are mosquitoes, flies, and biting gnats; the most repulsive are two species of cockroaches; and the most destructive are termites. All, incidentally, are said to have accompanied islanders in their wanderings and were brought to Pohnpei by man. Several other biting and stinging pests are not encountered as often: centipedes, lice, fleas, wasps, and scorpions.

Historically, mosquitoes *(amwise)* have been man's deadliest enemy among insects by spreading malaria, mainly in tropical areas. But fortunately not on Pohnpei. There is no malaria on the island, although the females of several species of mosquito found on Pohnpei are capable of carrying the disease. Cases of dengue fever transmitted by mosquitos and causing severe pains in muscles and joints occur, but the disease is never fatal. Most mosquitoes on Pohnpei are night-biting pests. They breed in stagnant water often found in tree holes, discarded coconut shells, snail shells, or anywhere that larvae can live and grow in water. Screening is probably the best protection from mosquitoes. Other methods of protection are lighted mosquito coils, aerosol sprays, mosquito nets, and clothing.

Any visitor to Pohnpei will immediately recognize the common housefly *(loahng)*, probably the most annoying and disease-spreading insect pest on the island. The fly is found in particular abundance around domesticated animals, and breeds in fresh excrement, fermenting vegetation such as rotting breadfruit, and in the carrions of squashed toads and snails on roadsides. Flies feed only on liquids, but often spread dysentery by lighting on filth and carrying it onto food. Control on Pohnpei is by eliminating breeding areas, screening, and the use of pesticides.

Biting gnats *(mahn en losapw)* live in the mud of mangrove swamps along the shoreline, and are so minute that they are barely visible. These gnats have a piercing, sucking mouth, an annoying bite that causes an itch, and they attack by battalions rather than individually. Biting midges, however, are not spreaders of disease. They are most active on Pohnpei shortly before sunset on evenings in which there is no rain and complete calm. The best protection from biting is a favorable wind, but aerosol sprays and clothing are also helpful.

Throughout the years, cockroaches *(kol)* have been the most frequent stowaways among larger insects brought to Pohnpei, and have survived wherever man has ventured from the arctic to the equator. They are most abundant, however, in the tropics. Roaches are said to be the most ancient of insects, estimated to have existed for 400 million years. On

Pohnpei there are two main types: the Australasian and the oriental. Both are capable of flying short distances, and are found throughout the island. Like the giant African snail, cockroaches will eat nearly anything. Those on Pohnpei are dark reddish-brown in color and range in size from about a half-inch to nearly three inches in length. Most live in decaying or rotting matter, but they also inhabit dark places and cracks and crevices in homes and are repelled by light. The best prevention on Pohnpei is pesticides, keeping food covered, and disposal of garbage. However, eliminating cockroaches from an area is a never-ending struggle.

Termites *(lohng)* flourish on Pohnpei, and are divided into two groups: subterranean insects and dry-wood termites. The latter are the dayfliers that are often seen, and which periodically shed their wings after a rain. They are about three-quarters of an inch in length. Subterranean termites live on or under the ground. Both species feed on wood so abundant on Pohnpei, or wood products such as paper, but will not feed on living trees. The best protection from termites is the use of building materials that are free of wood, or by coating wood with termite-resistant chemicals.

Centipedes *(meninrahn)*, usually found under stones, bark, leaf litter, in rocky crevices, or in thatch walls and roofs, are actually very shy and will avoid humans whenever possible. Their bites, however, cause a fiery pain, usually accompanied by swelling and fever. Centipedes measure about six inches in length and are reddish in color.

Lice *(likarak)* are carried by chickens, birds, and rats in addition to humans on the island, and they probably accompanied the first islanders in their wandering voyages throughout Oceania. The most common are head lice, although pubic lice are also found. The pesty head lice are common among female children, and definitely prefer long hair to short hair for their homes. A tropical bed bug is also found on the island. Fleas *(likarak)* are not a problem because of the damp environment. This same condition, however, encourages the breeding of flies. A species of flea is present that lives on dogs and cats.

A slow-flying wasp *(loangalap)* is seen more frequently. It is black in color and its slender body measures about an inch in length. Wasps build mud nests in structures such as a native thatch house or a *nahs* which have numerous openings. On Pohnpei wasps seldom sting humans. They are probably the most prevalent stinging insects in Micronesia.

Scorpions *(eskorpion)*, like the feared centipedes, a terrestrial arthropod, are night-crawlers and seldom seen. They travel alone and are only in pairs when mating. They are most frequently found under rocks or foliage in unexposed areas, but occasionally are found in homes on Pohnpei. Their bites are extremely painful, but scorpions avoid contact with humans if at all possible. They feed on insects using crab-like claws, but sting with their tails. The species on Pohnpei measures about two inches in length and is gray in color.

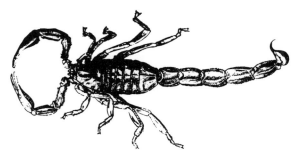

Scorpion

There have been a number of beetle pests (all beetles in Pohnpeian are called *kisin mahn,* or little animals) over the past years that have been destructive to crops. All have been brought to the island, usually by cargo vessels, and spread to local crops. Among the most serious are the rhinoceros beetle which attacks coconut palms, the banana root borer, and the Mariana (Saipan) coconut beetle. Alert eradication efforts by Japanese and U.S. Trust Territory agriculture departments have prevented serious damage on Pohnpei by introducing viruses, predators, or parasites to combat the beetles.

Rhinoceros
Beetle

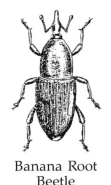
Banana Root
Beetle

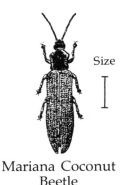
Size

Mariana Coconut
Beetle

(approximate size)

Birds

Oceanic birds	*menpihr en nansed*
Land birds	*menpihr en nansapw*

The best description of the birds of Pohnpei is in *The Avifauna of Micronesia, Its Origin, Evolution and Distribution,* by Rollin H. Baker. An informative source available locally is *Birds of Micronesia* by Harvey G. Segal, an instructor at the Community College of Micronesia.

Human activities have caused a decrease in the number of birds native to Pohnpei. At least five species formerly on Pohnpei are thought to be extinct because of a changing habitat since contact with western civilization began.

It is impossible to consider the birds of the island out of context of other areas of the Pacific because so many are migratory. The avifauna of Micronesia alone consists of 206 kinds of birds belonging to thirty-seven families and ninety-one genera. Ornithologists divide the birds into three main categories, then subdivide them further for classification. The main categories are oceanic birds; migratory shore birds; and land and freshwater birds.

There are thirty kinds of oceanic birds *(menpihr en nansed)* recorded in Micronesia, of which eighteen are said to be resident and twelve are visitors. These are divided into inshore and offshore varieties. The inshore birds prefer the area from the mangrove swamp on Pohnpei to the barrier reef, and search for food in the lagoon. However, they also come to shore frequently, and insects are part of their diet. Common on Pohnpei are the reef heron, the noddy tern, and the white (fairy) tern. The offshore birds spend considerable time at sea and inhabit an area from the barrier reef to distances well beyond the sight of land. On Pohnpei these offshore birds include the red-footed booby, frigate bird and the tropic bird.

Of the twenty-nine species of migratory shore birds seventeen species are regularly seen and twelve are uncommon. Migratory birds are believed to have reached the island from Polynesia, Melanesia, the Moluccas, Celebes, Philippines and Palearctica. On migratory flights, birds arrive by three specific routes: via Palau from Asia; south from the Sea of Japan via the Mariana Islands; and from the east via the Hawaiian Islands. The golden plover, the New Zealand cuckoo and the Polynesian tattler are frequently found on Pohnpei.

There are some 147 kinds of land and freshwater birds *(menpihr en nansapw)* in Micronesia, of which only six have been introduced by man. It is believed that Pohnpei's shore birds gradually spread from the eastern hemisphere rather than from the Americas. Important factors in the dispersal of bird life have been the direction and intensity of winds, the size of islands and their isolation, and the climate. Perhaps the most common bird found on Pohnpei is the noddy tern. Other prominent land birds are the Micronesian kingfisher and the reed warbler.

On Pohnpei there are a total of thirty-nine species. Included are heron, seven species of the snipe/sandpiper family; six gulls and terns; two doves and a pigeon; a lory; an owl; a kingfisher; and two starlings. There are historical accounts of Pohnpeians being provided with rifles and ammunition from visiting sailing vessels with which to hunt pigeons. At present, bird hunting is done mostly by youngsters who hurl stones with surprising accuracy. A pigeon hunting season, however, takes place in the month of December annually.

By an act of the Pohnpei State Legislature on October 22, 1981, the official state bird was designated as the Pohnpei Lorikeet *(serehd)*. This small five-inch parrot-like bird has a reddish coloring with a purple head and yellow tail feathers. It is sometimes found as a pet in Pohnpei households, although state laws have been enacted to protect the lorikeet from being hunted. Its feathers are used for decoration and also for lures made for tuna fishing. (In an informal survey among twenty Pohnpeians, none was able to name the official state bird. Most guessed, hopefully with tongues in cheeks, frozen chicken or turkey-tail, two popular protein meals in the Pohnpeian diet.)

Pohnpei Lorikeet

Fish and Sea Shells

Fish	*mwahmw*
Sea shells	*pwili*

Fish *(mwahmw)* is a major source of protein in the Pohnpeian diet, but is not a part of the prestige economy. There are more than 1,200 kinds of fish recorded in Pohnpei waters, only four of which are said to be inedible. Main fishes are bonito, yellow fin and skipjack tuna, mahi mahi, barracuda, sea bass, sharks, snappers, stone fish, parrotfish, flying fish, gobies, archer fish, flounder, butterfly fish, surgeon fish, trigger fish, marlin, and sailfish. Dolphins are abundant, but whales are few. Off of Ponhpei , fishing is mainly done in the lagoon, and so reefs, tides and water depth affect both the fishing techniques used and the type of fish that are caught. Generally, low islanders of Pohnpei State are better fishermen than native Pohnpeians because they are much more dependent on the sea for survival.

Years ago, the shells of mollusks or turtles were fashioned into fish hooks, and the fibers from coconut husks were woven into sennit for fishing lines. Since the Japanese administration, these have been entirely replaced by metal hooks and imported fishing line, except in the several tourist craft shops on the island.

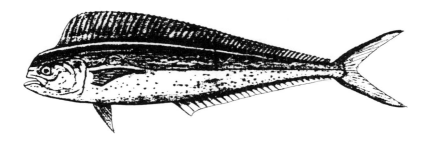

Mahi Mahi or Dolphin-Fish

Before World War II, a mini-fishing industry was established by the Japanese, and bonito fishing surpassed even copra in the value of exports. There were five small Okinawan companies and one large Japanese firm on the island in 1940. At present, there is no local commercial fishing industry that exports its product. A 160-ton capacity cold-storage facility was completed in March, 1986, at a cost of $1.7 million to encourage a local commercial fishing industry. It is located on the dock at Takatik Island adjacent to the airport.

Fishing takes place both day and night on Pohnpei. Hook and line fishing from canoes, motorboats, or from the shore is the most popular method. Net fishing was introduced by the Japanese. Formerly, Pohnpeians made their own nets out of purchased string and lead weights, but imported nylon nets have replaced them. A home-made dip net is still used to catch shrimp in mountain streams, however. Spear fishing used to be done with multiple-point wooden spears. Metal spears, usually propelled by a length of surgical tubing, have entirely replaced them.

To a visiting diver, sharks are a main concern, and they do appear often in Pohnpei's lagoon. However, of some 300 different species of sharks, only twenty-eight are known to attack swimmers. The most dangerous—the hammerhead, great white, tiger, and blue sharks—inhabit deep waters and are not found in Pohnpei's lagoon.

Lobster and mangrove crab, often called Pohnpeian crab or Samoan crab, are the most popular shell fish on the island. Mangrove crabs are caught with spears or forked sticks in the mangrove swamp. During the night of a full moon when the tide is very low, crabs can be picked up by hand in large numbers off of the fringing reef. Lobster fishing is done at the same time, usually on the barrier reef that surrounds the island. Lobster, incidentally, is a preferred shell fish by Americans on the island, but is not particularly appealing to Micronesians.

The waters around Pohnpei are "rented," usually to Japanese and Taiwanese purse seiners for tuna fishing, the second most important commercial fish in the world (after prawns and shrimp). Fees for fishing in the waters are charged for each single trip. Considered in the fee are the fish-catching facilities on the vessels and the current market value of the catches.

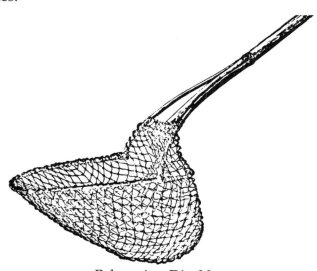

Pohnpeian Dip Net

There are eleven rather extensive, illustrated, books on sea shells and shell collecting available at the library of the Community College of Micronesia. For a beginning collector, the best book is probably *Marine Shells of the Pacific* by Walter O. Cernohorsky. For the more experienced collector, the two volumes of *Shells of the Western Pacific* by Tetsuaki Kira would be most suitable.

A year-round warm climate and comfortable water temperature are ideal conditions that Pohnpei provides to sea shell *(pwili)* collectors. However, the island's excessive rains and its forty to fifty percent annual cloud cover are disadvantageous. There are government restrictions only on trochus shelling off of the island.

The intertidal zone between the mangrove swamp and the barrier reef is the most fertile shelling ground. The majority of tropical Pacific species inhabit this region. Mollusks, however, are not easy to find. They shun sunlight and take cover in loose coral, weeds, sand, and cracks and crevices in coral heads. Cowrie shells are often covered by mantle, adding to their camouflage, and cone shells are frequently hidden in sand with only a small portion of shell exposed. The best conditions for shelling are clear days and low tides when reefs and coral heads are either exposed or under a few inches of water.

At least forty-one species of cowrie shells and thirty species of cone shells have been found off of Pohnpei. The most uncommon cowries are the jester, clandestine, sieve, zigzag, limicina, mole, eyed, egg, tortoise, and goodalli. Rather rare cone shells include the fly speck, admiral, pink, omaria, and striatus. Common shells found are the tiger, gold ringer, and money cowries, and the marble cone shell. The golden cowrie is one of the most coveted shells, and several are found off of Pohnpei and Ant each year. Depending on size and conditions, this shell can be sold for a hundred to a thousand dollars.

Cowrie Shells

The only commercial shelling that takes place on Pohnpei is with trochus shells *(dakasingal)*. In 1937 the Japanese fisheries department planted 12,000 shells in the lagoon. The war prevented development of the industry, which was originally intended for the manufacture of buttons and jewelry, however, and the shells were not exported in any significant numbers. They were harvested when eight centimeters in diameter, and most trochus were used for food by the Japanese in World War II. At present there is a trochus shelling season on Pohnpei in August and September and shells gathered by local residents are sold for export to Japan.

Trochus Shell

Scuba diving on Pohnpei is becoming increasingly popular, especially among expatriates and tourists. The reefs of the island have been described as "normally spectacular" by the dive-master of the adventure cruise vessel *S.S. Thorfinn*, but outliers Oroluk and Ant had top reviews. The manta rays of Oroluk have a spread of more than fifteen feet, and the atoll is nearly untouched by divers. The visibility, the sheer drop-offs and the colorful corals of Ant, along with the marine life, received raves. There are three businesses on Pohnpei that provide diving equipment and offer tours.

GOVERNMENT, ECONOMICS, AND EDUCATION

Government

Modern government on Pohnpei began with the arrival of the first American naval commander on the island, Captain Albert A. Momm. His initial military regulations published in Pohnpeian, Japanese, and English on September 19, 1945 guaranteed rights and freedoms that eventually were incorporated into the constitution of the Federated States of Micronesia thirty-eight years later. Among these were the right to due process of law if arrested, the prohibition of summary judgment by police, the elimination of compulsory labor, enforcement of property rights of Pohnpeians, and the prohibiting of detention without cause.

Government under military rule, begun by the Japanese in 1936, was continued by the American administration until 1951. After the Japanese surrender, the island was first given over to the Commander of the Marshall/Gilbert Islands in September, 1945, then to the Commanding General of the Occupation Forces in Truk in January, 1946, and finally to a separate military government unit on Pohnpei and Kosrae in May, 1946. By the following month, the entire government of what is now Pohnpei and Kosrae States consisted of one military government officer, one supply officer, and six enlisted men. This number was not to substantially increase until the end of 1946.

161

Pohnpei became a district of the United States Trust Territory of the Pacific Islands by an agreement between the United States and the United Nations Security Council which was approved on April 2nd and became effective on July 18th of 1947. Interim responsibility until civilian government could be established was given to the U.S. Department of the Navy. Until 1951, admirals of the navy—first Denfeld, then Ramsey, then Radford—would be the chief executives of the islands. The "strategic trusteeship" allowed the United States to govern and administer all of the former Japanese mandated islands in Micronesia, and also to establish military bases.

Administration of Pohnpei was transferred to the U.S. Department of the Interior in July, 1951. Elbert D. Thomas had been appointed as the first civilian high commissioner in January of 1951, however.

In May, 1952, a charter was written for the island of Pohnpei and the same year the first session of the Ponape Island Congress was convened. No previous regime had ever allowed local legislative bodies to exist. In 1958, the Ponape Island Congress became the Ponape District Congress, a unicameral body with representation from all municipalities in the district, the forerunner of the present Pohnpei State Legislature.

At present, Pohnpeians are governed on the municipal, state, and national level by elected executives and representatives.

The municipalities of Pohnpei are situated within the boundaries of the former kingdoms. These entities are more or less independent of the state government and can establish legislation for the betterment of their community residents so long as their laws do not conflict with those of the state or the national government. (An example is the regulation of the sale of alcoholic beverages.) All municipalities have the same political structure and consist of an elected executive and a municipal council. The titles of executives vary—in Madolenihmw it is high commissioner, in Kolonia town it is mayor, and in Sokehs it is chief magistrate. Municipal judges are appointed by the state governor upon recommendation of the people of the municipality and serve four-year terms that are renewable. In 1985-86, each of the eleven municipalities of the state held constitutional conventions and now each operates under its own individual constitution within the framework of the state government. At the municipal level, traditional hereditary leaders have considerable influence on who is elected to office, and more than a little influence on who is elected to state and national government offices. The six municipalities of Pohnpei proper and the five in the outer islands with their de facto populations in 1985 were as follows: Kolonia, 6,306; U, 2,603; Madolenihmw, 4,339; Kitti, 3,997; Sokehs, 5,060; Nett, 4,038; Mokil, 268; Pingelap, 738; Sapwuahfik, 566; Nukuoro, 395; and Kapingamarangi, 507. (Note: outlier Ant is part of Kitti municipality of Pohnpei, and Pakin is politically part of Sokehs. Outlier Oroluk is part of Kapingamarangi for voting purposes. About 3,200 residents of Kolonia vote in municipalities outside of town.)

On the state level, the state legislature was formed as an elected unicameral body in 1963 and called the Ponape District Legislature. The first elections were held in November/December of that year, and the first session was convened in January, 1964. The Ponape District Legislature became the Ponape State Legislature in 1979 without any substantial change in form. Its present composition is as follows: Madolenihmw, Sokehs and Kitti, four members each; U, Kolonia and Nett, two members each; and one member from each of the outer island municipalities. The twenty-three member legislature increases in number as the population of the state increases, and the position of Speaker of the Pohnpei State Legislature is considered to be the second most influential on the island.

The present Pohnpei State government consists of a governor, a lieutenant governor and a judiciary in addition to the legislature. The two executives and the legislators are elected to serve four-year terms. The legislators are elected from constituencies based on population and must simply receive more votes than their opponents in order to serve. The two executives, however, must each receive a majority vote to win, otherwise a runoff election will be held. (The gubernatorial elections of 1979 and 1983 both required runoffs for the office of governor.) The four judges in the judiciary are now appointed to twelve-year terms by the governor that are renewable with the consent of the state legislature.

The executive branch has seven departments whose heads are appointed by the governor, and who must be approved by the state legislature. These are the Departments of Land, Treasury, Justice, Education, Conservation and Resources Serveillance, Health Services, and Public Works.

Constitution Day for Pohnpei State is the Eighth of November (1984) when the state constitution first took effect. The state flag has six stars on a blue field to note the six municipalities of Pohnpei Island, and two olive branches representing peace. Quite appropriately for Pohnpeians, a cup to hold sakau is in the center of the design.

Pohnpei, Kosrae, Truk, and Yap districts of the U.S. Trust Territory of the Pacific Islands joined together to form the Federated States of Micronesia on May 10, 1979. The F.S.M. is located on a wavy line about 1,600 miles in length running east to west in the Western Pacific Ocean. It is bordered by the Commonwealth of the Northern Mariana Islands to the north, the Republic of Belau to the west, and the Republic of the Marshall Islands to the east. The closest southern neighbor is Papua New Guinea. The 100,000 people in its two million square mile ocean area are divided into five distinct ethnic groups with an equal number of different languages and several dialects in most languages. Central Carolinians,

mostly Trukese, compose the largest group, about fifty percent of the population. Other groups are Eastern Carolinians,
predominantly Pohnpeian, thirty percent, followed by Yapese,
twelve percent, Kosraean, six percent, and Polynesian, about
two percent. Slightly more than half of the people in the
F.S.M. live in the 49.2 square miles of Truk State which has
a population density of 970 people per square mile. (The density of Pohnpei State is 216 people per square mile.)

The government of the F.S.M. is a representative
democracy consisting of fourteen senators in a unicameral
legislature. One senator is elected at-large from each state.
These four legislators serve four-year terms. The other ten
senators are chosen by constituencies based on population,
similar to electing a congressman in the United States. They
serve two-year terms. In 1986, however, a proposal was made
in Congress to increase the two-year terms to four years,
requiring a constitutional amendment and a referendum in
each of the four states. The president and the vice-president
of the F.S.M. are selected from the four at-large senators by
their colleagues in the legislature. Pohnpei State sends four
senators to the F.S.M. Congress: one is the senator elected
at-large, one senator represents Madolenihmw and Kitti
municipalities, one represents U and Nett municipalities and
the outer island of Pingelap, and the other represents Sokehs
municipality, Kolonia town, and the remaining outer islands
of Pohnpei State. The rest of the F.S.M. Congress members
are six senators from Truk, two from Yap, and two from
Kosrae.

F.S.M. Presidential Seal

The judiciary of the F.S.M. consists of two supreme court judges, a chief justice and an associate justice. Both are appointed for life.

As mentioned above, the president and the vice president of the F.S.M. are chosen by the senate. The executive branch of the national government also consists of four departments. These are External Affairs; Resources and Development; Finance; and Transportation.

The temporary capital of the F.S.M. was spread throughout Kolonia—in a renovated former hospital, in offices above stores, and in a converted bar and hotel. A $14 million capital, however, was constructed in Palikir, five miles from Kolonia, and was completed by the end of the decade.

New F.S.M. Capital

Under terms of Secretarial Order 3039 from the U.S. Department of the Interior, the F.S.M. assumed full governmental and administrative authority from the Trust Territory of the Pacific Islands. In addition to the Constitution of the F.S.M., which was drafted in 1975 and ratified in a referendum on July 12, 1978, a Compact of Free Association with the United States was approved by the voters of the F.S.M. in a plebiscite in June, 1983. On its lurchy way through the U.S. Congress, the Compact was delayed by arguments and amendments, but finally passed in 1985. Early in 1986, it was signed by U.S. President Ronald Reagan. On May 29, 1986, the Compact was finally approved by the United Nations Trusteeship Council with only the Soviet Union objecting. The Council's resolution directed the United States to grant the new political status to the F.S.M.

Ten areas of agreement between the Federated States of Micronesia and the United States are stated in the Compact.

The initial sections deal with military matters. The first specifies U.S. armed forces land use and operating rights. Since the U.S. government has not sought land for major facilities in the F.S.M., this section mentions mostly the financial and operational arrangements for the U.S. Coast Guard Loran Station in Yap, and four U.S. military civic action teams, if these teams are requested by individual states. The second section of the Compact details the legal status, rights and responsibilities of the U.S. military and civilians working for the armed forces while they are present in the F.S.M.

The third agreement is mainly concerned with friendship, cooperation, and mutual security between the two governments. It includes provisions for the U.S. to defend the F.S.M. and its citizens, and also for the U.S. to provide financial assistance in the future to the government of the F.S.M. This section allows for denial by the U.S. of any third nation to use the F.S.M. for military purposes.

The fourth agreement of the Compact relates to the continued provision by the U.S. of postal and weather services, civil aviation safety and economic regulation services, and federal programs. It also sets forth rights and responsibilities of U.S. non-military agencies and contract personnel employed by these agencies.

The fifth section concerns an agreement on marine sovereignty. It reaffirms F.S.M. control over affairs relating to its two hundred mile maritime zone, and acknowledges the capacity of the F.S.M. to become a contracting party to the Law of the Sea Convention, rather than be represented by the U.S.

The sixth section clarifies mutual assistance and cooperation in law enforcement matters between the U.S. and F.S.M. It includes agreement on the pursuit, arrest, detention, and extradition of fugitives from justice, and the transfer of prisoners.

In the seventh section of the Compact, the U.S. government agrees to represent the interests of the F.S.M. before the International Telecommunications Union (ITU) until a time when the F.S.M. has personnel available to undertake this function.

The eighth section permits the U.S. to install and operate communications facilities in the F.S.M. if these facilities are necessary for the U.S. government to fulfill its defense programs and services, and other obligations of the Compact.

The ninth section requires that real or personal property of the U.S. government or the T.T.P.I. government located in the F.S.M. be transferred to the F.S.M. government without cost.

The final agreement of the Compact is a memorandum of understanding which provides that the F.S.M. and the U.S. agree to set forth in detail the procedures governing implementation of the financial provisions of the Compact.

As far back as 1970, U.S. commonwealth status and citizenship, and an offer of funding indefinitely was offered by the U.S. government and declined by the Congress of Micronesia. Thus began more than sixteen years of negotiations on the future political status of the Trust Territory of the Pacific Islands. During this period, the Mariana Islands district opted for U.S. commonwealth status, and Palau and the Marshall Islands districts chose not to be member entities of the F.S.M.

Consequently, the Compact of Free Association applies only to the former T.T.P.I. districts of Yap, Truk, Kosrae, and Pohnpei. The duration of the Compact is fifteen years, and then it will be renegotiated.

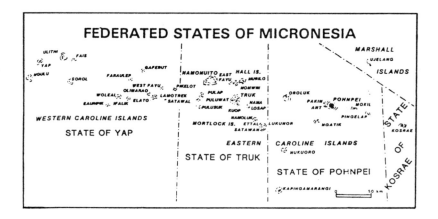

Economics

Economic development for the benefit of the ruling nation has always been a desire of imperial powers on Pohnpei. The road building program during the German Period that sparked an armed rebellion had strong economic motivation. Even the redistribution of land to individual Pohnpeians was done for economic reasons. Each deed-holder was required to plant ten coconut trees per month, along with other crops thought to be of commercial export value, by the government.

During the 20th Century, Pohnpei was closest to economic self-sufficiency during the Japanese Period than at any other time. The Japanese encouraged a thriving fishing industry and dried bonito was a major export of the island. Before World War II, more than 3.5 million pounds of tuna were exported annually. Coconuts for copra were also grown on plantations in Nett and Madolenihmw and about three thousand tons were exported annually before the war. The island was also self-sufficient in produce. During the last years of the war when imports ceased completely, the main shortage was of textiles and not food. A frequent criticism of the Japanese Period, however, is that it was only foreigners who prospered economically, and not the Pohnpeians.

The old Eastern proverb, "Be a mountain or join a mountain" is particularly appropriate in the Western Pacific. A lack of industry and development of resources, and a very low tax base, have caused the states of Micronesia to rely on funds from the United States to finance national and state governments. According to the F.S.M. Office of Budget, these funds totaled $83,798,000 in fiscal year 1985, $21,426,000 of which was given to Pohnpei from the following sources:

U.S. Special Grant (Operations)	$9,892,000
General Fund (Operations and Public Projects)	1,102,000
Federal Grants	4,062,000
CIP Grants	5,215,000
Special Operations and Maintenance	1,115,000

Nearly half of the imported commodities in the F.S.M. come to Pohnpei State. Of $33,158,000 in imports in 1984 (the last year in which complete statistics are available), fully $14,324,000 in imports came to Pohnpei's thirty percent of the F.S.M. population. As would be expected, food, beverages and tobacco were the largest imports, totaling $6,756,000. Other commercial imports to Pohnpei were: crude materials, $484,000; animal/vegetable fats, $2,000; chemicals, $887,000; manufactured goods, $1,899,000; machinery and vehicles, $2,898,000; miscellaneous manufactured items, $1,392,000; and not classified, $5,000. (Petroleum products imported into Pohnpei State are not included in the above.)

Exports from Pohnpei have not been a significant economic factor during the American Period. In FY 1984, for instance, they totaled less than a half of a million dollars in value. Copra has always been the largest export during the last four decades. On Pohnpei it is collected by the United Micronesian Development Association at designated locations and shipped to the Nichimen Corporation of Osaka, Japan, where it is sold to a subsidiary of the Fuji Oil Company, which processes it into coconut oil for use in the manufacture of candy, suntan lotion and high-grade lubricants. Unfortunately, the price of copra fluctuates radically. In recent years it has been as high as $650 per ton, but in 1986 it was down to $100 per ton. A small local coconut oil processing operation, Ponape Coconut Products, was begun in 1974 and now produces bath soap, marekeiso body oil, shampoo and liquid utility soaps for household uses. The company had a net profit of $25,000 in 1985. Small quantities of gourmet pepper ($80,117 in value) and handicraft ($47,552 in value) also contribute to the economy. Tourism, although not an export, contributed $1,229,040 to the island's economy with 5,121 of the F.S.M.'s ten thousand visitors and businessmen in 1985. The industry, however, is limited because of high air fares, few quality hotels available, and inadequate development of tourist attraction sites.

On Pohnpei, national and state planners, economists and lawyers far outnumber doctors, dentists and registered nurses. In the past decade, there has been no shortage of plans, ideas, and legal opinions, but implementation remains a problem. A footwear (zori) factory was started by an economic development officer in 1983, but slipped into oblivion in 1984. In the past three years, two small hotels on the island have closed and two have opened—with a net loss of fifteen rooms. Pohnpei's gourmet pepper industry remains at mean tide, and there has been little increase in acreage for pepper in the past few years. The fishing industry, Pohnpei's biggest natural resource, remains in foreign hands.

A most precious economic asset of Pohnpei is its youth. A significant problem, however, is that this economic asset is increasing at a streaker's pace. The population of Pohnpei was barely 20,000 in 1975; it is nearly 30,000 in 1986. The only higher education in the F.S.M. is offered at the Community College of Micronesia, a two-year post-secondary institution. In the Compact of Free Association mentioned above, however, there is no provision for financing the college.

The largest employer on Pohnpei is government (national, state, and municipal) with 2,120 people, or 26.5% of the labor force. Employees in the private sector total 21.3% and subsistence agriculturists total 30.8%. Of the labor force of 8,010, there were 21.4% unemployed in 1985. To reduce economic reliance on government employment, the state administration has attempted to involve the private sector in operations that have been under government control. Government vehicle repair service and coral digging for road work have been privatized. The electrical power system, the fresh-water distribution and the sewer maintenance operations were opened for bids to be taken over by the private sector in 1986. Competing with government employment is difficult for the private sector, however. The minimum wage for state employees is $1.50 per hour, but there is no minimum wage law for private employees. An inexperienced clerk in a store might receive seventy-five cents per hour and a starting laborer in construction could expect about a dollar an hour.

The construction industry is the largest non-government employer on the island. More than twelve hundred homes and businesses were built or renovated in 1985 and 1986. Local builders have been assisted with loans from the island's banks, the U.S. Farmers Home Administration, and have been aided by the Pohnpei State Housing Authority. The $24 million F.S.M. capital project will provide construction jobs on Pohnpei well into the 1990's. Skilled labor is trained by the Pohnpei Agriculture and Trade School, but not nearly enough graduate to meet current local needs. Foreign employees, particularly from the Philippine Islands, continue to be needed to supply middle-level manpower. A small Civic Action Team of thirteen U.S. Air Force Corps of Engineers, the only American military presence on Pohnpei, assists in state road building and construction projects, and also trains local workers.

There are four banks on Pohnpei, three are private, full-service banks and one is government operated. The most recently established bank is the Bank of the Federated States of Micronesia which opened its first branch on Kosrae in 1986.

The Bank of Guam began operations in 1982 and the Bank of Hawaii in 1964. The F.S.M. Development Bank was established by the Congress in 1979 and commenced commercial operations in 1982. It was set up to provide financing to accelerate economic development, particularly in agriculture, fisheries, manufacturing, and real estate.

Over the next fifteen years, hundreds of millions of dollars will flow into Pohnpei, Kosrae, Yap and Truk in U.S. Compact funds alone. The impact of this money on the social well-being and economic development of the people is unclear. What is not unclear, however, is that the F.S.M., and consequently Pohnpei State, will have more control over its economic destiny than at any time since the first Spaniards landed on the island a century ago.

Education

Formal education on Pohnpei dates from the arrival of the first Protestant missionaries in 1852. Before that time, of course, learning of traditional skills took place. Boys were taught fishing, house building, canoe construction, and farming. Girls learned the domestic skills of child care, cooking, weaving, and gardening. Specialized skills such as navigation, and the use of traditional medicines were also taught, but usually within individual families.

The first formal education was introduced during the Early Contact Period by American missionaries sent from Hawaii. In 1856, the first printing press was brought to the island and the initial publication was a single sheet with the Lord's Prayer and a hymn. Within a year, however, the first school book was produced, a twelve page primer. Also among the first publications that year were a new seventeen page book of hymns and a fifty-five page collection of stories from the Old Testament of the Bible. Nearly all teaching was done by the wives of the first Protestant missionaries on the island. Schools emphasized basic literacy for Bible study, domestic arts for girls, and manual skills for boys. The first Pohnpeian language orthography was begun at that time.

Education slumbered during the short Spanish Period (1886-1899). The only formal learning encouraged by the government was church related and no attempts were made to force the Spanish language on Pohnpeians or to interfere with their traditional institutions. What little education that took place was provided by American Protestant missionaries, but even this schooling ceased when the Americans were exiled to Mokil and Kusaie (Kosrae) by the Spanish Governor Cardarso in November, 1890.

The German Period (1899-1914) was a time of the changing of the guard in education as well as government. German Catholic Capuchin priests replaced the Spanish Franciscans in 1905, and began the first Catholic public education. American Protestant missionaries were allowed to return from exile. However, their work in education was considerably hampered when the German governor, Viktor Berg, issued a directive that German be the only foreign language taught in the schools. German Lutherans finally replaced the Americans in 1907.

Japan occupied Micronesia in a bloodless takeover in 1914, and Japanese civilians assumed the administration of Pohnpei in 1921. More educational development took place during the Japanese Period than during the Spanish and German Periods combined. As early as 1920, the government subsidized Congregational Protestant missions and, consequently, education. Spanish Jesuit priests were allowed to return to Pohnpei to continue the work of the German Capuchins. A criticism often heard that encouragement of Christian religions by the Japanese administration was a deliberate attempt to keep Pohnpeians pacified may be unfair. However, the Japanese Period was the time of least unrest in Pohnpei's history to date.

The curriculum in Japanese schools for Pohnpeian children stressed language, and half of the regular course consisted of Japanese. Other subjects taught were arithmetic, singing, physical education, manual work for boys, and housekeeping for girls. Children eight years of age and older were given three years of schooling. The academic year was forty-eight weeks in length and six days per week. A two-year advanced supplementary course for brighter students was also offered, into which about a third of the pupils were accepted. By 1937, attendance at schools had become mandatory for all students within walking distance of an elementary school, about seventy percent of those in the age group. Schools were segregated on the island and children of Japanese nationals were taught by qualified Japanese teachers. These pupils received six years of mandatory schooling and two supplementary years of advanced study.

Older Pohnpeians can be seen today using children to translate English for them. Quite often these same older Pohnpeians will be seen in conversation with Japanese visitors. Those Pohnpeians fifty years of age and above have retained their Japanese language ability to an amazing degree after forty years of American administration.

Education on Pohnpei continued during the initial years of World War II. Besides government schools, Protestant teaching was conducted by a Japanese minister, assisted by Pohnpeian pastors. The Catholic mission at the time consisted of three Spanish Jesuit priests, six brothers, eleven Spanish nuns, and one Pohnpeian sister. After February of 1944, when any standing structure became a choice target for American bombers, the children evacuated the schools.

The American occupation of Pohnpei began on September 11, 1945, and all Japanese nationals were repatriated by the end of the year. With their exodus, the population decreased from 19,930 to 5,600 and formal education once again came to a standstill.

An increase in education began in earnest with the civilian administration of Pohnpei in 1952. Attempts had been made to rapidly prepare Micronesian elementary school teachers in a new language and curriculum. Courses were instituted at a teacher training center sponsored by the U.S. Navy, and first established on Guam in 1947. The center, at that time called the Pacific Islands Teacher Training School, was moved to Truk the next year and offered a two-year course for potential teachers. The program was increased to three years in

1959 and moved to Pohnpei where a class of sixty teachers graduated in June of 1960. The school was renamed the Pacific Islands Central School in 1962. (Two of the first qualified Micronesian teachers at the school from Pohnpei district were Senator Bethwel Henry, Speaker of the F.S.M. Senate, and Bailey Olter, Vice President of the Federated States of Micronesia. Both joined the staff of the school in the early 1960's.) In 1964, PICS became a district high school and was renamed the Ponape Island Central School—without changing its initials. In the same year, the first election for the Congress of Micronesia took place. Nearly all of the elected senators and representatives to the new body were former teachers.

Pohnpei at present offers both public and private elementary and secondary education. Attendance at government elementary schools is free and compulsory, but entrance into secondary education is determined by an examination. (About a third of the children who complete elementary school go on to high school.) All private schools are church-affiliated. Elementary education is offered by the Calvary Baptist, Catholic, and Seventh Day Adventist sects. With a very large school-age population on Pohnpei, this educational service is particularly needed on the island at this time. There are also three private secondary schools, the high schools of the Baptists and the Seventh Day Adventists and Micronesia's premier vocational institution, the Pohnpei Agriculture and Trade School affiliated with the Jesuit Order of the Catholic Church in Madolenihmw Municipality. Elementary schools in Pohnpei State had a total enrollment of 7,032 pupils, and approximately 1,400 attended secondary school in the academic year 1985/86. Each permanantly inhabited outer island in the state has an elementary school, but their students must come to Pohnpei if they qualify for secondary education. The forty-one state-supported elementary schools had a pupil enrollment of 6,507 in school year 1985/86 and 390 teachers. Pohnpei Island Central School (PICS), the only state high school, had an enrollment of 1,050 students and fifty teachers. Nearly all teachers and administrators in the state system are Micronesian.

Higher education, like secondary education on Pohnpei, can trace its origins to teacher training. The Micronesian Teacher Education Center was established in 1963 to train in-service elementary school teachers. In 1970, MTEC became the Community College of Micronesia, which offered two-year programs leading to the Associate in Science Degree in Elementary Education. The college has since added programs in special education, business management, nursing, and liberal arts, and is now a fully accredited member of the Western Association of Schools and Colleges in the United States. CCM could well be the smallest college serving the largest area and most diversified population in the world. Students are selected from a two million square mile geographical area and eight different cultural groups. The college has a resident enrollment of about two hundred students and an extension enrollment of nearly a thousand. Since 1978, CCM has been a constituent of the College of Micronesia, which also has campuses in Palau and the Marshall Islands.

Logogram
Community College of Micronesia

TRADITIONAL CULTURE

Introduction

The best source of information on traditional culture is an informed Pohnpeian. It is a very complex subject on which volumes have been written. The best book on the subject translated into English and written by a Pohnpeian is *The Book of Luelen* by Luelen Bernart, and an excellent source by a non-Pohnpeian is *The Native Polity of Ponape* by Saul H. Riesenberg. Another good source on culture by an American is *Democracy in a Traditional Society: An Analysis of Socio-Political Development on Ponape* by the late Daniel T. Hughes. William R. Bascom's *Ponape: A Pacific Economy in Transition*, mentioned earlier, is also an excellent reference.

Kingdoms, Royalty and Titles, Families and Clans

KINGDOMS *(wehi)*

Five traditional entities exist on Pohnpei today. Different publications refer to them as kingdoms, tribes, districts, states, or municipalities. They are Madolenihmw, U, Kitti, Sokehs and Nett. The town of Kolonia, a separate administrative entity, was formerly a part of Nett.

Pohnpeian traditional history traces the origin of the present entities back some five centuries to the time when the island was ruled by a series of tyrannical kings, the Saudeleurs. A young warrior named Isokelekel conquered the Saudeleurs, established himself in Madolenihmw, and assumed the title of Nahnmwarki. The son of Isokelekel, Nahnlepenien, was given the title of Nahnken. In time this position became almost equal to the Nahnmwarki. One by one, sections broke away from each other to evolve into five municipalities on Pohnpei today.

Foreign administrations have influenced the traditional entities, particularly in the control and allocation of land. Until the German administration (1899-1914), all land was controlled by the traditional leaders. In 1912, land reform took place under the German District Administrator, Dr. Heinrick Kersting. Individual deeds of land ownership were issued and the principle of land inheritance through the patrilineal line was established. Although the Nahnmwarkis retained some authority by their rights to award titles, their strongest sanctions, the right to distribute or withhold land, was taken from them. Limited tribute was paid to royalty in form of a head tax from which they were given an annual salary. The German administration also withdrew the right of the Nahnmwarkis to impose the death penalty or to banish a deed holder from his land. During this period the Nahnmwarki of Nett was installed.

The Japanese occupied Pohnpei only two years after District Administrator Kersting's land reforms. They did not strictly enforce the German rule of inheritance through the patrilineal line, but decided land cases on an individual basis. Although they did not enforce restrictions of tribute laid down by the Germans, they continued the head tax to pay royalty (a sum of money, or fifteen days of public work per year). During the Japanese administration, the fifth and final position of top royalty existing today, the Nahnmwarki of Sokehs, was established.

The influence of the American administration on the traditional structure has been mainly political. The kingdoms were renamed municipalities in 1947, and a chief magistrate was elected as the highest executive official in each. A council was also elected as the legislative body for each municipality. Although the real power of the traditional leaders has diminished, they still retain considerable influence on the municipal level. Great deference behavior is given to traditional leaders in both etiquette and language.

Each municipality is divided into some twenty or thirty sections ((*kousapw*), whose heads are appointed by traditional leaders. These sections whenever possible have access to both highlands and the sea. The larger sections contain twenty-five to thirty-five farmsteads with about two hundred people, but the smaller ones might contain only four or five

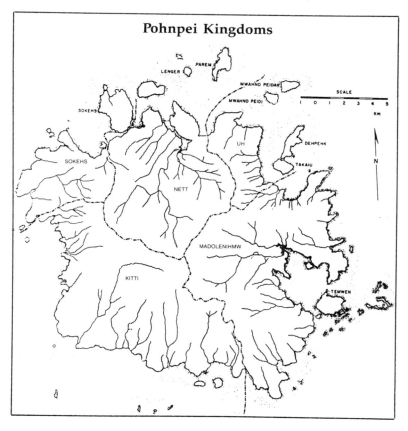

Pohnpei Kingdoms

families. Section chiefs look out for the interests of the higher municipality leaders and keep an eye on the productive ability of farmsteads. They also allocate tribute responsibilities of food brought to feasts and other functions. They are the link that transmits the wishes of the traditional leaders to the individual farmers.

There are no villages per se on Pohnpei, unless the town of Kolonia is considered a village. (If one drives through the "village" of Awak, only the Catholic church would let one know.) Sections, however, provide functions that otherwise would be in village centers. Boundaries of sections are precise, and often ancient. Each contains a *nahs* or feast house near the home of the section chief around which community activities take place. The exact number of sections changes from time to time. Sections may split over leadership, or two sections might combine for a particular purpose. Combined sections are usually designated with the Pohnpeian *powe* for the upper part and *pah* for the lower. Riesenberg in 1968 tabulated 125 sections of Pohnpei: Kitti had 37, Madolenihmw, 28; Nett, 23; Sokehs, 21; U, 15; and off-shore Pakin, one.

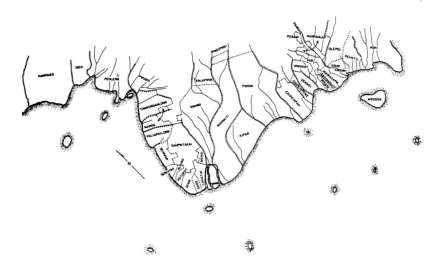

Sections *(kousapw)* in Kitti

Each municipality has three social ranks to one of which all Pohnpeians belong. At the top is the highest titled royalty, or nobility, who belong to one of two ruling sub-clans. To be a member of this rank, both of one's parents must be members of these groups. Below the top royalty is another social rank in which one parent belongs to one of the ruling sub-clans. The lowest social ranking, and by far the largest, is occupied by commoners, neither of whose parents belong to a ruling sub-clan.

The Nahnmwarki and the Nahnken in each municipality are the two principal chiefs. Below each is a ranked series of eleven, or in some cases more, titleholders considered to be the most important in the municipality. Each series contains many more than the top group, however, and could include as many as two hundred titles.

Some titles appear in all five municipalities, but the titleholders are not necessarily of equal rank because municipalities are ranked. Madolenihmw is highest followed in order by U, Kitti, Sokehs and Nett, and this ranking further contributies to the inequality of titles.

Titles have feminine equivalents which are assumed by women upon marriage to a title-holder. Some chiefly titles are also reserved for sisters or daughters of several Nahnmwarkis on the island. A man may acquire a higher title by marrying one of these ladies. He is then called "Big Bones," *(tihlap)*, because he must work harder than others at feasts, and excel in other forms of service in order to prove his worth.

The highest titles are acquired through birth, but lesser ones are most often earned by various forms of service. Titles may also be acquired through merit, or an individual may be promoted from one title to a higher one. In the top group, this may transpire because of the death of a higher titleholder. In lesser titles, promotion might come about because of loyalty, personality, relative age, physical ability, community position outside of the municipality, exploits, industry and obedience. All enter into rising in titles and promotion. About ninety-five percent of Pohnpeians hold a municipal or section title on the island. Many hold both wehi and kousapw titles.

FAMILIES *(Peneinei)* AND CLANS *(Kienik)*

Every Pohnpeian is born into three kinship units, as well as into a traditional kingdom. These are the nuclear family, the extended family, and the clan.

The nuclear family occupies a single household that usually includes relatives other than the father, mother and sons and daughters of the basic unit. On Pohnpei, a household averages six or seven members. With the Pohnpeian nuclear family one finds much stronger authority in the hands of the father than one usually finds elsewhere. Children are expected to be obedient to him without question throughout their lives. If a child grows to be an adult of sixty-five years of age and has his own grandchildren, he still must be obedient to his father and even accept beatings from him without putting up a defense.

Within the nuclear family, there is a special relationship, one of protectiveness, between brothers and sisters. A stranger might compliment one's sisters for being talented or attractive in the United States. Not so on Pohnpei. It would show a familiarity with the girls that is not at all appreciated from strangers, and not tolerated from other Pohnpeians. The first-born son is usually favored in a nuclear family and is given preferential treatment over other children by parents, and deference by his younger brothers and sisters. He is being groomed to one day have the responsibility as the leader of the family.

The father dominates the nuclear family and the mother is usually subservient to him. (*"Sohte ohl kin masak lih,"*—

no man is afraid of a woman and a man should not let his wife rule his life.) Although clanship is passed through the mother, inheritance, usually land, is determined by the father.

The second kinship unit, the extended family, consists of several generations held together through the patrilineal line. They may occupy a common residential area, which could be a large section with separate houses for each of the smaller groups, or they could have individual houses grouped together in a smaller area. The older male in the family is head of the establishment and maintains overall supervision of the group. There are usually separate and clearly defined rights and duties for each member of this basic subsistence unit.

The larger kinship unit, consisting of a number of extended families who consider themselves descendants of a common female ancestor, is the clan. There are nearly twenty such groups on Pohnpei, and they are now spread throughout the municipalities. Clans have no overall chiefs. However, they are divided into sub-clans and ranked by seniority within each clan. (The highest ranked is the sub-clan that had the first descendant from the common female ancestor.) The senior male in each sub-clan is its chief, and his functions are less political than social and economic.

Clans are matrilineal, and so clanship is inherited through the female line. Consequently, a father and his children are of different clans. Some clans have totems such as an animal, bird, or fish that are looked upon as actual clan ancestors. These creatures cannot be killed and eaten by clan members. Examples are the Turtle, Black Bird, White Bird, Soto Bird, and Great Eel clans. Others are named after places, such as Pwok on Pohnpei, Maraki in the Gilbert Islands, and the Clan from the Other Side of the Water. One clan, Luhk, is named after an accident deity.

It is difficult to find a Pohnpeian who could name all of the clans on the island, or the exact number of clans, for that matter. It is known that during the smallpox epidemic of 1854, entire clans ceased to exist because clan members would not desert those who were infected with the disease.

Nahs Feast House

POHNPEIAN PERSONALITY

"A deep sense of pride that cannot be express-
ed openly, a hunger for praise when it is deserv-
ed, a retiring modesty, tolerance and patience,
together with a quiet dignity, are dominant
characteristics of the Ponapean personality. The
people of Ponape have a character, as well as a
history and a set of traditions, that is their own.
Americans who come to Ponape from the Marshalls, confident that they 'understand natives'
from their previous experience, must either revise
their opinions or, as has usually been the case in
the past, leave without meeting the Ponapeans on
common ground."

William R. Bascom
Ponape: A Pacific Economy in Transition

Childbirth, Marriage and Funeral Customs

Customs relating to childbirth, land, food, and eating habits, marriage, traditional beliefs, skills, and funerals on Pohnpei are presented in *Some Things of Value, Micronesian Customs and Beliefs*. The book was written at the Community College of Micronesia and is available locally. Parts of the customs on childbirth, marriage, and funerals are taken from this source.

CHILDBIRTH (neitik)

Expectant mothers, especially those having their first child, are treated with great care on Pohnpei, and are never left alone. They are provided with anything they desire. It is thought that failure to do so would cause the expectant mother to have great pain in childbirth.

After six or seven months of pregnancy, the woman and her husband visit her parents for a feast called *kamweng kasapw*. On this occasion, half of the foods are donated by both the wife's and the husband's families. Historically, *kamweng kasapw* was a farewell feast for an expectant mother in case she did not survive the birth of her child.

At the time of the birth of the child, procedures and customs vary, depending on whether the birth takes place at a home or in the hospital. In both places, however, it is considered quite shameful for the expectant mother to show pain by crying out during labor or the actual birth. Consequently, the woman's relatives are usually present during the delivery as an incentive to silence. To show pain to outsiders is especially shameful.

All celebrations, foods donated and gifts presented after the birth of the child are called *pilen dihdi*, or watery breast. In the past, the term referred only to gifts that could be consumed.

When the mother regains her strength, a ceremony is held, and the husband is responsible for organizing it. Members of the family must fish for four days, and search particularly for two types of shellfish and clams: *kemei* and *lipwei*. These are thought to develop rich milk in the mother's breasts. Those who remain behind prepare local foods for the large feast that is held.

At a time following the fourth day after the birth, the family will usually take the child to be baptized at either a Catholic or Protestant church. After the baptism, another feast takes place.

The largest birthday ceremony in the life of a Pohnpeian child usually takes place a year after the birth. The party is especially lavish if the child is first-born, and is male. Infant mortality was much more common in the past than at present. After a year of life, however, it is felt that the child is strong enough to survive, and serious illness or death would be unlikely.

A child is born into firmly established traditional social and political structures. He is a welcome member of the nuclear family, whether the mother is married or not, and is also a member of the extended family of the father (or that of the mother if no marriage has taken place). He is a member of a clan through his mother's line. He is also a part of an historic kingdom, of which he will later become quite aware. All of this, in addition to being a Pohnpeian and a citizen of the Federated States of Micronesia.

Now I bathe in the leaping, in the running, in the beautiful water.

Go away now what is evil from my child!

Return now what is good of my child!

Thus I bathe in the leaping, in the running, in the beautiful water! Ue!

(A chant by the woman who knows charms when first bathing an infant in a river at age three months.)

MARRIAGE (inou sarawi)

Christianity has influenced marriage on Pohnpei, and some customs practiced before the arrival of missionaries in the mid-1850's have been discontinued. Pohnpeians have always been monogamous, and Christianity did not introduce this practice. Polygamy was only practiced by a few high chiefs. Even among the polygamous royalty, one wife, the first, was always considered the "real" wife. Others were more or less considered as concubines or secondary wives.

In the past, the time for marriage and the attainment of adulthood was often symbolized by tattooing of both men and women. Men usually tattooed their arms and thighs while women tattooed their lower limbs. Neither men nor women tattooed their faces.

Marriage on Pohnpei usually takes place outside of one's clan (exogamous). In the past this custom was more strictly enforced than at present. Often property and social factors were considerations in selecting partners. Arranged marriages, where parents or other close relatives determine the marriage partners, take place on Pohnpei, but are not nearly as common now as in the past.

There is almost no open dating as practiced in the United States in Pohnpeian society. Traditionally, couples meet secretly, continually, until they decide that they wish to marry. The man and the woman might then inform their parents, but quite commonly, only the man will inform his family. If the parents agree, they will plan a date on which to visit the home of the lady.

When asking for the marriage, the parents of the man will be accompanied by prominent relatives and will bring *sakau*. After the sakau is pounded, the first cup is given to the relative who will ask for the marriage. He in turn will offer the drink to the father of the potential bride and explain the purpose of the visit. If a marriage is agreed upon, the couple is then considered to be married. A date will be set for a formal wedding with a very large feast to follow. The bride certainly does not leave her family completely, but she then owes her obligations to her husband and his family.

Unions in which a couple reside together without having had a formal or legal marriage are common on Pohnpei. Also, it is not at all uncommon for Micronesians to marry non-Micronesians on the island.

"Uhn seu ieu pwopwoud."

(A clump of sugarcane falls apart unless bound
together. A man and his wife should not be
apart for long periods of time.)

Pohnpeian proverb

FUNERALS (mehla)

When a death occurs, the family of the deceased will notify the local Soumas. He will then contact the Nahnmwarki of the municipality for permission to bury the body, and to request his attendance at the funeral. The Soumas will bring with him two stalks of sugarcane. If one is presented, only permission to bury the body is requested; if both are offered, attendance of the Nahnmwarki at the funeral is requested as well. The Soumas holds the cane so that its leaves are facing toward the Nahnmwarki. Permission for burial is always granted as the Nahnmwarki would never refuse this. For various reasons, however, he might not be able to attend the funeral and would send a titled representative in his place.

Deaths become known in the local area immediately by word of mouth, and then are announced by the radio station when news reaches Kolonia. Friends and relatives flock to the home of the deceased bringing rice, biscuits, sugar, canned meat, and any other food that can be prepared quickly to serve to the mourners during the night. As visitors approach the coffin, attending women cry and wail, and female visitors join in the crying. When enough people have gathered, men will pound sakau while women prepare food for the group. Since guests continue to arrive, cooking and pounding sakau continue throughout the night. Very often a choir will arrive to sing hymns. At daybreak, most of the men return to their homes to gather yams, breadfruit, pigs, and dogs for the feast that will be given after the funeral.

Burial always takes place the day after a death occurs, unless there are unusual circumstances to prevent it. When friends and relatives again assemble at the home of the deceased, the coffin is closed and nailed shut and a great deal of crying, wailing and moaning takes place, but only by females. The coffin is then escorted to the grave. (Nearly all burials take place on private homesteads rather than in cemeteries.) At the burial site, the coffin is lowered into the grave. Friends and relatives then throw a small piece of earth, a stone, or perhaps a branch into the grave for a final farewell. Often a choir also attends the burial.

The mourners leave the grave to be marked and decorated later, and gather at a *nahs* or the home of the deceased for a funeral feast. It is important that the family of the person who has died spares no expense in preparing this activity, as it reflects directly on their feelings for their dead relative. A quantity of food is set aside for titled guests, and the rest is served to others attending. It is common for those attending to take a plate of food with them when they leave. After a discreet period of time, most mourners will leave, but members of the extended family will remain together and prepare an *uhmw* for the following day.

Close family members stay together for four days. On the fourth day after the death, some men will go fishing while other family members remain behind to prepare another feast. When the fishermen return, one of them will be chosen to place part of the catch near the grave. The fishermen will be rubbed with coconut oil and given *mwaramwars*, flowered garlands, and will also be served sakau. Active mourning might take place for up to forty days by some members of the family.

There are naturally some variations in customs depending on individual family preferences. Also, factors such as employment and schooling have adjusted funeral responsibilities for some family members.

To a western observer, several aspects of funerals on Pohnpei may seem unique, if not contradictory. In a society of very strong inter-personal relationships where deaths are felt poignantly, a funeral often resembles a party or an Irish wake. Tricks are played on mourners and practical jokes are common after the burial. Also, those closest to the deceased in family relationships are often the busiest with welcoming guests, cooking, and serving food and beverages. If a woman falls asleep during her all-night vigil, she may well awaken to find her face painted comically with charcoal or mud. The idea behind this apparent frivolity, however, is a serious and planned attempt to cheer up those close to the deceased, and in some slight way to relieve their sorrows.

Languages

Like all languages, Pohnpeian has changed over the years. However, it has changed much less rapidly since the first writing system was developed by American Protestant missionaries in the 1850's. Initially, written Pohnpeian was used for publishing school readers, hymn books, and translations of parts of the New Testament. For a study of the major grammatical features of the language, see *Ponapean Reference Grammar*, by Kenneth L. Rehg. The most recent, and most complete, *Ponapean-English Dictionary* was published in 1981 and was written by Rehg and Damian G. Sohl. Both books are on sale locally. The orthography of Pohnpeian is still being developed, however, and the same word is often seen spelled differently by different writers.

If the president of the Federated States of Micronesia met with his vice president, his attorney general and the governor of Pohnpei, and all spoke their native languages, chatter would be heard in Trukese, English, Pohnpeian and Mokilese. There are six Micronesian languages spoken in the Federated States, most with regional dialects, and nine spoken in the former Trust Territory of the Pacific Islands. The official language of the F.S.M. and Pohnpei State is English.

All Micronesian languages are members of the Austronesian family, which includes several hundred languages spread from Madagascar to the most western of the Pacific islands. In Micronesia are found Nauruan, Kosraean, Marshallese/Gilbertese, Chamorro, Woleaian, Palauan, Yapese, Trukese, and Polynesian, as well as Pohnpeian. None are mutually intelligible, although some are more closely related than others. (Trukese learn Pohnpeian easily, for instance, but only Yapese easily learn Yapese.)

Despite four foreign administrations, the Pohnpeian language has not changed significantly. The vocabulary has been increased, rather than replaced by foreign contributions. From the Spanish Period, the additions that are retained are mostly words relating to the church; additions from the German Period are quite minimal. The *Ponapean-English Dictionary* lists about four hundred words borrowed during the Japanese Period. The American Period in language might be considered in two different centuries, the whalers and missionaries of the 1800's and the post World War II years. Consequently, some five hundred borrowings into Pohnpeian have come from English.

About three quarters of the people on Pohnpei are native speakers of Pohnpeian. Other sizable language groups are Kapingamarangans (Polynesians) in Kolonia and several thousand Mortlockese, mostly in Sokehs and Madolenihmw. Groups residing on Pohnpei from the outer islands of Pohnpei State, other than Nukuoro and Kapingamarangi, speak languages mutually intelligible with Pohnpeian, to varying degrees.

Children on Pohnpei begin public primary school at about

age six. The language used for instruction is Pohnpeian, and elementary oral English is taught as a subject. Instruction in Pohnpeian continues during the first two years of school. In grade three, pupils begin basic reading in English. The grade in which English is used as a medium of instruction in all subjects of primary school varies from place to place, but is usually about grade four. From the upper grades of primary school through secondary school and the Community College of Micronesia, English is the medium of instruction in all subjects.

Pohnpeian has two dialects: one is referred to as the Kitti dialect and the other is the main, or northern dialect. They are distinguished by their vowel sounds, particularly in the use of the letter *e*. There is also a "high" Pohnpeian language used in speaking to traditional leaders, and a "low" or common language. They are differentiated by the particular words used, and by markers, or determiners, used somewhat like affixes, when speaking the "high" language.

Written Pohnpeian employs a phonemic writing system basically, where one letter symbolizes only one possible sound. (As a contrast, the letters *e* and *u* in English each have four possible sounds.) Pronunciation varies between the Kitti and the northern dialect, as mentioned above, with the latter considered to be the standard only because most speakers of Pohnpeian use it. Vowels are somewhat similar to French or Spanish. The *t* sound has a "tch" and the *d* has a sound somewhere between a *d* and a *t*. The alphabet of Pohnpeian employs twenty symbols, sixteen single letters and four double letters or digraphs. The most unusual features of the alphabet to a visitor are the digraphs *oa*, *mw*, and *pw*, and also the letter *h*, signaling the lengthening of a vowel, which seems to appear everywhere.

Kala*h*ngan o*h* kasele*h*lie,
Thank you and goodbye

An excellent guide to sounds of Pohnpeian letters is provided on a chart on pages *xix* and *xx* of the *Ponapean-English*

Dictionary (Honolulu, University Press of Hawaii) by Kenneth L. Rehg and Damian G. Sohl. (See page *xiii* for another language sound chart.)

Just a few words...

English	Pohnpeian	Mokilese	Kapingamarangan
one	*ehu*	*ehd*	*dihi*
two	*riau*	*ari*	*lau*
three	*siluh*	*esil*	*dolu*
four	*pahieu*	*oapoang*	*haa*
five	*limau*	*alim*	*lima*
six	*wenou*	*ohn*	*ono*
seven	*isuh*	*eis*	*hidu*
eight	*waleu*	*awal*	*walu*
nine	*duwau*	*adu*	*hiva*
ten	*eisek*	*eisek*	*matangahoru*
hello/goodbye	*kaselehlie*	*kasalehlia*	*malia goe*
thank you	*kalahngan/menlau*	*menlau*	*dime poro koe*
good	*mwahu*	*mwehu*	*malia*
bad	*sakanakan*	*nauna*	*huaidu*
yes	*ei*	*eh*	*uaa*
no	*soh*	*soah*	*deeai*
come	*kohdo mahs*	*kampare*	*loomoi*
go	*kohla mahs*	*inla*	*looadu*
stop	*udi mahs*	*kauhdi*	*hanganoho*
wait	*awi mahs*	*sousou*	*whoa*
America	*Amerika*	*Amerka*	*Baalangi*
What is your name?	*Ia edomw?*	*Ia oadoamw en?*	*Toingo la koai?*
My name is_____	*Edei_____*	*Ia_____*	*Tokuingo la ko___*
Where is_____?	*Ia_____?*	*Ia_____?*	*Tehe la, Ihee_____?*

In conversation, wit and innuendo frequently dominate, or at least contend for attention with factual information. Humorous double meanings in words, often suggestive but seldom crude or vulgar, keep speaker and listener constantly alert in verbal sparring matches.

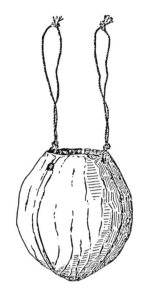

Coconut Liquid Container

Legends

Often doctoral students and other researchers into Pohnpeian culture are stymied by incomplete answers from Pohnpeian informants. Traditionally, to tell all that one knows about a subject or a story is thought to cause the informant to lose part of himself. Legends, like knowledge of traditional medical cures told by elders, might only be passed on in their complete forms to selected family members, oftentimes the youngest male member. Since it is unlikely that the youngest will inherit land, the secret knowledge could be his legacy from the family.

The following legends were part of a rich oral tradition even before the arrival of Europeans and Americans on the island. Few Pohnpeians are unfamiliar with them, but they are told with some variations by different groups. The best published source of Pohnpeian legends is a traditional history of the island written by Luelen Bernart and translated by Saul H. Riesenberg, the late John L. Fischer, and Marjorie G. Whiting, *The Book of Luelen*. (For legends on Pohnpei's outliers, see *Pohnpei State Outlying Islands*, pp.224-246.)

HOW POHNPEI WAS FORMED

If early Pohnpeians had had their own Bible, Book One would begin with the story of Sapkini and the creation of Pohnpei. Like the Bible, there are versions of the story, in this case thirteen variations.

On a far off island, Sapkini viewed his universe as a gigantic canopy, or a big roof with long, sloping eaves, in which he and his people were the center. The canopy-roof was the sky. Where it touched the sea, Sapkini knew land would be found beyond it, just as a canopy or extended eaves touch ground.

Sapkini selected wisely his crew of women and men with whom he would sail into the unknown to find a new land. All were endowed with particular necessary skills or magical qualities for sailing or working land. Among the women were Lipalikini, Woman Hewing; and Litorkini, Woman Weaving; and there was Lisapikini, Woman of Little Rain; and Lieulele, Woman of Clear Weather; and there was Lipeuktakalan, Woman Raising Up to Heaven. Sapkini also took with him two Women Earth, Lioramanpuel and Lijaramanpuel, and also the woman Limuetu, who was later to become very important. And Lijapikini, Woman Turning Over Wood, also went on the voyage. The men selected were Saupeleti, Master of Hewing Down; and Saupelata, Master of Hewing Up; and Satakono, Master of the Waves; and two others, Lanperen and Perenu. There was also Nipalatakenlan, Man of Heaven.

For the journey, a large, strong, deep-hulled canoe was

needed. So Lipalikini hewed out a hull and Lijapikini carved designs and fashioned the outrigger. Litorkini wove the sails from fiber of the outside layers of the trunk of banana plants.

When their preparations were completed, the adventurers sailed toward the distant horizon where the sky touched the sea, guided only by birds. Lienkatautik summoned the wind for the sails and Lieulele provided a smooth sea. Then, somewhere in lost mid-ocean, the voyagers met an octopus named Lidakika and greeted him humbly. Lidakika was

friendly to the group and directed them to a distant shallow reef on which a small coral head, completely barren, was exposed. They named it Tierenjap, meaning bit of land, because it was no larger than the distance between the canoe and its outrigger. From this bit of coral, the island of Pohnpei was to grow.

By magic, stones and boulders were called to Tierenjap from other places, but the earth and soil was continually being washed away by waves from the sea. So Katenenior was called, Stabiliser of the Shore, to surround the land and create a barrier reef for protection. Then Katinanik was summoned to cause mangrove trees to take root and hold the shore in place. When the people saw trees growing in saltwater by the shore, they shouted "Ahk," and the word has been used for mangrove ever since. After the shore was secure, Lioramanpuel and Lijaramanpuel dug earth and piled it on a platform. And so the platform became very large and made a place they named *pei* (stone altar). Everything on top of it was called *pohn*—Pohnpei, upon the stone altar.

When their work was completed and their new island was fully formed, the voyagers began to look homeward. Finally they all decided to leave except for the woman Limuetu and her husband, said to have been Perenu, who remained behind to guard the new land. The couple bore many children and populated the island. They had little food except dry-land taro, however, and did not even know how to weave clothes.

After some time, another canoe arrived with Konopuel and his wife Lakarepuel, who knew how to work the land and grow different crops. No one knew how to build houses, though, so all of the people lived in caves and under rocks.

Later a third voyage to Pohnpei brought four men, Pakilap, Pakitik, Solap, and Sotik from a high island, probably Kosrae, and these men began to construct houses. There was no thatch for roofing as only arrowroot, wild yams and taro, grass and other small plants were growing at the time. But a later voyage brought Meteriap, who propagated ivory-nut palms and provided the thatch needed to complete the houses.

So the island today called Pohnpei was created. Later, the canoe which brought the first voyagers returned to see to its condition and the well being of Limuetu. They found her safe and happy and urged her to return to her real home. But for Limuetu, Pohnpei had become her real home, and so she remained with her children until she died.

HOW POHNPEI WAS CONQUERED

The first traditional historical age of Pohnpei was during its creation. In the second historical period, the island was ruled by a series of tyrannical chiefs, the Sau Deleurs (Sau is a title much like Lord, and Deleur is a location, in this case, Pohnpei). At the end of this period, the dynasty was overthrown by an invasion from the east led by a warrior named Isokelekel.

The last Saudeleur was an arrogant tyrant, so belligerent that he was rude and insulting even to his titled subordinates. The Saudeleur was uncontrollable because he felt that he had to pay homage to no one. He even had the audacity to imprison Nansapwe, the Thunder God. Nansapwe, however, escaped and left Pohnpei. Some say the Saudeleur freed the Thunder God from prison and sent him away because the God was roaring continuously while a captive. The Thunder God sailed to the east in his royal canoe. However, the boat sank in mid-ocean. To save the Thunder God, a passing sea bass transformed a taro flower into a needlefish which saved the God by skipping him over the waves to land.

The Thunder God arrived at the "land upwind." Some say this was one of the islands of the Ratak Chain of the Marshall Islands, but most believe that it was Kosrae. There he visited a clanmate, an old lady named Lipanmai, of the Under the Breadfruit Clan. He fed a bitter lime to Lipanmai and she shuddered and became pregnant.

Lipanmai bore a son who was named Isokelekel. As the child grew up, he continually heard stories of how the Saudeleur had insulted and offended the Thunder God. When mature, the young man determined to take revenge on the Saudeleur by invading and conquering his island.

With friends, Isokelekel sailed to Pohnpei. When some distance offshore, they saw what appeared to be a population of giants guarding the shoreline and the hills. The potential invaders made a hasty retreat back to Kosrae. There, they were told that it was not giants they had seen, but spear-palm trees that from a distance resembled giant men in skirts.

On the next attempt to sail to Pohnpei, Isokelekel made better preparations. He sailed with a fleet of women and children and 333 warriors by way of Sapwuahfik to Pohnpei's offshore atoll of Ant. There they rested and learned all they could about the language, Pohnpei, and the Saudeleur. Finally they sailed around Pohnpei to the harbor of Madolenihmw where they anchored.

The Saudeleur was disturbed by the news of the fleet of strangers. Still, he sent a delegation to welcome the newcomers onto the island while he made his plans. On Pohnpei, Isokelekel's soldiers acted peacefully and all took young, beautiful Pohnpeian wives,. Isokelekel's lieutenant Nahnsen, however, took an older, experienced woman from whom he knew he could learn more to help him with his eventual conquest. Isokelekel's identity as leader was always concealed from the Pohnpeians, incidentally, so he could move about without drawing much attention. At Pohnpeian feasts he would sit with commoners, and if a Pohnpeian happened to be present at his feasts, he would not sit at the front of the group.

There is disagreement about how the actual fighting began. Most believe it started rather innocently with children of Pohnpeians quarreling with children of Isokelekel's group. Adults from both groups took sides, feelings intensified, and the war was on.

In battle, Pohnpeian soldiers proved to be brave, but reckless. Isokelekel's warriors, on the other hand, were cautious and clever. The weapons of both sides were the same: long spears, javelins, slings with small stones, shafts with stingray points for stabbing, and stones for throwing. All of the action took place at or around Nan Madol.

As the war intensified, Isokelekel's forces retreated. At the height of the struggle, Isokelekel was wounded by a stone thrown by a young Pohnpeian named Taukir. It is said that the wound stimulated Isokelekel to fight fiercely — "Thank you! Until now I did not know we were fighting. It seemed like playing," he said. With the invader's forces in near rout, a lieutenant of Isokelekel's named Nahnsen refused to fall back further. He thrust a spear through his foot impaling it to the ground in order to stem the retreat. Seeing this unusually brave act, Isokelekel's soldiers rallied and attacked, scattering the enemy. The Saudeleur was driven into the Sanipan River and transformed into a small, blue freshwater fish called a Palaiaw, that is in the river to this day. It is never eaten by Pohnpeians.

After the victory, Nahnsen was credited with stimulating Isokelekel's forces to win the battle. He could have been appointed the Nahnmwarki, but he insisted that Isokelekel have this highest title. In a benevolent gesture, Isokelekel rewarded Taukir for wounding him by giving the young man land and a high title. The two became very good friends, just as two people who have fought each other often become fast friends today.

(The war ended the second traditional period on Pohnpei. Isokelekel became the first Nahnmwarki, or paramount chief, and ushered in the third historical period, the last before the arrival of non-Micronesians on the island.)

Traditional Tattoo Designs

HOW THE ROCK OF ISOSEURI WAS NAMED ON POHNPEI

Several centuries ago there lived a man named Isoseuri in a section of Pohnpei called Kepinne in Kitti Municipality. One day he heard that a clan named Dipwinmeniso had invaded and captured Peidiker, the home of his relatives and clan. To be sure that this was true, Isoseuri journeyed to Peidiker. There he was met by two men on guard. One man was right-handed and the other was left-handed. When they threw rocks at him at the same time, Isoseuri knew indeed that Peidiker had been taken. Isoseuri then returned to Kepinne to spread the news to his remaining relatives. They planned their revenge for the next day.

All of the men with their spears left for Peidiker early the next morning. Among them was Kadehnkan, the best drum-beater in Kitti and also a man who carried a torch of fire. When they arrived at Peidiker, Isoseuri leaped onto a large rock. The rock went rolling down to the river, but Isoseuri rode it all the way until it stopped. He then told his forces to attack and win the battle.

The two sides fought fiercely, and those from Kepinne thirsted for revenge. The torch-carrier set fire to all the huts as the two sides fought. Finally the Dipwinmeniso clan was defeated and ran from the scene of battle. Kadehnkan pounded on his drum. When the people of Kitti heard this, they knew that Isoseuri had won the battle.

The relatives of Isoseuri had two clans, the Dipwinmen, and the Nahniek. Isoseuri divided the land captured into two parts so that each clan had a section. To the Dipwinmen he gave a section called Enpeinpah, and to the Nahniek clan he gave a section called Enpeinpewe. In these two sections only people from these clans have high traditional titles.

HOW DECEPTION SAVED U FROM BEING CAPTURED

According to legend, Isokelekel consolidated his power at Nan Madol in Madolenihmw after defeating the Saudeleur. He then set out to defeat all the tribes of Pohnpei.

There was a warrior of giant size named Taukatar living at U. He was such a large man that he had to bend over when speaking to people. Because of his large size, he was greatly respected and considered to be the protector of the people of U. Also, he possessed magic powers. His home was under a rock at Awak.

Isokelekel and his companions first sailed to Saladak in U and started to land, but suddenly saw Taukatar standing on the shore holding a huge club and wearing a yellow grass skirt. Isokelekel feared that the men of Saladak were all as large as this man with the yellow grass skirt, and so he sailed on to find an easier enemy.

Taukatar immediately hurried down the coast ahead of Isokelekel. When the canoe again tried to land at U, they saw a very large warrior holding a club and wearing a blue grass skirt. Since the skirt was a different color, Isokelekel did not know that this warrior was the same Taukatar. Fearing that these men also were too large to defeat, he sailed without landing again.

Taukatar again moved away quickly to Awak, where Isokelekel was headed. By magic, he changed his grass skirt to a red color this time. When Isokelekel again saw the large warrior, he did not know that he was the same Taukatar and he again sailed on without landing. Because of Taukatar's deception, Isokelekel did not set foot on the soil of U.

Isokelekel eventually captured most of Pohnpei Island. Without the courage, deception and magic of Taukatar, however, he would have added the people of U to his domain.

HOW SAKAU WAS FIRST GROWN ON POHNPEI

Uitannar was an old man who had always served and worshipped a god named Luk. When Uitannar was tired, weak, and nearly blind from old age, Luk appeared before Uitannar and offered to take the old man on a journey. But Uitannar was exhausted from age and poor health and could not move from his mat. Luk took hold of his hand, and Uitannar felt strength return to his body, and his blind eyes were able to see again. By trail and by canoe, Uitannar and Luk went to the island of Na. Then they journeyed further into Madolenihmw. Along the way they met a married woman who took a liking to Luk and gave him a love present of a necklace. To return the kindness, Luk took the skin from the heel of Uitannar and gave it to the woman. She was told to bury it and an amazing plant would grow in its place, the juice from which would change people's lives. This was done, and the first plant of sakau was grown and its liquid consumed. People were amazed to see rats nibbling at the plant roots become immobile, sick and drunk. They named the plant "joko," which is "soakoa" in the Kitti dialect of Pohnpeian and "sakau" in the northern dialect.

In the meantime, up above, two people of heaven were watching the earth people enjoy sakau, and they were curious about it, so they descended to earth and stole a root of the plant and took it back to heaven. There, they presented it to two Lords of Eels, who planted it in the Garden Plot of Heaven. It grew immediately. The gods then pounded the sakau plant, and a piece of it flew off of the pounding stone, out of heaven, and floated down to the home of Uitannar where it took root and sprouted. And this is how the sakau plant began multiplying throughout all of the areas of Pohnpei where it can be found today.

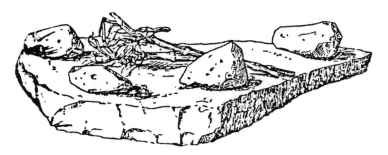

Sakau Pounding Stone *(peitehl)*

(For a description of sakau, its ceremonial preparation, and its effect, see *Flora of Pohnpei*, pp.125-129)

Values and Beliefs

(from the frivolous to the philosophical)

PROVERBS

There is a refuge sure in Pohnpeian proverbs. Very often actions are justified by a proverb that condones a principle or particular behavior. Just as often, non-action can be justified in the same way. Proverbs are also used to excuse unacceptable behavior. Face must be saved in Pohnpeian society and islanders are particularly sensitive to public criticism and embarrassment. Proverbs may be used for proving points or for winning arguments. They also offer advice or warnings by stating a particular truth known to Pohnpeians. Proverbs are characterized by brevity of language and frequent use of elliptical sentences rather than meter and rhyme as in English. It is not unusual for one proverb to cancel out another by directly contradicting it. Consequently, one must always be careful when making generalizations about Pohnpeian attitudes based solely on a fragmentary knowledge of witty proverbial statements. A few well-known witty proverbial statements follow.

"Tehn keleu marahra."
(He is a light hibiscus leaf. His ideas and opinions are disoriented like a hibiscus fluttering in the wind.)

"Nan awatail me kitail kin pitkihla."
(Clever words can help us to get out of difficult situations.)

"Eluak reirei sapwasapw."
(If you miss out on something desirable, there is always a chance that it will come again, because life is a long journey.)

"Me kin wia, kin dolung."
(What you sow, you reap. If I steal someone's money, someone will steal mine.)

"Ke dehr wonohn en pahn oahs amwahu."
(Don't just lie there when there is work to be done. You are acting as though you are asleep and have nothing to do.)

"Sohte ohl kin mihmi pahn emen ohl."
(No man should consider himself less skilled or beneath another.)

"Kiris ieu ohl."
(Do not act too high, proud or snobbish.
A man can slip or fall.)

"Nan Kepdau en Pahleng me diren pehwehwe."
(At the reef entrance in Pahleng there are plenty of manta
rays. There are many fish in the sea, or many girls available.)

"Lik sansal."
(Never judge a person from outer features
or outside appearances.)

"Mweleng en ohl."
(There are many things contained in a man,
but he will not let anyone know all of them.)

"Joh mehkij jampah joh kin janjal."
(Don't worry about secrets. There is nothing
in the world that is unknown.)

*"Sohte ohl kin musekihla mehkot ahm pil pwurehng
kangala."*
(No man vomits up something and then
swallows it down again. A man should not have
to swallow the words he has spoken.)

"Sohte ohl kin sansara mahl."
(No man should open his mouth without a purpose.
Loud conversation and laughter are female traits.)

"Se kin damasang saut, damehng samat."
(When a choice is to be made between our matrilinial
clansmen and our father, we take the side of our father.
We stop being an outrigger float for our clansmen.)

"Pilen pahn mweli."
(Criticism of traditional leaders is meaningless activity,
like water flowing through underground rocks.)

"Kedehr karuahla peinkarat amah."
(Don't be in a hurry for the banana to ripen. Do not
introduce sexual activity to girls who are immature.)

"Tohtohn kol."
(A multitude of cockroaches. Plenty, but worthless.)

"Selin peneinei sohte kin ohla."
(A man may love his wife, but she is second after
children. A man and wife may split,
but children remain attached to parents.)

"Sohte pelen kot madau."
(There are no taboos across the sea. What is not
accepted at home may be accepted when far away.)

"Nennenin sarau kommwoad."
(A man should be like a barracuda, waiting quiet and
motionless and then strike violently when attacking.)

"Ser en mwanakapw."
(The light of a young man is darkness. He can
move in the dark without fear and nothing
is particularly difficult for him.)

"Mweli-ieu ohl."
(A man should have the characteristics of a boulder,
heavy and hard to move in both thoughts and ideas.)

"Mwpuladadahn tuw rengireng."
(Warmed by flaring firewood. Dry wood flares quickly,
makes a big flame, and then dies in a short time.)

"Uht sohte kin wa mahi."
(The banana plant does not bear breadfruit. Like comes
from like. A son will be like his father.)

"Kadohdo mwurin wahrsereh."
(It makes no sense to swim after a fish that has escaped.)

"Wasahn mehla wasa koaros."
(Everywhere is a place for death, so a real man should not worry and should act without fear.)

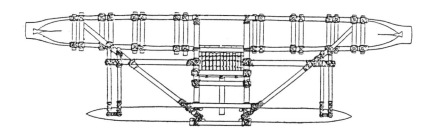

Superstitions, Omens and Taboos

English speakers have their lucky sevens and their unlucky broken mirrors, leaning ladders, and black cats in well-known superstitions. Pohnpeians have omens and taboos that are put into maxims and aphorisms. Most are concerned with basics of island living — fishing, birds and animals, weather, visiting, and childbirth, marriage and death. All of the sayings included here are known locally and a number of them are familiar to young people throughout Micronesia. Some would not be unfamiliar to children as far away as Hawaii, or even central Iowa, for that matter.

FISH AND FISHING

Pointing a finger at a flock of birds following a school of fish should never be done because the fish will disappear.

If you look back while trolling, you will not catch a fish.

Drinking water just before going fishing will cause a lot of rain to fall.

If one steps on human excrement before going fishing, one will catch no fish.

One must not eat raw fish or cooked fish before going fishing or no fish will be caught.

The first fish that bites should be caught or the fisherman will catch few fish.

If a fisherman dreams about blood, many fish will be caught.

If one finds coins in one's pocket while fishing, they should be thrown into the sea.

Never kill and eat a seabird before going fishing.

Stepping on a blue starfish will bring bad luck to a fisherman.

If you repeatedly eat the tails of fish, you will live away from your home.

Never allow women to sit in or on your canoe before going fishing.

Eating dolphin will cause one to lose one's teeth.

Do not take meat with you when you go fishing, or you will catch no fish.

A thread-small fishing line can never drag a large fish ashore.

If you see a cat licking its paws, you will catch many fish.

If you make noise while fishing, ghosts of the dead will join you and scare all of the fish away.

If you are in the water fishing and you see a fish jump into the air, you won't catch any fish.

Never eat chicken before going fishing.

It is bad luck to yawn while fishing.

You will soon eat some fish if a falling breadfruit leaf hits you.

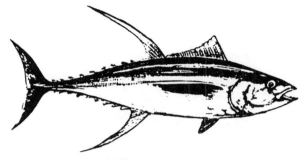

Yellowfin Tuna

BIRDS AND ANIMALS

A dog howling at night means that someone has died.

A cat licking its face means that rain is coming.

A rat running across your path will bring bad luck.

A chicken flapping its wings means a visitor is coming.

A blackbird flying across your path will bring bad luck.

A butterfly seen while fishing will bring bad luck.

A grasshopper flying at night means that rain is coming.

A worm seen in a puddle in a rain means you will get meat later.

A gecko crackling at your back door means a friend is coming.

A turtle seen while fishing will cause no fish to be caught.

A bird singing at night will bring bad luck.

A spider leaving its web means that a typhoon is coming.

A rooster crowing at midnight means bad news will soon arrive.

Golden Plover

WEATHER

If one goes on a journey on a rainy day, one will be sure to return.

If it is raining and the sun is shining at the same time, someone has just died.

If you point a finger at a rainbow, your finger may be permanently bent.

Throwing rocks into a river will cause the river to flood.

Sneezing four times in a row means that lots of rain is coming.

If one kills a seabird, bad weather will come.

Blowing on a horn will bring rain.

A red sky in the evening means that rain will fall the next day.

If you turn over a starfish, bad weather will follow.

If you visit a friend and it is raining, it is said that you brought the rain.

If rain falls when the moon is shining, a ship will soon arrive.

When one hears thunder, it is the god Nahnsapwe speaking.

A gecko crackling in the center of your ceiling means rain will come.

If you point your finger at a waterfall, it will cause rain to fall.

VISITING AND TRAVELING

If a gecko is crackling near the front door, a stranger is about to arrive.

Sweeping a floor at night will cause a member of your family to leave.

A wide space between your teeth means you will live away from your parents.

If a butterfly or a dragonfly comes into your house, an important visitor will soon arrive.

If a cat cries at night, a ship will arrive the next day.

If you leave on a trip and then immediately return home, you will have bad luck when you again leave.

Two coconuts falling to the ground at the same time means a ship is coming soon.

If you continually bump into your friend while walking, you will soon part.

If a red bird flies over your house, a visitor will arrive with news.

If you get a boil on your leg, you will be traveling soon.

A white spot on your fingernail means that you will soon take a trip.

When everyone in the household is sleeping and you sneeze, a member of the family will soon leave.

Bending a reed or a large blade of grass along your path will cause your journey to be shortened.

PREGNANCY AND CHILDREN

If food is not cooked well in a traditional oven *(uhmw)*, it means that the wife is pregnant.

It is bad luck for a pregnant woman to wear flowers.

When traveling, a pregnant woman should always have a cover on her head.

A lot of pain in a pregnant woman's womb means that she will have a male child.

If a pregnant woman dreams of death, she will have a miscarriage.

If a pregnant woman goes out a lot at night, her baby will cry excessively.

If you dream about flowers, someone you know is pregnant.

A pregnant woman should never walk in the rain.

If a pregnant woman eats while walking, she will have a difficult and painful delivery.

If one dreams about mangoes, a relative is pregnant.

If a woman in her first pregnancy does not receive all of the best care, she will experience a difficult delivery.

Acquiring anything for a baby before the birth might cause the unborn baby to die.

It is shameful for a woman to show pain during a delivery.

It will bring bad luck if a woman eats while holding an infant.

If you have more than five long lines in your hand, you will have many children.

It is bad manners to brag about the intelligence or ability of your children.

A woman craving for green mangoes, limes, or anything very sour means she is pregnant.

A pregnant woman should never argue or be cross lest she give birth to a child who will be incorrigible.

A child who gives you the most grief early in life will be the one closest to you in later life.

Coconut Frond Basket

A man must not have sexual relations with his wife before going fishing, or no fish will be caught.

If a wife steps over her husband's fishing equipment, her husband will catch no fish.

A wife to a husband is like an outrigger to a canoe.

If a man combs his wife's hair, it means they will soon divorce.

If you marry someone from a different culture, it means no one from your culture will marry you.

Weaving a mat while your husband is away fishing will cause him to catch no fish.

If a girl accidentally chews a lock of her hair while eating, someone will propose marriage to her.

If a husband and a wife say the same word at the same time, they will soon part from each other.

A man should never take his wife fishing with him or they will catch no fish.

A girl who has many boyfriends will be the last to marry.

A man may love his wife, but she is second after children are born.

If a girl wears an old mwaramwar, she will marry an old man.

If a star is seen close to the moon, someone will soon be asked to marry.

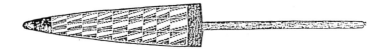

Dance Paddle

If a person tells all that he knows about Pohnpeian lore and legends, he will become empty and die.

A star within a ring around the moon is a sign of death.

If you take back a gift you have given, your father will die at sea.

If a crab crawls into your home, a funeral will take place there.

If you feel like scratching the sole of your foot with a knife, someone in your family has died.

If a seabird cries on your roof, someone has died.

If you see a lizard die, one of your relatives will die.

If a child resembles the father too closely, the father will die.

Sharpening a knife before going to a funeral should never be done.

If a person gets a high traditional title and is unworthy of it, he will have an early death.

When the wind keeps changing directions, someone is going to die.

Making a noise with a hammer at night is a call for death.

If one dreams of flowers and can actually smell them upon awakening, death is near.

Naming a child after one's self is calling for a replacement and so death might come.

Two geckos making crackling noise while fighting means that someone has died.

Winds coming to Pohnpei from the south bring death with them.

POHNPEI STATE OUTLYING ISLANDS

Introduction

The first question asked to Pohnpeians by many visitors is, "Where are the beaches?" The answer has to be, "On the outer islands." The state of Pohnpei contains eight outlying atolls in addition to the capital island: Ant, Pakin, Oroluk, Sapwuahfik (Ngatik), Nukuoro, Kapingamarangi, Mokil, and Pingelap. (Until 1977, Kosrae Island was a part of the U.S. Trust Territory district that included Pohnpei and the outliers.) The land area of the atolls and the main island is 133.4 square miles, making Pohnpei nearly as large as Kosrae (42.3 square miles), Truk (49.2 square miles), and Yap (45.9 square miles) states combined.

Each outer island is a municipality of Pohnpei State, or is a part of a municipality of Pohnpei Island. Ant is administratively part of Kitti municipality, Pakin is part of Sokehs, and Oroluk is administratively joined to Kapingamarangi. Each municipality is governed by an elected chief executive and a council of elected members. Since 1985-86 when each municipality drafted its own constitution, some laws have been different from one municipality to another. All atolls are represented in the state legislature.

Populations of the outlying islands are deceptive. The numbers resident on the islands are far smaller than those who consider themselves as natives of the particular islands. For example, Pingelap Atoll has a de facto population of 712, but fully 1,352 Pingelapese are in Pohnpei State. Those off of the island are usually working on Pohnpei. A very large percent of the legal residents of the outer islands live away from their municipalities. Those actually living on location in the islands total 8.6 percent of Pohnpei's people, but outer islanders comprise 14 percent of the population.

The land area of the outliers is small, only a total of 3.18 square miles combined. Each bit of land, however, has its own physical and cultural characteristics, history, and its own unique story to tell.

Ant

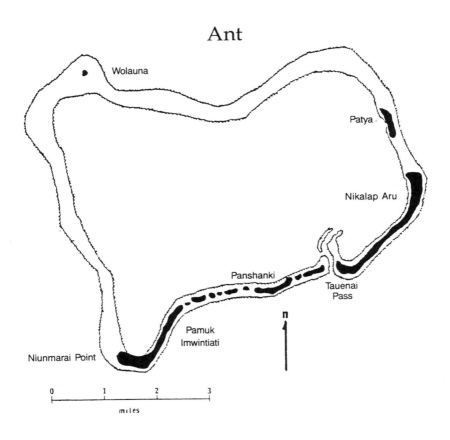

Type of island: Luxuriant atoll.
Number of islets: 13.
Land area: 0.72 sq. mi.
Lagoon size: 28.70 sq. mi.
Main islet: Niakalap Aru.
Population: Transient from
  Pohnpei.

Language: Pohnpeian.
Island group: Senyavin Islands.
Cultural group: Eastern Carolinian.
Main religion: *(See Pohnpei)*
Political: Part of Kitti municipality
  of Pohnpei.
First recorded foreign contact:
  1529.

Other names: Andema, Fraser, William the Fourth Group, Anto To.
Distance from Pohnpei: 8 nautical miles southwest, from pass to pass.

6° 45' 00" north
158° 00' 00" east

With a land area of only 0.72 square miles and thirteen small islets, Ant is the largest of Pohnpei's outliers. It is inhabited throughout the year by Pohnpeians. Although a part of Kitti municipality of Pohnpei, the island is owned by the Nanpei family of Pohnpei. It is the only privately owned outer island in the F.S.M.

Ant is part of the Senyavin Islands group. The name was given to Pohnpei, Ant, and neighboring Pakin by a Russian captain, Fedor Lütke, while on a scientific expedition around the world in 1828 aboard the *Senyavin*.

Because of its proximity to Pohnpei, Ant has always been a coveted jewel in the Senyavin Islands crown. The atoll's channel is a short eight miles southwest of Pohnpei, and it is said that Ant is the isle where Nahnesen, a young lieutenant of Isokelekel who defeated the Saudeleurs, lived for a time. It was on Ant that Nahnesen courted an elderly woman who supposedly provided the strategy for winning the battle at Nan Madol, and ushered in the third Pohnpeian historical period with the defeat of the Saudeleurs. Lütke in 1828 found the island uninhabited and very nearly went aground.

Ant is truly a mariner's dream of an island paradise, and deserves a far more picturesque name than it has. The atoll is undeveloped, and very nearly untouched. It is moist, luxuriant, and covered with tropical vegetation except on its expansive sandy beaches. Ant's waters are teeming with marine life, and some of the best scuba diving and snorkeling in the area are around its reefs. Ant is truly the tropic isle of romantic novels, movies, and dreamers.

The Nahnken Isoani of Kitti willed the atoll to the first Henry Nanpei in the middle of the last century. Nanpei's land claim was later recognized by the Spanish governor Pidal in 1896 and by the German district administrator Dr. Albert Hahl in 1899. Over the years, Ant's main economic function has been to produce copra.

Soulik en Ant and Naruhpe

At Lohd, in Madolenihmw, there was a woman who had three daughters. The youngest was the most beautiful among all the girls of Pohnpei. She had a particular pond in which she would bathe daily and the pond flowed into the sea. Whenever she would bathe, fragrant oil from her skin would float away into the ocean.

There lived at that time on Ant Atoll a man named Soulik en Ant who was very cruel. One day the oil from the skin of the lovely woman floated all the way to Ant and was found by Soulik en Ant. He was so excited by the oil that he decided to sail to Pohnpei and take its owner for his wife. He then assembled all of his men to accompany him to Madolenihmw.

Many canoes sailed from Ant to Pohnpei. When they arrived, Soulik en Ant sent a messenger to the old woman telling her that he was taking her youngest daughter for his wife. But the mother loved her daughter dearly, so she sent her eldest daughter as a bride to deceive Soulik en Ant. But the man from Ant was not fooled, and he sent the eldest daughter back to the old lady. The mother then sent her next oldest daughter to be the wife of Soulik en Ant. But again he was not fooled and he sent the woman back to her mother and demanded the youngest daughter. The poor old lady could do nothing but obey the wishes of Soulik en Ant.

After the arrival of the lovely young girl, all of the canoes then sailed back toward Ant. On the way back, Soulik en Ant became more and more furious because he had been deceived by the old woman, so he threw the young girl into the sea. As she was sinking, her long hair became tangled in the outrigger of the canoe of a man named Kanikin en Ant. Sharks immediately attacked and her whole body was devoured except for her lovely face.

Kaniki en Ant felt such love and pity for the girl that he pulled her head from the sea. When he returned to Ant he took the head to his house and wrapped it in taro leaves and hid it in a different house. A few days passed and Kaniki en Ant went to the house again to see the lovely face of the dead girl. When he opened the door he was startled to see that the girl had come back to life and was sitting combing her long hair. He was so happy to see her that he took her for his wife.

The evil Soulik en Ant heard what had happened. He was so jealous that he planned a cruel deception. He would hold a feast and invite everyone so that Kaniki en Ant could not fail to come. Then he would murder him and reclaim the young girl for his wife.

The feast took place and everyone attended, including Kanikin en Ant and his bride. But the girl knew of Soulik en Ant's evil plan and so she did not participate in any of the activities. All she did was put more and more coconut husks on the fire. When the smoke was very dark and thick, she and Kaniki en Ant leaped into it and the smoke carried them together back to Lohd. There they happily stayed together for the rest of their lives.

This legend is known to be true in Madolenihmw. The young girl's name was Naruhpe, and her bathing pool and the nearby taro patch can be seen clearly in Lohd to this day.

Pakin

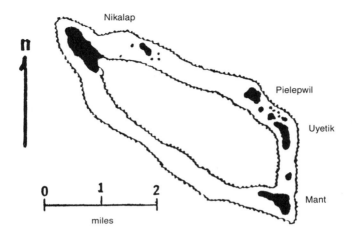

Nikalap

n

Pielepwil

Uyetik

0   1   2   Mant

miles

Type of island: Dry-forest atoll.
Number of islets: 16.
Land area: 0.42 sq. mi.
 Lagoon size: 5.50 sq. mi
Main islet: Nikalap.
Population: sparsely inhabited
 intermittently by Pohnpeians.

Language: Pohnpeian.
Island group: Senyavin Islands.
Cultural group: Eastern
 Carolinian.
Main religion: (See *Pohnpei*.)
Political: Part of Sokehs munici-
 pality of Pohnpei.
First recorded foreign contact: 1529.

Other Names: Pegenema, Paguenema Group, Pakeen, Pakin To.
Distance from Pohnpei: 18 nautical miles west.

7° 05' 30" north
157° 46' 30" east

Pakin has always been an afterthought in the history of
Pohnpei, even though mentioned as one of Pohnpei's satellite
atolls by navigators from Quiros to Lutke. (The Russian's name
for the atoll, incidentally, was "Paghenema.") During the
Sokehs Rebellion of 1910-1911, a small group of insurgents
chose Pakin as a refuge from German wrath, but were found
and exiled to Palau. Today, the atoll is occupied by
Pohnpeians.

With a land area of only 0.42 square miles, Pakin is the smallest of the Senyavin group, and the second smallest atoll of Pohnpei's outliers. Its sixteen islets are administered by Sokehs municipality of Pohnpei, eighteen nautical miles to the southeast.

Pakin's lagoon is five and a half square miles in area, but has no entrance passage. It can be entered, however, by small boats at high tide, with care. Fishing is excellent in the area and a small boat with a 200 h.p. motor can reach Pakin from Kolonia in an hour and a half. In past years, Pakin has served as a haven of sorts, and a number of fishermen thought lost after being blown or swept away from Pohnpei have turned up safe in Pakin's tiny islets. On a clear day, the atoll can be seen from the hills of Pohnpei.

Sapwuahfik (Ngatik)

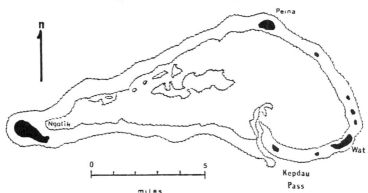

Island type: Luxuriant atoll.
Number of islets: 9.
Land area: 0.67 sq. mi.
Lagoon size: 30.43 sq. mi.
Main islet: Ngatik.
Population, 1985: 566.

Language: Pohnpeian/Ngatikese.
Island group: Eastern Carolines.
Cultural group: Eastern Carolinian.
Main religion: Evenly split between Protestant and Catholic
Political: A municipality of Pohnpei State.
First recorded foreign contact: 1773.

Other Names: Islas de la Pasion, Raven, Seven Islands, Nachikku To, Ngatik.
Distance from Pohnpei: 75 nautical miles southwest.

5° 47′ 15″ north
157° 90′ 15″ east

According to Pacific scholar Saul Riesenberg, the population of Sapwuahfik in 1855 consisted of seven Gilbertese women, one Pohnpeian man and woman, fifteen Sapwuahfik women and four men, eight children of uncertain parentage, and two whites. "From these mixed origins, the present population is descended." A total of 734 people in Pohnpei State claim origins from this group.

One of the most tragic incidents in Oceania history took place on Sapwuahfik in 1837 when the crew of the British cutter *Lambton* invaded the island and slaughtered every male they could find. The attack was in reprisal for a purported attack on two *Lambton* crewmen the previous year. The booty stolen after the massacre was twenty pounds of turtle shell. Despite British admiralty investigations, none of the attackers ever paid any penalty for their outrages (see *History*, p.42).

Sapwuahfik is shaped somewhat like an arrowhead with its main islet at the tip pointed eastward. The channel entering the 30.43 square mile lagoon resembles a French curve gone awry and is eight miles from Ngatik Islet. The atoll's main islets are quite distant from each other and total 0.67 square miles in land area.

Sapwuahfik was first recorded in 1773 by a Spaniard with the unlikely name of Felipe Tompson aboard the *Nuestra Senora de Consolacion*. However, Quiros in 1595 probably saw the atoll.

In 1985, the delegates to the constitutional convention of Ngatik Atoll renamed it Sapwuahfik, a name that even Sapwuahfikese have difficulty pronouncing. The main islet, however, retains the name of Ngatik.

Limenarleng of Sapwuahfik

There is a small islet called Paina nine miles from the main islet of Ngatik on Sapwuahfik Atoll. This islet is known because the daughter of a king was rejected by her parents.

On Ngatik long ago lived a king and queen with a daughter named Limenarleng. In those days women wove skirts and mats from the fronds of palms, and even the queen would go with the village women throughout the island gathering material for their weaving.

One day Limenarleng was resting on the beach because she was pregnant. The queen brought palm leaves and the King's "tor," a grass skirt, and left them for Limenarleng to dry in the sun. She told her daughter to look after the leaves and the tor and to be sure that they did not get wet. Then the queen left with the other women. Limenarleng was drowsy and soon she fell asleep, and when she awoke later, the tide had risen and everything was soaking wet.

The king and queen discovered what had happened and they abused and scolded their pregnant daughter, which is very much against custom on Sapwuahfik. Then they told her to leave their home. So Limenarleng left Ngatik when the tide was very low and walked toward the beach. Since the tide was out she walked and walked until she reached Paina. She took with her only a single coconut which she planted on the newly-found islet.

Back on Ngatik the king and the queen were melancholy and lonely, for their daughter had been gone many months. They searched everywhere, but Limenarleng was nowhere to be found.

The month of Limenarleng's delivery arrived and she gave birth to a son. When the boy matured and was old enough to sail a canoe, his mother built one for him and told him to sail off to Ngatik and visit his grandparents. Before he left she told him that if the fronds of their coconut palms turned yellow in his absence, then he would know that she had died.

The boy sailed his canoe to Ngatik, but when he arrived, he was beaten by the people and cast into the sea because he did not know the custom of how a strange canoe should approach the island. He was left to drown when an old lady, who happened to be one of the king's maids, came to the shore and rescued him. She then took the boy to her home.

The king and queen soon discovered that the strange boy was their grandson, for he sang songs about his mother and why he came to Ngatik that only Limenarleng's son could know. All of the people were happy and a royal feast was prepared in the boy's honor.

Soon, the boy told his grandparents that he must return to Paina because his mother was left there alone. So the king and queen prepared to accompany the boy and ordered all of the people to come with them. They all sailed to Paina the next day. When the island was sighted, the boy began to weep, for he saw that the fronds of their trees had turned from green to yellow. He knew that his mother had died. And even today on the small island of Paina, yellow fronds are found as a reminder of Limenarleng and her son.

Nukuoro

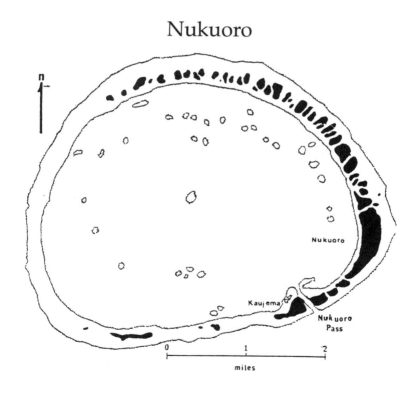

Island type: Luxuriant atoll.
Number of islets: 46.
Land area: 0.64 sq. mi.
Lagoon size: 10.52 sq. mi.
Main islet: Nukuoro.
Population, 1985: 395.

Language: Nukuoran (Polynesian).
Island group: Eastern Carolines.
Cultural group: Polynesian.
Main religion: Protestant.
Political: A municipality of Pohnpei.
First recorded foreign contact: 1801.

Other Names: Dunkin, Monteverdeson's Group,
Monteverde Islands, Nugoro To.
Distance from Pohnpei: 251 nautical miles southwest.

3° 50' 30" north
154° 58' 15" east

When visiting Nukuoro in 1806, a crewman of the Spanish vessel *Pala* remarked that the "inhabitants are of the most pacific disposition." But dispositions change like tides. In 1830, the schooner *Antarctic* of New York was attacked by Nukuorans. Only with cannon fire and muskets were the crewmen able to repel the attack, after killing or wounding more than twenty natives.

The island of Nukuoro shines in Pohnpei State as a classic example of the most luxuriant moist atoll. It almost seems to have been created so that romantic writers can practice using superlatives. Nukuoro's circular reef contains forty-five small islets in addition to the large islet of Nukuoro, mostly sitting on an eastern half moon. At low tide, one can walk between islets from the most northern to the pass at the southern extremity of the atoll. The lagoon of Nukuoro, however, is one of the deepest in the entire Pacific.

An American, Captain Moses Barnard, aboard the *Lydia* recorded Nukuoro in 1801. Since then, this Polynesian member of a Micronesian state has mainly been left to splendid isolation. Its nearest neighbors are Sapwuahfik, 160 nautical miles north, and Kapingamarangi, 165 wet miles south. The young ladies of Nukuoro are some of the most beautiful in the islands, or anywhere else, for that matter. If this fact were publicized, Nukuoro's splendid isolation would undoubtedly cease immediately.

Nukuoro retained its isolation during World War II and neither the Japanese nor the Allies occupied the island. According to a longtime resident, occasional American reconnaissance flights took place, however. Also, a Japanese pilot crash-landed and was later rescued from Nukuoro by his countrymen.

As a municipality of Pohnpei State, created in 1958, Nukuoro is administered by an elected chief executive and represented in the Pohnpei State Legislature. The Polynesian language spoken on the island is not similar to Pohnpeian, but is closely related to the language spoken on Kapingamarangi.

Hadulehu of Nukuoro

There is a large indentation in the reef of Nukuoro that is clearly visible to this day. It is said that it was caused by a spirit long ago who punished a cruel man for his horrible deeds.

Hadulehu was a frightful man who lived in a concealed hole in the ground at a place called Taghidihidi. His entire body from head to foot was covered with sharp teeth. He was not afraid of any living person and only feared the ghost Deiaogausema and the Lady of Ladi. Whenever unsuspecting people wandered close to his hole, Hadulehu would wait in ambush and pull them into it. He could eat an entire person in a matter of a few seconds, and he ate many.

Soon, word spread throughout Nukuoro about Hadulehu's activities. The ghostly spirit Massagumani heard about the cruel deeds and set out for Honpei to report them to Deiaogausema. The spirit Deiaogausema had been dead and buried in Demmen Channel for some time when Massagumani arrived, but Massagumani through magic was able to communicate with him. When Deiaogausema heard of Hadulehu's behavior, he was very disturbed and rose from his watery grave. He hurried straight to Taghidihidi, found Hadulehu's hideaway, and stomped his foot on it, crushing

Hadulehu into the hard coral of the barrier reef, leaving the large dent that we see in Taghidihidi today.

Kapingamarangi

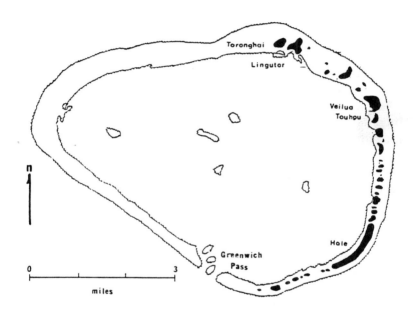

Island type: Luxuriant atoll.
Number of islets: 33.
Land area: 0.52 sq. mi.
Lagoon size: 22.01 sq. mi.
Main islet: Touhou.
Population, 1985: 507.

Language: Kapingamarangan (Polynesian)
Island group: Eastern Carolines.
Cultural group: Polynesian.
Main religion: Protestant.
Political: A municipality of Pohnpei State.

First recorded foreign contact: 1809.
Other Names: Constantin, Greenwich, Pikiram, Gurinitchi To.
Distance from Pohnpei: 415 nautical miles southwest.

1° 04′ 45″ north
154° 48′ 30″ east

There are two Kapingamarangis. One is located in Porakiet village in Kolonia, and one is the island 415 nautical miles south of Pohnpei Island (see *Sights and Sites*, p.259). The village was established early in the Japanese administration when ninety Kapingamarangans were moved to Pohnpei following a 1916 to 1918 drought. The island was first recorded by Captain Edmund Fanning aboard the *Tonquin of New York* in 1809 and named "Equator." The name "Greenwich" was mostly used in the last century and the passage into the lagoon still bears this name. English writing, incidentally, also called the Kapingamarangi settlement on Pohnpei "Greenwich Village."

At a degree plus a bit above the equator, Polynesian Kapingamarangi is the most southern of Micronesia's atolls, sixty-four miles north of the line. New Ireland and Rabaul 350 miles away in the South Pacific are closer to the island than is Pohnpei. East or west for nine hundred miles each way, no land breaks the ocean's surface.

According to oral history, Kapingamarangi's first ancestral chief was named Utamatau and he came to the island by accident. Utamatau was sailing his canoe in search of his wife, Roua, who had swum off despondent because of her husband's wandering ways. Utamatau found Roua shortly before she would have drowned, and they were both eventually washed up at Kapingamarangi.

Two tragic events are recalled in the history of the island. One occurred in 1870 when eight large Marshallese canoes, lost at sea, arrived at Kapingamarangi. The Marshallese massacred the people there for no apparent reason and the population of pacific Kapingamarangi was reduced from five to six hundred to about one hundred. The Marshallese sailed off twenty months after their arrival with a number of prisoners and were never heard from again. The second event was a natural disaster. The drought mentioned above that occurred from 1916 to 1918 caused the death of about sixty people on the island before the Japanese on Pohnpei evacuated part of the population. Tragically, half of those evacuated died of dysentery on Pohnpei.

During World War II, fifty Japanese military occupied the island to operate a weather station and man a small seaplane base. During Allied bombings of 1943 and 1944, many of the Japanese were killed, but the natives suffered no casualties. Fifty Kapingamarangans, however, were taken away for forced labor on Pohnpei. The Japanese evacuated the island in July, 1944, about a year before the end of the war.

The position of Kapingamarangi's thirty-three islets resembles a crescent on a pear-shaped coral reef. The largest islet, Hale, is nearly uninhabited, and a smaller one, Touhou, contains most of the population. The Kapingamarangan people living in the colony on Pohnpei are roughly equal in number to that on the home island.

Known throughout the Pacific as expert carvers and weavers, Kapingamarangans are also some of the best fishermen in Pohnpei State. According to John L. Fischer in *The Eastern Carolines*, Kosraeans in Micronesia wear the most clothes. Kapingamarangans wear the least.

Touhou of Kapingamarangi

Most of the people on the tiny Polynesian atoll of Kapingamarangi live on a small islet called Touhou. This islet is different from others on the atoll, and there is little doubt that it was made by man rather than nature. A story is told in Kapingamarangi about how this came about.

Long ago, during the time when idols and images were worshipped, it was decided by the people to build an island on the coral reef. It was planned that all of the people should work during the daylight hours, but never during the night. Then the people came together to pray and ask their gods for help.

On the first day they gathered large chunks of coral and put them together in piles. When the sun began to set, all of the workers returned to their homes to rest from the day's labor. The following morning when they returned to work, they were startled to find that the pile of rocks was very much larger than when they had left it the previous evening. They knew that something supernatural must be happening because all of the men had been at their homes sleeping during the night. They discussed this, and decided that it must be the work of their gods that were assisting them.

Day after day the people continued to work at building their island, and night after night the gods helped them. Finally, the islet was completed. It was high above the sea and was the most beautiful islet of the whole atoll.

The people planted different food crops and built a very large hut in which they could worship their gods. After all of the planting and building was completed, they looked at their lovely new home and named it Touhou. (In the language of Kapingamarangi, "tou" means island and "hou" means new.)

An anchor was needed to keep Touhou from drifting away, and so a very large stone was brought by the gods from a distant island for this purpose. It was a volcanic stone, and the people placed it on the windward side closest to the breaking surf.

When all was completed, the people feasted, danced, and shouted for joy. They knew that so long as the stone anchor remained in its place, the island of Touhou would not drift away. And so it is today, and any visitor to Kapingamarangi can see Touhou held firmly in place, prevented from drifting away by the stone that the gods brought for an anchor.

Mokil

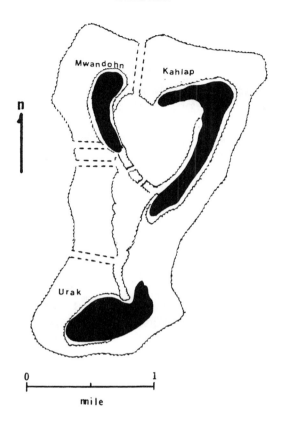

Island type: Luxuriant atoll.
Number of islets: 3.
Land area: 0.48 sq. mi.
Lagoon size: 2.61 sq. mi.
Main islet: Kahlap.
Population, 1985: 268.

Language: Mokilese/Pohnpeian
Island group: Eastern Carolines.
Cultural group: Eastern Carolinian.
Main religion: Protestant.
Political: A municipality of Pohnpei
  State
First recorded foreign contact: 1815.
Other Names: Duperry, Wellington, Mwekil, Mokiiru To.
Distance from Pohnpei: 88 nautical miles.

6° 41′ 00″ north
159° 47′ 15″ east

There are more Mokilese on Pohnpei than on Mokil Atoll. In the census of 1985, Mokil had the fewest people (268) of any outlier other than Oroluk. The Mokilese colony on Pohnpei increased when the German administration settled a number of Mokilese on Pohnpei after a devastating typhoon in 1905. Throughout Pohnpei State, however, there are 644 Mokilese.

The Wellington Group is the name given to Mokil by Captain G. Betham in 1815 aboard the *Marquis of Wellington*. A later name, "Duperrey," was more popular during the last century. At that time, many people were living on Mokil's Mwandohn islet to be near the visiting whaling ships. The center today is on Kahlap. The population has remained rather constant over the past fifty years: 1935 - 258; 1958 - 338; 1973 - 231; 1980 - 289; and 1985 - 268. (One N.J. Anderson in 1852 numbered the population at eighty-seven.)

Like most of Pohnpei's outliers, the highest elected official on the island is a chief magistrate, and Mokil sends one representative to the state legislature. The language of Mokil is closely related to Pohnpeian, but more closely to the language of Pingelap.

Pohnpeians are known for yam farming, Nukuorans for fishing, Kapingamarangans for carving and weaving, and Mokilese for carpentry. Their particular preeminence is in building a kind of whale boat, known on Pohnpei simply as a Mokilese boat. Breadfruit, coconut and some twelve other woods are used in boat building, certain woods being especially suitable for specific parts of the craft. Each piece is fashioned by hand and about ten men might work together with no pay involved. Each worker, however, keeps a rough calculation of the time he has spent on the project and can expect the boat owner to repay him in kind at a future time.

An airstrip on Mokil's fringe reef was scheduled for completion in late-1986. However, a seriously burned accident victim required an immediate air evacuation in March. Pilot Peter

Reichert of Pacific Missionary Aviation on Pohnpei along with Dr. Steve Ostroff successfully landed on the half-completed runway and were the first ever to land on the atoll.

A bit of a footnote on Mokil. The small island undoubtedly has the largest percentage of any ethnic group serving in the United States Marine Corps. Four are presently in the Corps.

Lodup of Mokil

People of Mokil have great respect for strong men, and Lodup was one of the strongest ever known. Lodup was a giant of a man who lived with his wife and their two sons. His feats of strength are still famous on the island. He had a taro patch on Kahlap, one of the islets of Mokil, and it is said that Lodup made this patch by picking up a large stone by himself and throwing it from the middle of Kahlap into the sea.

Another story showing the strength of Lodup is often told. In this story, he saved all of the people of Mokil from a force of invading canoes. It seems that Lodup was sound asleep on the neighboring islet of Mwandohn when the people saw an uncountable number of canoes heading toward Mokil. The islanders knew that only Lodup could defeat this large enemy, so they hurried to Mwandohn to awaken him. But Lodup had been asleep for fully three weeks and the people were unable to awaken him from his slumber. They became so worried that they lost hope, and then they remembered Lodup's bell made from mountainous stone. They rang the bell two times, shouting Lodup's name twice, and then paused. They did this repeatedly until the huge, strong man began to stir. Finally Lodup was wide awake and saw the fleet of canoes approaching. He grabbed the two tallest coconut trees on the island and pulled them out by their roots without effort. Then he tied each of his sons to one of the trees with coconut fronds and swung them effortlessly over the attacking canoes. As he did this, his sons were able to kill all of the invaders and sink their canoes. The people of Mokil were then safe and Lodup was respected and admired even more than before.

One day the islanders thought that they might be able to beat Lodup at diving, so they set up a competition. It was decided that everyone would dive into the sea and stay underwater as along as possible. The last one to surface would win the competition. So the competitors all dived into the lagoon, but Lodup chose to dive into the deep water beyond the reef. When the last man could hold his breath no longer, he surfaced, but Lodup remained submerged. Finally, the people thought that Lodup had drowned and that they had finally beaten him at something, but Lodup was still holding his breath at the bottom of the sea. In fact, he remained there for nearly five years. When he tried to move, he found he was anchored in place by coral that had grown on top of him over the years, and so Lodup drowned. Before he died he shook himself. This caused the whole island to shake and trees to topple and houses to tumble. It also showed to all the people that it is a mistake to think that they could beat Lodup at anything.

Pingelap

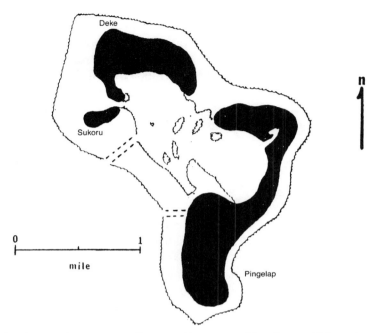

Island type: Luxuriant atoll.
Number of islets: 3.
Land area: 0.68 sq. mi.
Lagoon size: 0.46 sq. mi.
Main islet: Pingelap.
Population, 1985: 738.

Language: Pingelapese/Pohnpeian.
Island group: Eastern Carolines.
Cultural group: Eastern Carolinian.
Main religion: Protestant.
Political: A municipality of Pohnpei
State, F.S.M.
First recorded foreign contact: 1793.

Other Names: MacAskill, Musgrave, Pelelap, Pingerappu To.
Distance from Pohnpei: 163 nautical miles east southeast.

6° 12′ 30″ north
160° 42′ 30″ east

Pingelap is the only Pohnpei outlier with a lagoon smaller than its land area. The lagoon measures only 0.47 square miles while the three islets combine to a land area of 0.68 square miles.

241

Ethnohistorians suggest that Pingelap was first settled at about AD 1,000 from Pohnpei, but there have been no archaeological excavations on the island. Oral history of Pingelap recounts two devastating typhoons which hit the island during precontact times, the second at about the year 1775. In both disasters the population was reduced to some thirty survivors. A severe typhoon struck in 1905 during German times which caused a major evacuation to Pohnpei, and a destructive storm occurred as recently as 1972.

In 1793, Captain Musgrave, aboard the vessel *Sugar Cane* enroute from Australia to China found Pingelap, and felt no qualms about naming the island "Musgrave." Later, a Captain MacAskill in 1809 aboard the *Lady Barlow* called the island MacAskill's Island, the name that Pingelap retained throughout the 1800's.

The early 19th Century was a time of isolation for the people of Pingelap—their last ever—even though the island had been accurately charted by a number of navigators. Pingelap was unpopular because it provided no deep water harbor, its people were inhospitable to strangers, and Pohnpei and Kosrae, only a few days sail away, were high islands and much more appealing. The first missionaries visited Pingelap shortly after mid-century, partly to mitigate the influence of the infamous Bully Hayes. Continuous missionary activity, however, is dated from 1873. By 1881, Pingelap had a Congregational church with 271 members.

Nearly the entire present population of Pingelap is divided into four clans determined by descent from original female ancestors. According to legend, Sou was the father of three daughters, Dipwinwai, Serawik, and Kipar. The fourth ancestor, Sapwenapik, was the granddaughter of one of the three daughters of Sou. The main function, or possibly the only real function, of clans on Pingelap, is to regulate marriage.

There are seventeen aristocratic titles on the island, twelve of which have Pohnpeian names. The highest title, which bears the Pohnpeian designation of Nahnmwarki, can be traced back twenty-five generations.

Unlike Pohnpeians, but similar to all other outer islanders, Pingelapese live in a village rather than scattered throughout the three islets. Their settlement on the largest islet is near a four-hectare taro patch and contains a store, school, municipal office, and the heart of the Pingelapese community, the Protestant church.

The Japanese called Pingelap Pingerappu To, but only occupied the island temporarily. As mentioned above, the Pingalapese language is understandable to Pohnpeians, but more understandable to Mokilese.

Isopaw of Pingelap

A stretch of lagoon sits between the islets of Deke and Sukoru on Pingelap Atoll at present. At one time, however, these islets were a single piece of land. They became separated when a god from the Marshall Islands visited the atoll and caused the lagoon to form.

On the western side of Jaluit Atoll in the Marshalls, at an area sticking out from the rest of the land, sits an islet named Pingelap. It has this name because it is placed at the exact spot where the god took sand from Pingelap in Pohnpei State and deposited it at Jaluit.

Long ago the people of Pingelap worshipped a god named Isopaw. He was a lazy god and his greatest pleasure was sleeping away the days. He would only awaken briefly at night. On a day while Isopaw was sleeping, another god from Jaluit appeared on Deke. He was careful not to awaken Isopaw, and he took a gigantic handful of sand from the area causing a trench to form that became a lagoon between Deke and Sukoru. The people watched this unusual happening, and then they immediately awakened Isopaw and told him the news. Isopaw asked in what direction the other god had gone, and was told it was directly to the east. Isopaw then hurried after the strange god.

By the time that Isopaw caught up with the other god, they had traveled all the way to Jaluit. When the Marshallese god saw Isopaw, he dropped all of the sand that he was carrying and hurried away. The sand was spread over such a large area of the reef that Isopaw could not hope to pick it all up, so he left it all on Jaluit and returned to Pingelap.

From that time onward, a lagoon has separated Deke from Sukoru. This is at the exact place where the Marshallese god scooped up the sand while Isopaw slept. Also, there is an islet on Jaluit that is named after this incident, and this is where the god dropped the sand when being chased by Isopaw. It is named "Pinglap" Islet.

Oroluk

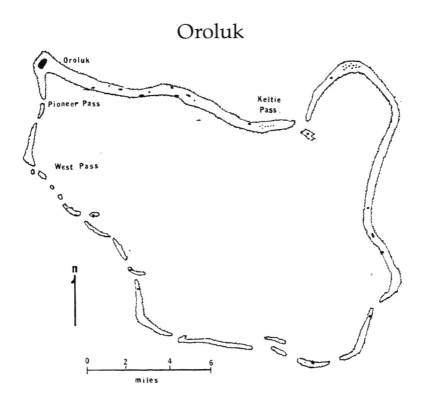

Type of island: Dry-forest atoll.
Number of islets: 19.
Land area: 0.19 sq. mi.
Lagoon size: 162.35 sq. mi.
Main islet: Oroluk.
Population, 1985: 2.

Language: Kapingamarangan (Polynesian).
Island group: Eastern Carolines.
Cultural group: Polynesian.
Political: Kapingamarangi municipality of Pohnpei State.
First recorded foreign contact: 1824.

Other Names: Baxotrista, Cambellriff, San Augustino, Ororukku To.
Distance from Pohnpei: 164 nautical miles west northwest.

7° 35′ 45″ north
155° 09′ 50″ east

Sea turtles are much more plentiful on Oroluk than people. With only 0.19 square miles of land, it is Pohnpei's smallest outlier, but also has the largest lagoon at 162 square miles. Oroluk has about nineteen islets, depending on the tide level.

According to a Pohnpeian story, Oroluk was a thriving atoll at one time until most of the land was washed away in a typhoon. Later, it became a stop for trading canoes sailing to Truk, and still later, a source of coconuts and turtles for Japanese merchants.

American Captain William Worth aboard *Rambler* in 1824 is credited with making Oroluk known to the outside world. He named his find Tucker's Island. The atoll's long and almost circular reef, uncharted in the last century, was often a navigator's tragic surprise. It was on Oroluk that the Belgian sailing vessel *Constance* went aground. While enroute to the Philippines in small boats, the crew used two of their number for survival food. As late as 1973 a Japanese skip-jack fishing vessel discovered Oroluk's reef, and remains there to this day—firmly.

Since population figures have been kept, Oroluk's have varied from tiny to none: 1935 - 42; 1958 - 0; 1973 - 0; 1980 - 10; and 1985 - 2. (In the F.S.M. Senate election of 1985, Oroluk's vote was split. One vote went to the winner, Bethwel Henry, and one vote went to his opponent.) Since 1974, the atoll has been inhabited by Kapingamarangans.

Minto Reef

8° 08′ north
154° 18′ east

There is a part of Pohnpei State, the most northerly and the most westerly, that is heard more than it is seen because of pounding surf and breaking waves. Minto Reef is an atoll-shaped, submerged coral formation northwest of Oroluk Atoll. It contains a few feet of sand bank, often awash, and no vegetation.

Minto has had other names in the past: Wishard Reef, Costello Reef, Minto Sho, and Minto Breakers. In 1980, a transient double-ender yacht out of Pohnpei named *Tar Baby*, single-handed by American Robert Venable, sailed westward. Two weeks later, in calm weather, the vessel was spotted in prime condition, fully rigged, hard on Minto Reef by a passing cruise ship, the *Lindblad Explorer*. A boarding party found only the sound of the waves on Minto, but not a living soul on board.

(Distance from Pohnpei: 265 nautical miles west northwest.)

SIGHTS AND SITES

Kolonia Town
Porakiet, Kapingamarangi Village
Spanish Wall and Park
Administration Area
Japanese Agriculture and Weather Station
Catholic Center and Bell Tower
Protestant Church
College of Micronesia
German Munitions Cave
Nanyo Boeki Kaisha Store
Sokehs Rebellion Mass Grave Site
German Cemetery
Pohnpei State Legislature, Capital Hill
Pre-World War II Tanks

...in Kolonia

Introduction

The tropics are forever unkind to historical relics, artifacts, and structures made from materials other than stone, brick, or cement. Rainfall, humidity and erosion attacking metal and wood have always been enemies of archaeologists. Even the anthropologist's favorite contributors, garbage pits, have yielded little of historical significance on Pohnpei. The most enduring structures on the island are the basalt rock ruins of Nan Madol, the crumbling stone and mortar Spanish Wall, and the brick bell tower of the old Catholic church.

There are numerous concrete platforms and foundations from times past, especially the sites around Kolonia. Most, however, are covered by more recently built structures. Whenever possible, the Germans built on Spanish foundations, the Japanese on German foundations, and Pohnpeians after World War II, on all three. Also, structures have often served several flags or purposes over the years. The present renovated television broadcasting station was the island jail until 1974, but was originally built as the residence of the chief Japanese agriculturist in the 1920's. The office of the president of the Federated States of Micronesia is a building that was a pediatrics ward of the Ponape District Hospital until 1977, and was originally an elementary school for Pohnpeian

children during the Japanese Period; and the stone foundation and steps in front of the Police Station were once, quite
appropriately, part of the Japanese judo club.

The most enduring remains of Pohnpeian structures from
the Early Contact Period and before are the stone foundations of buildings. According to Rev. Luther Gulick, writing
in 1857, Pohnpeians "lay stone most admirably. The foundations of their houses are to this day of stone. They are of
course laid by eye, yet the angles are square, and the faces
plumb. . ."

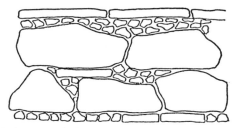

Pohnpeian Stone Masonry, circa 1908

Kolonia Town

> *"Kolonia is anything but beautiful: a cluster of weathering
> wood and rusting corrugated buildings strung anyhow along
> a wide street. . . Kolonia, indeed, reminds me of nothing so much
> as an American frontier town."*
> > Georgia Hess
> > San Francisco Examiner

> *"The main street of Kolonia. . . looks like a scene out of
> 'Gunsmoke.' The only thing missing is the horses."*
> > David Shapiro
> > Gannet, Honolulu

> *"Downtown Kolonia. . . looks like a small, seedy western
> town, with a ramshackle mix of wood and corrugated tin."*
> > George Cruys
> > Pacific Travel News

251

Except from frontier buffs, the capital of the State of Pohnpei and the Federated States of Micronesia seems to have had a rather bad press. Yet, how many western frontier towns have survived under four foreign flags in a century, and have been completely flattened three times, once by B-24 *Liberator* bombers and the sixteen inch guns of six American battleships?

Most of the early contact with western traders, whalers and missionaries took place at either the harbor of Madolenihmw or further south at Ronkiti. Robert Fulton was indirectly responsible for Kolonia's assuming importance. The advent of the steam engine allowed large vessels to sail directly to the windward and to negotiate channels in which sailing craft could not navigate.

The Pohnpeian name for the area of Kolonia is Mesenieng, literally translated as "the eye of the wind." According to one Pohnpeian legend, it is considered a sacred place. Lütke, on his voyage to Pohnpei in 1828 referred to the area as "the harbor of bad reception" because the hostile welcome he received did not allow him to land.

Protestant missionary activity began in the area with the arrival of Rev. Edward T. Doane from the mission station in Madolenihmw in 1865. Within two years a mission house was completed. By 1871, the first manually operated sawmill was constructed. This facilitated the completion of Kolonia's first mission church, a structure consisting of a basement for prayers and a school, and an upper meeting room. The cost of materials was $500. The mission was called the biblical Canaan, but to Pohnpeians it was "Kenan."

On April 19, 1887, the town of Santiago de'l Ascension was officially founded by the Spanish, and immediately referred to as "La Colonia." However, Rev. Doane claimed that the area was legally his, and produced a paper dated July 26, 1880 and signed by a local leader as proof. The issue was only settled after Rev. Doane was deported to Manila for a hearing in 1887. There the Governor General overruled the Pohnpei authorities on the grounds that Doane was not provided an opportunity to speak for himself. Doane was released and returned to Pohnpei. By the time a second inquiry took place in 1892, Doane had died.

Under Spanish rule, the town was little more than a walled, fortified compound from which soldiers sortied. It was thoroughly unsafe for any Spaniard to leave the area without an armed escort.

Germany purchased Spain's Micronesian possessions (except for Guam) for 17,500,000 German marks, or about $4,250,000 at the time. Spanish Governor Ricardo de Castro y Gandara transferred the town to the Governor von Bennigsen from the German protectorate in New Guinea on October 13, 1899. La Colonia became die Kolonie. The Germans found the structures of the town, recently vacated by 389 Spanish troops, to be in such worn and dilapidated condition that they were promptly razed. The new government closed the brothels, opened the area to all Pohnpeians, and tore down many of the fortifications built by the Spanish. The administration also encouraged commerce and built a new hospital and an agriculture station. By 1901, there were 173 foreigners in the town area, quite an international mixture: forty-one Malays; thirty-three Americans; twenty-eight Filipinos; twenty-two Germans; seventeen Japanese; twelve Spanish; ten English; eight Chinese; one Chamorro; and one Hawaiian. In 1902, thirty vessels called at die Kolonie.

The town was leveled for a second time in six years on April 20, 1905, by a devastating typhoon. German documents record all structures in the colony destroyed except for a six-cornered building left from Spanish times. Public and private losses were estimated at half a million marks (about $135,000 at the time). It was several years before the town was completely rebuilt.

From late October, 1910, until early January, 1911, die Kolonie was effectively blockaded by insurgents during the Sokehs Rebellion. Fortifications torn down from the Spanish Period were hurriedly rebuilt, and the town again resembled the walled, armed camp of the Spanish.

A squadron of six Japanese warships arrived at Kolonia Harbor on October 7, 1914 and raised the third foreign flag in two decades over the town. Japan later assumed legal control over all of German Micronesia by a League of Nations Mandate in 1920.

The town was the administrative, cultural, and business center for some ten thousand Japanese and Okinawans in the mid-1930's, and enjoyed its golden hour. There was reliable water and electricity, and there were telephones that worked. Businesses, mostly operated by non-Micronesians, included seven shops selling ice cakes and ice sticks, seven bakeries, more than twenty restaurants where a full meal of fish and rice cost fifteen sen (about four American cents at the time), and a dairy. There was a slaughter house and butcher shops, a pharmacy and more than fifteen dispensers of non-prescription medicines, in addition to barber shops, laundries, second-hand stores, curio shops, and licensed liquor dealers. Nearly all facilities were segregated and few Pohnpeians lived within the limits of the town. The administration did hire some thirty-seven Pohnpeians as policemen, medics, nightwatchmen, janitors, and translators, however, and about fifty domestics were also employed. Contact between Japanese women and Pohnpeian men was prohibited even in the nine Japanese brothels.

If Kolonia enjoyed its shining hour in the mid-1930's, its darkest hour arrived early in 1944. From February to May, twenty-five years of development was flattened by United States B-24 *Liberator* bombers and six American battleships. On September 11 of the following year, General Masao Watanabe surrendered Pohnpei to U.S. forces aboard the destroyer *Hyman* in Kolonia Harbor. The exodus of Japanese and Okinawans that year decreased the population of the island from 19,353 to about 6,000. During 1945, the first year of American occupation, Pohnpeians were allowed to tear down and remove what remained of some 940 bombed-out structures, completing the destruction of the town and allowing Kolonia to lapse into an extended slumber.

The rebuilding of Kolonia has been almost too gradual since 1945, when only the Protestant church, the bell tower of the Catholic church, and a building housing the Japanese weather station were the largest buildings standing. Politically, in May of 1965, Kolonia parted from Nett municipality and was given the autonomy of a separate local government unit by the High Commissioner of the Trust Territory. The town government now consists of a mayor and a town council, all of whom serve a four-year term.

At present, Kolonia occupies 450 acres of land on a peninsula on the northern side of the island. During the last census (1985) there was a population of 6,306 in the town. However, only 3,152 people were legal residents of the town. The other 3,154 were voting residents of other municipalities, or expatriate workers.

Nearly eighty percent of the land in Kolonia is leased to citizens for residential or commercial purposes. Leases last for twenty years and include an option to renew. The amount of rent paid by a leasee varies, and depends on when the land was actually leased. In all cases, however, the rent is nominal.

During the Japanese administration of Kolonia, streets had specific names. At present, however, they are called by what they are—waterfront road, or main street; or where they go—PICS Road, the road to Sokehs—but there is not a street name sign anywhere. There are no specific addresses, and places are identified by their proximity to familiar locations. Thus, the Palm Terrace is "next to the Agriculture Station," and the tennis court is "across from the Police Station." Still, older residents of Pohnpei remember well the former street names, and main remains Namiki Dori.

Eight residential or commercial sections in Kolonia are identified by Pohnpeian or Japanese names that tell of a feature or characteristic of the area that may or may not still exist. The most northern point of town is *Kumwunlaid*, or fishing point, and *Tewenneu* is the channel of the stonefish. *Mapusi* is the name of a Japanese civilian engineer corps which once had facilities in that area, and *Ohmine* is named for a company which once produced a rice-based liquor there. *Pwunso* is Japanese for agriculture station. Other designations familiar to senior Pohnpeians, and often used when specific locations are needed are *Kaingandori*, the fishing cooperative; *Hachikendori*, the tennis court; *Ishii Nojyo*, area of P.I.C.S. High School; *Mitsukawadori*, the road past the college; and *Pohnlik*, the Catholic Mission property.

Nicknames and unofficial designations are also used by the residents—*Chinatown* is an area off of the waterfront that is especially crowded with outer islanders, and the *Kosraean "Village"* centers around a small church just below the Community College of Micronesia.

History has moved rapidly in Kolonia since Pohnpei joined the former Trust Territory of the Pacific Islands districts of Yap, Truk and Kosrae to form the Federated States of Micronesia on May 10, 1979. Construction of both government facilities and private residences has increased considerably after Kolonia was designated the new capital, in order to accommodate the F.S.M. work force of some 550. In 1985 alone, 650 residences and businesses were either built or renovated on Pohnpei, mostly in the Kolonia area. Although plans have been drawn to relocate the capital to the Palikir section of Sokehs municipality, Kolonia will remain the seat of government for both the State of Pohnpei and the F.S.M. throughout the 1980s.

The town is also the educational center for the island, and in one respect for the entire F.S.M. The two largest public elementary schools and the largest private school are located within or near the town limits, and the largest secondary school is located a few hundred yards south of Kolonia. The combined enrollment of these schools is about 2,000 pupils. The Community College of Micronesia, the only institution of higher education in the F.S.M., is located in the center of town.

Even without government facilities, the town will continue to be the center for business, commerce and social functions for the nearly thirty thousand residents and for most tourists as well. Nine of the twelve larger retail stores, or more appropriately, general stores, on the island are located on or adjacent to two somewhat parallel roads in Kolonia, the waterfront road and the main street through the town. All are within a short walk of each other, and most have formal names that are hardly known and never used by locals. The first name of the owner usually designates the store. Thus, the *S-Mart Way Market* is forever Martin's, *The Family Store* remains Annes', and *Panuelo's Store* is Dr. Alex's. Other popular large businesses are Ambros's, Jerry's, Leo's, Carlos', and Bernard's, regardless of their formal names. The prices at these stores vary, but they are all high—fifty to a hundred percent higher for most items than at a supermarket on the U.S. mainland.

Over a hundred hotel rooms are available in six hotels in the Kolonia area, all within walking distance of each other. Some hotels are more popular than others and the quality of cleanliness and services varies. The most popular hotel on Pohnpei, The Village, is located five bumpy miles to the east of the town. Thirteen restaurants are available in the town

area, specializing in Micronesian, American, or oriental food. There is little advertising, and not a neon sign or traffic light to be seen this side of Honolulu. The most popular meal for local residents in Kolonia is a verb turned into a noun. A "take-out" is usually several pieces of fried chicken, spare ribs or fish, a liberal portion of rice, and a locally grown vegetable or starch often served with a coconut, and sold for less than $2.00. The larger bars in Kolonia are all part of a hotel or serve some food, but not by law. Drinks are reasonably priced by U.S. standards. The most popular locally-made drink, sakau en Pohnpei, is steeped in tradition, and there are nine bars in the town area. (See *Flora of Pohnpei*, pp. 125-129.)

Kolonia is a part of Pohnpei, but somehow apart from Pohnpeian traditional lifestyle. Towns are foreign to most residents and they still prefer to live on fertile farmsteads or in tiny family hamlets. Mesenieng and even Santiago de'l Ascension are much closer to a Pohnpeian's way of life than was the colony of the Japanese and Germans or the Kolonia of today.

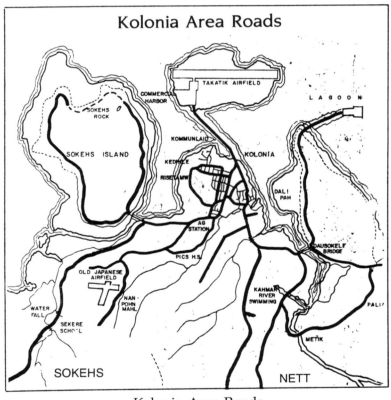

Kolonia Area Roads
(Kolonia Historical Map, p. 271)

Porakiet, Kapingamarangi Village

The largest minority group in a concentrated area in Kolonia is the five hundred or so residents of Porakiet Village. The settlement was founded nearly seventy years ago on eighteen acres of land on the western side of Kolonia, and called *Porakiet*, a name meaning "rocky place." Half of the village occupies a steep, rocky cliff facing Sokehs Island, and rises a hundred feet above a shallow bay.

A severe drought on Kapingamarangi, an atoll located one degree north of the equator and 450 miles south of Pohnpei, began in 1916 and lasted until 1918. Some trees stopped bearing and sixty members of the small community died. To alleviate the population pressure, ninety people were shipped to Pohnpei to be employed in making copra and as stevedores. Some were also sent to Nett and Madolenihmw to collect and process hibiscus bark for a hat factory. Within a year of their arrival, half of the Kapingamarangans had died from a dysentery epidemic. The survivors were brought to Kolonia where the Japanese governor agreed to allow them a portion of land on a long-term lease basis. Most of the Kapingamarangans at the time were young, in their twenties and early thirties, and about forty percent were married. Within twenty years, the original number doubled. By 1964, according to anthropologist Mike Lieber, a core of families was living in Porakiet who considered themselves permanent residents of Kolonia. Yet, even today, the social relationships and organization of the community remain those of a traditional Polynesian atoll culture.

Perhaps the single best-known export items of Pohnpei are not produced by Pohnpeians, but by the Kapingamarangan carvers and weavers. Handicraft of the island are made almost exclusively by the Polynesian community in Porakiet and on the home atoll to the south. Popular items carved from mangrove wood are traditional canoes, fish mobiles, and particularly sharks and dolphins. Woven items include handbags and purses, hairpins, fans, trays, coasters and artificial flowers.

259

Spanish Wall and Park

A map of Kolonia drawn in 1890 shows a compound bordered by a lagoon to the east and north, and a wall on the west and the south. The size of the colony was about one fifth the size of the present town (see *History*, page 57). The remains of the Spanish Wall, one of the most visible historical sites in Kolonia, almost encircle the state and F.S.M. administrative offices.

Immediately after the first Pohnpeian rebellion against the Spanish in 1887, a large stone and mortar wall was hastily built. The wall enclosed two blockhouses on a knoll with weapons to prevent approaches from the sea, Fort Alphonse XIII facing west toward Sokehs, the governor's house and other residences, a hospital, government workshops and offices, and barracks. Originally the wall was fronted by a protective ditch and a large field of fire was cleared to prevent surprise attacks.

During the German administration, the wall was partially demolished as a show of confidence by the administration, and also to allow freer access into the area. It was rapidly rebuilt in 1910 during the Sokehs Rebellion, however.

During the Japanese administration much of the wall was removed. On a remaining portion, directly across from the state administration offices, the Japanese built a small platform facing their homeland which was used for praying. The platform, called the Omiya, is gone but its access stairs remain at the wall.

Much of what was left of Kolonia following the bombing and shelling of World War II, including part of the Spanish Wall, was bulldozed into dust. In 1975, however, a small restoration project on a part of the wall near the government offices was completed.

The most accessible history in Kolonia is the Spanish Wall Park. The rectangular area, about the size of an average city block, is bordered by the Spanish Wall and government offices to the east and the Catholic Center to the north. At present, however, the facilities in the park—benches and tables, a basketball court, and children's playground apparatus—have fallen into disrepair.

The park has the largest concentration of memorials on Pohnpei (two), a defaced Japanese monument with a pig and a rooster; and a statue and plaque erected by the Japan-Ponape Association in 1979 in memory of those who died during the war on the island. Dominating the area, and just beyond the park, is what might be considered the largest memorial on Pohnpei, the bell tower of the ruined Catholic church (see *Catholic Center* below).

Just adjacent to the park is the largest cemetery on the island where several hundred Spanish soldiers are buried. Its precise location is unknown. Paul Hambruch, a noted German anthropologist writing in 1908 observed, "The cemetery lies in front of the northwestern fortification gate. Cocoanut [sic] palms shade it. Great is the number of graves and peculiar their appearance. In long rows the Spanish officers and soldiers lie here who had to give their lives in fights against the rebellious natives. They are poor looking graves, cemented sarcophagus-like heaps decorated with broken pieces of beer bottles." Certainly, a large number of residences and businesses on the western side of the park cover the bones of these long-forgotten Spanish infantrymen.

Golden Gate or Central Park it is not. Yet a peacefulness pervades the area during the day. It is uncrowded, with large shade trees, memorials and expansive (for Pohnpei) spaces. And the history of Spanish and German times hangs heavily on the gun ports and portals of the crumbling Spanish Wall beyond.

Administrative Area

The former Spanish plaza and German and Japanese administrative compounds is now a baseball field surrounded on two sides by state and F.S.M. government buildings, on another side by the Catholic mission, and on the remaining side by an old Spanish fortification. It is doubtful that any baseball diamond, anywhere, has a more historic center field fence than Kolonia's—the famous Spanish Wall built in 1887. Along the first base line is an area occupied by the Pohnpei State administration. Directly behind home plate are the former state and F.S.M. courts. This same site was used for administration during the German Period, and was the location of the governor's residence during the Spanish Period.

A homerun down the right field line would hit the former office of the mayor of Kolonia. A ball hit some fifty feet further, and a big foul, would land on the two-story office building vacated by the Congress of the F.S.M., formerly Kaselehlia Inn, the first government hotel on the island.

Parallel to the third base line is a group of buildings formerly used by the F.S.M., including the offices of the president and the vice president. During the Japanese Period, an elementary school for Pohnpeian children occupied the site. Following World War II, the buildings were made into a hospital, originally staffed by an American physician and Micronesian nurses. In 1977, the hospital was relocated, the buildings were renovated, and several more were built.

The administrative area continues to be transitory, and the only consistency is young male and female ballplayers seen on the field almost daily throughout the year. (Since there are no seasons on Pohnpei, there is no single baseball season.) The state offices are in the process of moving to a former housing area in Kolonia, "Capital Hill," and by 1991, all F.S.M. offices are expected to be relocated to the new national capital site at Palikir.

Japanese Agriculture and Weather Station

The three-story building, plus a piece, at the State Agriculture Station appears to be from another era—and it is. The site was acquired for agriculture during the German administration and called the Agricultural Experiment Station. It was expanded by the Japanese and named the Tropical Industries Research Institute, Pohnpei Branch, and the top section was used as a weather station. From the mid-1920's until the outbreak of World War II, a number of trained experts from imperial Japanese universities worked in its departments of agriculture, livestock, and dendrology.

The gray building is somewhat hidden behind a forest of Polynesian breadfruit trees at the eighteen-acre Agriculture Station. It is one of only three main structures missed by American bombs and naval gunfire during World War II. The former weather station at the top used to provide one of the best views of Kolonia on the island, and it probably still does. The building, however, was condemned in 1976 and is now used only for storage.

Catholic Center and Bell Tower

The Catholic Mission on Pohnpei can trace its origin to the six Capuchin missionaries who landed on the island with the first Spanish governor in 1886. On the grounds are a number of foundations and partial walls remaining from the German Period, as well as the tall gray, brick bell tower.

Probably the most photographed historical site on Pohnpei is the bell tower of the old church. On land acquired by the Spanish in the nineteenth century, the Germans built a church in 1909, that was blown apart by the Japanese in 1944, just before the American occupation in 1945. The dynamited stone and brick were used for road materials and defense facilities after the evacuation of Kolonia. (It is somewhat ironic that the Japanese partially destroyed one of the only three large structures missed by allied attacks during the war.)

A small, well-kept cemetery sits near the entrance to the Center just beyond a break in the Spanish Wall, and in the shadow of the bell tower. The sixteen graves include priests and brothers who died during both Spanish and German times. A few yards beyond the small cemetery enclosure is the grave of Col. Sr. D. Isidro Guiterrez de Soto, a distinguished Spanish officer who was killed on September 17, 1890, assassinated by a Pohnpeian warrior while asleep.

In 1984, the crumbling bell tower was renovated to prevent falling masonry from injuring visitors. There are also plans to restore the bell at the top of the old tower that has been silent for several decades.

Catholic Bell Tower Ruins

Protestant Church

Protestant missionaries first arrived on Pohnpei from Hawaii in September, 1852, to counteract the influence of visiting whalers. They initially established themselves in Madolenihmw and Kitti, and Protestant missionary activities have been continuous ever since.

The largest Protestant church on Pohnpei is located on the waterfront road across from the largest retail cooperative department store on the island. The land on which the church is located has been church property since the first Protestant missionaries arrived from Madolenihmw to start the Canaan mission in Kolonia in 1865. The church was built by a Japanese missionary group in the early 1930's and was one of the three main structures left standing in Kolonia at the end of World War II.

On the grounds of the church are an air-raid shelter cave and three sets of stairs. During the War, the church was used as a barracks and a warehouse until the town was abandoned. Two hundred feet of the concrete floor were removed in addition to wooden doors and window frames to use in building shelters outside of Kolonia.

In front of the church is a grave. It is the final resting place of Rev. Minoru Louis, a prominent local clergyman who died in 1979.

First Protestant Mission in Kolonia

College of Micronesia

The College of Micronesia is the only opportunity for higher education in the F.S.M. It consists of four constituent institutions: The Community College of Micronesia on

Pohnpei; the Micronesian Occupational College in Palau; the C.C.M. College of Nursing that was recently relocated from Saipan to Majuro in the Marshall Islands; and the College of Tropical Agriculture and Science, a U.S. Land Grant college also on Pohnpei.

The Community College of Micronesia (CCM) grew out of an inservice teacher training institution, the Micronesia Teacher Education Center, and was established in 1970. Since 1978, the College has been a fully accredited member of the Western Association of Schools and Colleges in the United States. CCM has a resident enrollment of about two hundred full-time students. Two-year programs are offered in General Studies/Liberal Arts, Elementary Education, Special Education, and General Business, at the Pohnpei campus.

The College is located in dilapidated structures near the center of Kolonia. According to David Shapiro, writing for Gannett newspapers, "At the Community College of Micronesia, students attend classes in World War II quonset huts and live in dormitories with rundown rooms and toilet facilities that would incite a riot in any American prison." Mr. Shapiro is more than partially correct. However, all of the facilities presently used at CCM have been enlarged or renovated during the past twenty years, and there are also plans for a new $8,000,000 campus to be located in the Palikir area of Sokehs municipality.

(Directly overlooking the men's dormitory at the college are four large, partly concealed, Japanese concrete bunkers—ghost-like structures remaining from World War II. Whatever spirits that the bunkers hide, however, do not seem to deter students from their nocturnal visits there to seek privacy.)

German Munitions Cave

One of the few structures remaining from the German Period and still in use is a large brick chamber built in 1910. The chamber is dug into the side of a hill just off of the road a few yards up from the Community College of Micronesia and Kolonia Elementary School. It was used by both the Germans and the Japanese for storage of explosives and is presently used by the Pohnpei Transportation Authority for storing dynamite. Right next to the chamber are nine small caves, often hidden by underbrush or half buried, that were used by the Japanese as air-raid shelters during World War II. (One might tend to question the wisdom of putting shelters next to a munitions cave during the Japanese Period, and also having two schools nearly on top of a cave used for dynamite storage at present. The chamber is almost beneath the Pohnpei State Legislature building. Guy Fawkes would have loved the setup.)

In 1981, a cage-like grating similar to a prison cell was built in front of the steel door of the chamber to provide added security. It seems that a disgruntled resident had broken into the chamber and stolen dynamite caps with which he tried to blow up the Pohnpei District Court building. More damage was done to the amateur dynamiter, however, than to the court building.

Nanyo Boeki Kaisha Store

Nearly all publications note that the only three structures in Kolonia to survive the bombing and naval gunfire in 1944 were the Protestant church, the Catholic bell tower, and the main building at the Agriculture Station. However, a structure that formerly housed the Nanyo Boeki Kaisha Department Store also survived somewhat intact.

The building is located on the waterfront road across from the generator plant and the Public Market and was rebuilt after the war. Older residents remember the roof of the building being used by Japanese to enjoy the cooling breezes from the east during most evenings. Until recently, the structure was used as the electric shop for the Public Works Department.

Sokehs Rebellion Mass Grave Site

There are no large cemeteries on Pohnpei. Burial usually takes place on one's own land or that of a relative in the extended family. There are, however, several small cemeteries scattered about the island, the most ancient being at Nan Madol. Also of some historical significance are the cemetery at the Catholic Center (mentioned above), the Sokehs Rebellion mass grave, and a German cemetery.

The *Sokehs Rebellion Mass Grave* site is located near the tip of Piedra Point in the Kumwunlaid section of Kolonia. There, fifteen of seventeen condemned Pohnpeians were executed by a firing squad of Melanesian soldiers under German officers for their part in the slaying of German district administrator Gustav Boeder (see *History*, page 67). The execution took place on February 24, 1911. The condemned men were led to the execution area where a large, deep hole had been prepared, and mangrove poles were nailed between coconut trees to provide a grating on which to tie them. A young, condemned Pohnpeian, Manindokalong, the smallest in the group, reportedly looked into the hole and said, "So that's where they are going to put us. There's water inside." Then, showing no fear whatsoever, he was tied to the improvised fence and awaited calmly his execution.

The grave site consists of an area about twenty by twenty feet surrounded by a low concrete enclosure. In 1911, the execution site was some distance from the population center, but it is now in a residential area. Although bordered by the road, the site is often nearly hidden by underbrush.

German Cemetery

The *German Cemetery* has been somwhat of an itinerant on the island. Its original site was just west of the present location of Ambros' Department Store. In 1938, the Japanese administration moved a number of the remains to the present site near the base of the Kumwunlaid peninsula in order to provide land for newly arrived immigrants.

Two large black marble tombstones inscribed in German dominate the small graveyard. One is said to mark the grave of Viktor Berg, the German administrator who died suddenly the day after desecrating ancient graves at Nan Madol. Another is in memory of Gustav Boeder, the district administrator whose death sparked the Sokehs Rebellion. And here also, only a`long stone's throw from the grave of young Manindokalong, lie young German sailors—Josef Kneides, SMS *Emden*, Born 13 March, 1892, Died at Nan Kiop, 26 January, 1911. There are also some ten unmarked graves, and only one tombstone inscribed in English:

In Memory of
Ling
A Native of Yap
Died
June 15, 1900
A faithful servant and
an honest man

The cemetery is located in the shadow of the new Congregational Church just below the South Park Hotel.

Pohnpei State Legislature, Capital Hill

The Pohnpei State Legislature chamber was built in 1970 and is aesthetically the most pleasing architectural structure in Kolonia. It is located in an area popularly known as Capital Hill, bordered by the main street just south of the center of town. The hill is in the highest elevation in Kolonia and the building can actually be seen from a number of miles at sea. Next to the chamber is a recently constructed office building.

Because of its elevation, the area has always been popular and has had historical significance. A map drawn during the Spanish Period shows a fortified structure, Ft. Alphonse XIII, dominating its heights, and a photograph taken in 1911 shows the German district administrator's home where the legislature chamber is today. Besides the chamber, there are ten government homes that are gradually being renovated and turned into administrative offices. Among them are the offices of the governor and the lieutenant governor of Pohnpei.

The hill is pleasant, with its open, spacious and manicured grounds. A nice view all the way to the commercial port and beyond to the barrier reef is provided at the north end just outside of the chamber. Four flag poles stand there that formerly flew the flags of the United States, the United Nations, The Federated States of Micronesia, and the State of Pohnpei. Embedded in the concrete base is a metal plaque seldom seen by even local residents: the emblem of the U.S. Navy Seabees.

Pre-World War II Tanks

About seventeen pre-World War II army tank vehicles are rusting in peace in an area off of the main road just beyond Ace Commercial Center. The tanks are in various stages of disintegration, and some are better hidden now by underbrush than they ever were in World War II. The Japanese called the area *Yashirin* in reference to the nearby coconut plantation, and it was bombed heavily during the war. Remains of entrance posts, old pieces of machinery, building foundations, wheels, rails, generators and other scrap are still strewn about. It was used by the U.S. Navy as a headquarters after the war, and is now the property of the Etscheit family.

The tanks are a model called Type 95, Light by the Japanese. They were designed in 1935 and built from 1936 to 1943. The vehicles carried a crew of three small people and were armed with a 37 mm cannon and two machine guns. The 7.4 ton tanks were powered by a six cylinder diesel engine and could reach a speed of forty m.p.h.

The Japanese tanks are partly German. They have German-made engines and the vehicles were brought to the island in the late 1930's. One tank was taken off of the island, restored in Japan, and returned to Pohnpei in 1981. In a nuclear age, it looks rather harmless, sitting beside the Tourist

Information Commission in Kolonia. Hollywood might well appreciate its rather artistic camouflage colors. The tanks were originally colored a dark, ugly but functional, brown, however.

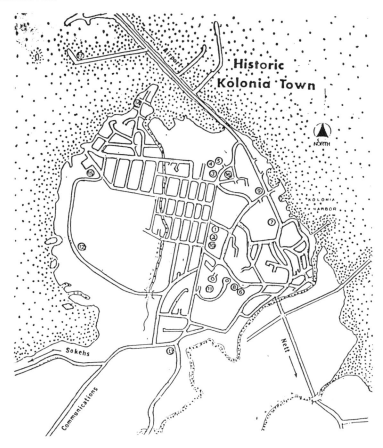

1. F.S.M. Post Office
2. Tourist Information Office
3. Spanish Wall and Park
4. Kubary Plaque Pedestal
5. Catholic Mission Tower
6. Community College
   of Micronesia
7. Protestant Church
8. German Munitions Chamber

9. Nanyo Boeki Kaisha Store
10. Pre-World War II Tanks
11. State Government, Capital Hill
12. Porakiet, Kapingamarangi Village
13. Agriculture Station
14. Sokehs Rebellion Mass Grave Site
15. German Cemetery
16. Baseball Field
17. Lidakika Beach

Sights and Sites

Takatik Island
Langar Island
Sokehs Island
Grounded Landing Craft
Lidakika Beach
Barrier Reef Islets
Circular Island Road
Nett Point
Nan Pohn Mal World War II Airfield
Pohnpei Agriculture and Trade School (PATS)
Nan Madol
Kepirohi and Liduhduhniap Falls
Nanpil Dam
Henry Nanpei Statue
Pwisehn Malek Volcanic Rock
Oomoto Foundation Plaques

...beyond Kolonia

Introduction

Every place is a place of interest to one who has never seen it before, and quite often to those who have. The recently completed road around the island has opened a cornucopia of sights and sites, a few of the most prominent of which are listed above. The list, however, is nearly inexhaustible, and is only limited to the curiosity of the visitor.

Lagoon Islands

The harbors of Pohnpei were often unkind to deep-draught vessels in the last century. Contrary winds, uncharted reefs and coral heads were a constant threat to arriving mariners. Also, castaway seamen who offered their services as pilots to incoming vessels were often more of a danger than the natural conditions. Until the last quarter of the 1800's, the main harbor was on the eastern side of the island at Madolenihmw because of its size and Pohnpei's dominant northeast winds. Ronkiti harbor in the south was also a center of foreign activity. Between 1850 and 1860, 238 vessels, mostly whalers, are recorded to have stopped for varying lengths of time at these harbors. The Spanish settlement at Kolonia (then known as Santiago) and the development of steam-powered vessels that could navigate in channels to the windward, contributed to the prominence of the present harbor.

Directly off-shore from Pohnpei are numerous alluvial islets. The number depends on the height of the tide. There are also twenty-three basaltic islands, about thirty coral islets on the barrier reef, and the historic artificial islets of Nan Madol. Within sight of Pohnpei are also the atolls of Pakin and Ant that complete the Senyavin group.

Islands off of Pohnpei are politically part of municipalities whose jurisdiction extends from the mountainous interior, through the intertidal area to the barrier reef, and even beyond the island. All municipalities contain alluvial, basaltic, and reef islands. Sokehs and Kitti municipalities contain Pakin and Ant respectively, atolls a number of miles distant from their outer reefs. The ninety-two artificial islets of Nan Madol are part of Madolenihmw municipality.

There are a number of large basaltic islands in the lagoons that are permanently inhabited. Parem Island off of Kolonia, for instance, is larger in land area than any of the outer islands of Pohnpei State. Other large inhabited islands are Mwahnd and Dehpehk Islands in U, and Nanue and Na Islands near the Nan Madol ruins in Madolenihmw. There are also reef islets with sandy beaches located at a number of places some distance from Pohnpei proper.

Takatik Island

The longest straight stretch of road in the Federated States of Micronesia is the one-mile long causeway heading north into the harbor from Kolonia to the Pohnpei air terminal on Takatik Island. The road was constructed in the late 1960's by dredging coral from the harbor, but was not paved until 1982.

From Kolonia, the causeway passes the Catholic Center (formerly the Catholic Mission), Piedra Point in Kolonia, and Lidakika Beach (which isn't a beach) to the Mobil Oil storage facility on the southeastern corner of Takatik Island. There are two tunnels under the causeway to allow for the flow of water, only one of which is large enough for small boats to pass through.

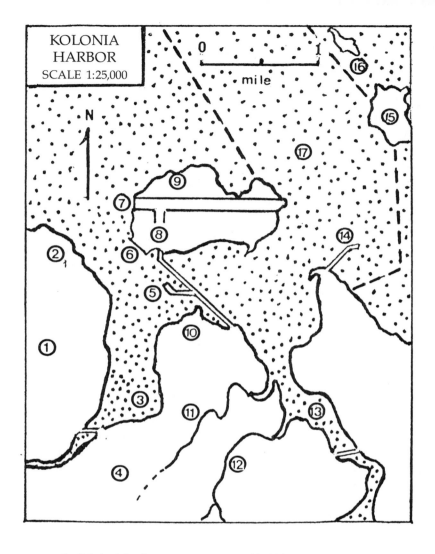

KOLONIA
HARBOR
SCALE 1:25,000

0   1
mile

N

1. Sokehs Island
2. Sokehs Rock (Peipalap)
3. Sokehs Yacht Basin
4. Nan Pohn Mal
5. Lidakika Beach
6. Commercial Dock
7. Airfield
8. Pohnpei Terminal
9. Takatik Island

10. Kolonia Town
11. Tewenneu River
12. Liwy River
13. Dausokele River
14. Nett Point
15. Langar Island
16. Sapwtik Island
17. Kolonia Harbor Limits
    (broken line)

Adjacent to Mobil is the only deep-water anchorage and docking area presently in use on Pohnpei. The wharf can accommodate two large vessels at a time in water thirty-three feet deep. The 901 foot dock contains two offices, three large warehouses, and the Pohnpei State Marine Resources Department. In 1982, the bottom by the vessel berths was dredged and the dock area was paved at a cost of $2,300,000.

Takatik itself is one of a number of alluvial islets off of Pohnpei, and was originally a large mangrove forest in the middle of the harbor. The 6,200 foot runway, like the causeway, was constructed on dredged coral from the harbor floor. The airport was officially opened in February, 1970, but was not paved until ten years later. (Before the runway was opened, the only inter-island or international air transportation was a frontier-type flight on an SA-16 seaplane.)

Dredging of sand from Pohnpei's lagoon and depositing it on the western corner of Takatik has formed the largest beach on beachless Pohnpei. There are two thatched huts for shelter, and the area is the prime water-skiing course in the Kolonia area. (See map, p. 275.)

Langar Island

The first land occupied by the Japanese when they annexed Pohnpei on October 7, 1914, was Langar Island, where the Germans had shops and rather large coconut groves.

The Japanese raised turtles in pens on Langar's sandy beach before World War II. During the war the island was used as a defensive position with artillery covering the two passages leading to the harbor, and it also provided a small but complete seaplane base with large underground fuel and water storage tanks. Langar was neutralized by bombs and naval gunfire early in 1944. However, it was used again during the American administration as a seaplane facility until the runway on Takatik Island was completed in 1970.

Bomb craters and cave shelters are a reminder of the punishment inflicted during World War II. The seaplane ramp on Langar, however, built nearly a half century ago, is still in excellent condition, and the roads to the north of the island, swept by the Japanese in 1933, are still free of coral heads. Hidden in the jungle at the base of Langar's dominant hill is the skeleton of a seaplane hangar, covered by vines and offering a quiet, cathedral-like effect. The island is very popular for day or weekend outings, and the roar of revving seaplane engines has been replaced forever by the shouts of picnicking Pohnpeian children.

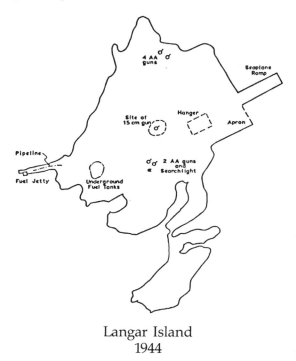

Langar Island
1944

Sokehs Island

Although not considered a harbor island, Sokehs, or Jokaj, Island and Rock dominate the area. The rock has been called the "Diamond Head of Micronesia" in tourist brochures, and its basaltic face shoots straight up 662 feet from the harbor. (The long ridge on the island, not nearly as spectacular, reaches an altitude of nine hundred feet.) In the

Spanish Period, the top of Sokehs was a refuge for Pohnpeians escaping from government troops. During the Sokehs Rebellion, Pohnpeians attempted to occupy the rock, but were dislodged by the more sophisticated artillery of the Germans.

Sokehs Rock (Peipalap) has been climbed very often by Pohnpeian youngsters, occasionally by hardy adults, and once by a hang-glider pilot in 1977. The pilot, a mechanic for the defunct Ponape Air Service, was to attempt a glide from atop Sokehs to either Takatik Island or the causeway. He was no

158° 12'E

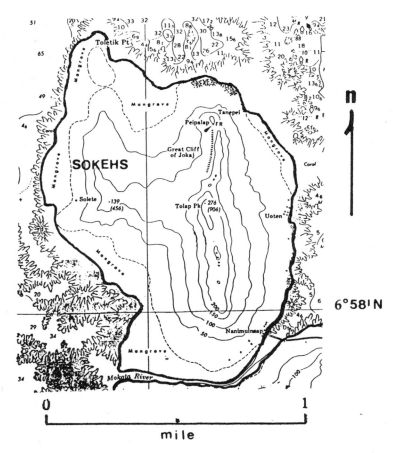

6°58'N

0   1

mile

sooner airborne than he was slammed against the rock's face by swirling and contrary winds. Fortunately, the pilot recovered from the experience—after being emergency air evacuated from Pohnpei, and spending five months in a hospital in Hawaii.

Sokehs has the largest non-Pohnpeian Micronesian population on the island. There are settlements of Mortlockese, Pingelapese, Sapwuahfikese, and Mokilese, with areas named after the origins of the immigrant families. In total population, Sokehs municipality is the largest on Pohnpei.

A walk around Sokehs Island takes a very interesting half day. The road is unpaved, and not completed for automobile traffic at the northern end. A small boat trip around the island takes about two to three hours, and the varying views of Sokehs Rock are startling.

Grounded Landing Craft

On the barrier reef just east of Sokehs passage is a grounded World War II vintage landing craft. Until 1974, the vessel was anchored in front of the present F.S.M. Congress offices, a building that was formerly the Kaselehlia Inn. The craft was towed that year to be sunk beyond the channel, the tow-line parted, and the vessel has found a permanent berth on the barrier reef ever since. She sits high and dry in about six feet of water at mean tide. The vessel is an excellent place for a picnic. She is beyond housefly and ant range, a fire can be built, and the cooling northeastern breezes are fresh and constant. Swimming and snorkeling are outstanding off of the landing craft, and she provides an ideal platform from which to investigate the barrier reef with scuba equipment.

It takes about thirty minutes from Kolonia to reach the vessel in a small boat with only an eight h.p. outboard motor. But nearly forty years in the tropics have taken their toll on the craft. She is quite rusted and care must be exercised when walking, particularly on the forward section of her deck.

Lidakika Beach

Lidakika was a legendary octopus that once inhabited the sea around Pohnpei, as any school child on the island will tell you.

The Lidakika Beach project began as an attempt to create a beach on beachless Pohnpei by a number of private citizens and contractors in 1975. It is located a quarter of a mile north of Kolonia off of the causeway leading to the Pohnpei air terminal, on a coral shelf dredged during construction of the airport runway. Originally, a small dock was repaired at the site, sand was dumped for a beach, and two thatch-roofed shelters were built on the three hundred foot, island-like area. "The best laid plans of mice and men. . ." Unnatural beaches seldom survive and so the sand was washed away; the shelters were built with the side of the roofs to the windward, and were blown down in a teaspoon typhoon; and the dock was partially destroyed by heavy equipment operating in the area.

Lidakika Beach is in temporary disrepair. Yet, like the legend of the octopus, it still survives, and is visited often by residents of Kolonia. It is a pleasant area for a picnic with perpetual cooling breezes and is nice for children's swimming at any tide level. And for sundowners it can be enchanting, with a remarkable view of the sun setting behind Sokehs Rock.

Barrier Reef Islets

Many visitors come to Pohnpei simply to get away from it all. Many residents of Pohnpei get away from it all by visiting a reef islet off of the main island for a few days. In addition to Pohnpei's twenty-three larger inhabited basaltic islands, there are about thirty coral islets dotting the barrier reef, mainly on the south and the southeastern sides. They vary in size from "large" Nahpali at .062 square miles to parts of Nan Pwil that are underwater during a high tide. To allow

Pohnpei residents to get away from it all—but not completely or too far—several of the islets provide basic conveniences at nominal rates.

Nahnningi (Joy Island) is operated by the Joy Restaurant in Kolonia and is located near the Pohnpei Agriculture and Trade School. It is also a short canoe ride from Nan Madol. Twelve thatched-roof cottages are available and two barbecue cooking areas. The circular islet is a bumpy hour-and-a-half drive, plus a twenty minute boat ride from Kolonia. It is planted on the only section of the barrier reef that is joined to Pohnpei proper on the southeast section of the island. Laiap (Rainbow Island) is a hundred yard long boomerang-shaped islet on the southern side of Pohnpei that becomes three small islets at high tide. It is located next to a channel break in the barrier reef and so diving and fishing are excellent. Laiap is leased by Pohnpei's largest hotel, the Cliff-Rainbow, and six unfurnished thatch cottages and barbecue facilities are provided. Kehpara Islet, on the southwest corner of the barrier reef, is privately owned and six thatched cottages are available. One of the largest and most historical reef islets is Nahpali, located at the entrance to Madolenihmw Harbor. It is owned by local entrepreneur Ambros Senda, who plans to develop the islet commercially (Fantasy Island) in the future.

Living on a reef islet, even for a short period of time, is the unique South Seas experience of artists and writers, and beachcombers and dreamers. The islets are often deserted, perpetual cooling breezes air-condition them, and the sound of the pounding surf on the barrier reef lulls, or stimulates, the mind continually.

Circular Island Road

Round islands seem to demand circular roads, and for nearly a century, administrations on Pohnpei have planned for one. A coordinated effort to build the circular road, however, did not begin until the late 1960's. The road was completed on the centennial of the Spanish occupation of

Pohnpei in 1986. There has actually been no mystery to a trek around the island on foot trails. Pohnpeian insurgent Soumadau en Sokehs in 1910 circled Pohnpei in a few days during his escape from the Germans. Boat travel, however, has usually been more convenient.

During the Spanish administration, work began on a segment of the road that wound east from the colony toward Awak. Some of the stone work can still be seen. The German administration's forced-labor policy on road work was partly responsible for the last armed revolt against foreign rule on the island. During the Japanese administration, roads were built in segments on the northern and eastern sections

of Pohnpei. During World War II, however, the roads were left to deteriorate in order to hinder a mechanized invasion. At the beginning of the American Period in 1945, the only roads were a mile and a half section from Kolonia into Nett and a five mile section into Sokehs. There was a two mile road in Madolenihmw and a four mile road to U, none of which were paved.

When serious road construction began in 1966, there was a problem of whether to begin on the east side or the west. A compromise was reached by beginning on both sides simultaneously and joining them at the southern end of the island. The biggest engineering headache was road construction through marshy mangrove forests.

The road is the most lengthy in the F.S.M., and possibly the longest 48.6 miles in the Pacific (over fifty-four miles including the paved section in the Kolonia area). It crosses thirty bridges, and a leisurely drive around the island takes about four hours, depending on road conditions.

Nett Point

Nett Point is the most northern tip of the Pohnpei mainland, although a number of lagoon islands extend further northward. From the point, a causeway extends about a quarter of a mile northeastward into the lagoon to a pier that was once a U.S. Navy fueling station. This site was also used as a main commercial deepwater dock for large vessels before facilities at Takatik were built in the late 1960's.

The four and a half mile trip to Nett Point is lovely, whether walking or riding from Kolonia. The road is shaded on the way and mostly level, with just a few soft hills. Along the roadside are nearly all of the flora mentioned in Chapter 4, and also examples of all structures on Pohnpei, from the traditional *nahs* to a most modern western-style home. There is an outstanding view of Kolonia and Sokehs Island along the way.

A single-lane road on a narrow causeway leads to the pier which sits some twelve feet above sea level at mean tide.

A large warehouse used by the Micronesia Bound Program is on the 150 foot dock. The breezes are continual and comfortable. There are steps down to a concrete platform from which one can enter the water, which is about twenty-five feet in depth, clear and clean.

Nett Point is a pleasant place for a picnic. There is a nice view of the northern lagoon islands and the distant Village Hotel to the east. The area is particularly popular with college students on weekends, but is usually deserted except for a few fishermen on weekdays. (See map, p. 275.)

Nan Pohn Mal, World War II Airfield

The former Japanese airfield at Nan Pohn Mal is located off of the right side of a paved road heading south from Kolonia. The 100,000 square meter base, built between 1935 and 1940, is one of three air facilities used by the Japanese during the war. It was completely destroyed, however, by American bombing and shelling in the first half of 1944.

Today, the area has become somewhat of a suburb of Kolonia in Nett municipality, but during the war it was a restricted area for Pohnpeians. Locating the past is somewhat like a treasure hunt because underbrush has claimed much of the area. In 1944, Nan Pohn Mal contained two aircraft runways of about two thousand feet each in length, one running north to south and the other east to west. These runways, complete with bomb craters, can still be seen. Also quite evident is a large service apron with the rusting skeleton of a hangar. The facility also contained gun emplacements, trenches, a network of tunnels, fuel and water storage tanks, and seventeen large buildings.

A quarter of a mile before arriving at the rusted hangar, a road turns off to the Pohnpei State Communications Station. A number of aqueducts, still serviceable after fifty years, can be seen along the short road. Also along the road can be seen one of the most beautiful views of the western side of Sokehs Island that can be found on Pohnpei.

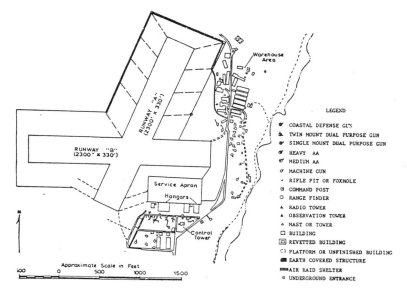

LEGEND

Nan Pohn Mal, 1943

Pohnpei Agriculture and Trade School (PATS)

Pohnpei Agriculture and Trade School is a private secondary school located in Madolenihmw, but accepts students from throughout Micronesia. The institution offers four-year programs in agriculture, agriculture/business, construction technology, and mechanics along with regular non-technical high school courses. PATS is only able to accept about ten percent of those who apply for admission annually, however.

PATS and Fr. Hugh F. Costigan, S.J., are synonymous on Pohnpei with dedication and quality education. The recently-retired director of the school initiated the planning, and clearing of the land and construction in 1958. From the first graduating class of thirty-seven students in 1965, Fr. Costigan has spiritually and physically guided the institution until his retirement in 1982. The work of Fr. Costigan was acknowledged in a letter from President Ronald Reagan to the emeritus director.

The student enrollment of PATS in the 1985/1986 school year was about 150. The staff members are both Micronesian and expatriate. Among the latter are volunteer graduates, mostly from Jesuit colleges, who teach non-technical subjects, several teaching priests, and a number of active and retired professionals in agriculture, construction, and mechanics.

The campus of PATS occupies a rather isolated two hundred acre site, originally chosen because it was the largest piece of Catholic church property available at the time. It contains more than fifty concrete structures consisting of classrooms, shops, animal shelters, warehouses, a new student center and cafeteria, and staff homes. Originally, all building materials for the school had to be brought to the site by small boats and barges. Recently a road constructed around the island has passed PATS, and the school is now accessible by land transportation.

PATS is the most beautiful campus in Micronesia. It is, however, a private school and permission to visit should be obtained in advance from the school administration (Box 39, Pohnpei, 96941).

Nan Madol

"The massive ruins of Ponape. . .speak in their weird loneliness of some dead, forgotten race."

Frederick J. Moss
Through Atolls, 1899

Since 1979, a fee of a few dollars per person has been charged to visit the ancient ruins of Nan Madol. This is hardly a new idea, and it is one of the few prices that had decreased with time. According to F.W. Christian writing in 1896, "We obtained a sullen and grudging permission to explore the ruins, for which, however, a fee of five dollars was demanded . . .I handed him five Spanish dollars which he eyed doubtfully, weighed, smelt, and nipped between his teeth, to make sure I had not palmed off lead on him."

Fantasy and fact are partners in the oral history of Micronesia's most historic site (Nan Matal, City of Matalanim, Nammatoru To). Located near Madolenihmw Harbor on a fringe reef just off of Temwen Island on the eastern side of Pohnpei, Nan Madol is one of archaeology's best kept secrets. The site consists of ninety-three man-made islets, mostly rectangular in shape. They range in size from about 350 square meters to 8,400. The entire site covers nearly 150 acres, about a third of a square mile, in shallow water a foot deep at low tide.

Radiocarbon dating of material from one of the Nan Madol islets indicates that the area was under construction in the year 1200 A.D. Recent diggings and excavations below the tidal level, however, indicate occupation in the area as early as 200 B.C. As deeper and more extensive excavations continue, this date will undoubtedly recede further into antiquity.

The origin of the huge basalt slabs that comprise most of the structures at Nan Madol is unknown. The quarries are not located within the immediate vicinity of the ruins, however. One corner stone on the islet of Nandauwas is estimated to weigh fifty tons: A two-ton sakau pounding stone has been located, and one-ton slabs are commonplace. It is believed that the slabs were transported to Nan Madol by rafts and could have come from the opposite side of Pohnpei. They were raised into place on inclined palm tree trunks. The generally hexagonal slabs are natural and not shaped by human hands. The criss-cross formations of the unworked basalt columns and blocks in the outer walls are filled with coral rubble available in the immediate vicinity, and reach to a height of fifty feet on Pohnwi Islet. The construction indicates an organized effort by thousands of workers over centuries.

Pohnpeian oral history tells of a warrior, Isokelekel, who came from Kosrae with 333 men and overthrew the ruling dynasty in battle at Nan Madol. He was installed as king, the first Nahnmwarki, in about 1628. Following Isokelekel, five succeeding Nahnmwarkis occupied Nan Madol, the last in about 1725. After that year, the area was occupied only intermittently by royalty.

During its prime, a thousand or more people occupied the artificial islands. Nan Madol was not actually a town, however, but more of a center for the residences of elite royalty and their retainers. It is generally divided into two sections: Madol Pah, or lower area in the western half, was the administrative center; Madol Powe, the upper town in the east was the ritual and religious center. The original name of Nan Madol was *"Soun Nan-leng,"* the Reef of Heaven. The Pohnpeian word *"madol"* refers to spaces between structures, in this case, canals. Thus, the romantic Venice of the Pacific.

The reason for abandonment of Nan Madol can only be speculated. Pohnpeian oral history offers no real clue. Paul Hambruch writing in 1910 said the adoption of new rituals and customs brought by American missionaries in the 1850's caused the abandonment. One of the first missionaries on Pohnpei, Luther Gulick, however, wrote that Nan Madol was already vacated when he arrived in 1852. More likely than religion, the reason for departure was depopulation caused by contact with outsiders who spread foreign diseases. Another reason was social. As high chiefs began to lose their absolute power, commoners became more independent. The tribute needed to sustain such a settlement without natural resources was no longer forthcoming. The high chiefs fled from the islets to firm, productive agricultural land, where they remain today.

In September, 1985, the ruins were designated by the U.S. Department of Interior as a National Historical Landmark, the only site in the F.S.M. with this distinction. This new status places the ruins on the U.S. National Register of Historic Places and extends a number of safeguards and benefits of U.S. historical protection laws to the site. In December, 1985, an issue of F.S.M. postage stamps was produced to further commemorate the ruins. Foreign administrations of Pohnpei have always considered Nan Madol to be public (government) land. The traditional owner of the area is the paramount chief, the Nahnmwarki of Madolenihmw, however, and it would be difficult to find a Pohnpeian who would dispute this.

The ruins of Nan Madol have crumbled and been neglected more during the past two centuries than historic sites elsewhere. Until recently, no care had been taken to preserve them. Typhoons have blown their share of history into the sea, and restless roots growing below the earth's surface have caused walls to fall, albeit in crumbled splendor. But then in the end, like the Acropolis in Athens, ruins must be ruined in order to be ruins, even at the Reef of Heaven.

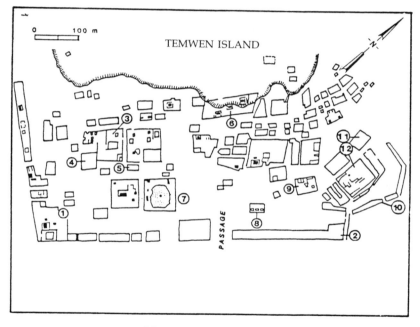

Nan Madol Ruins

1. Pahnwi	7. Darong
2. Kariahn	8. Peinering
3. Pahn Kadira	9. Pehikapw Sapwawas
4. Kelepwei	10. Nan Mwoluhsei
5. Idehd	11. Konderek
6. Pehi en Kitel	12. Nan Dowas

Kepirohi and Liduhduhniap Waterfalls

The four hundred plus inches of annual rain in Pohnpei's highlands contribute to numerous waterfalls on the island. Many of the more isolated falls are spectacular, especially after a recent heavy rain, but are accessible only when accompanied by a guide.

The most popular, and the most photographed, of the larger waterfalls on the island is Kepirohi in Madolenihmw. It is located on the eastern side of Pohnpei about twenty-five miles from Kolonia. Most of the journey can now be made by automobile. A pleasant trip to the falls from Kolonia and back, however, is by small boat through the lagoon islands, but the trip takes a full day.

The falls of Kepirohi are about seventy feet high with a large fresh water pool at its base. The temptation to climb to the top should be resisted, however. The slippery rocks have been the cause of frequent accidents. A visit to the falls is often included in a trip to the ancient ruins of Nan Madol. There is an entrance fee of $1.00 charged to visit Kepirohi.

Liduhduniap Falls are located in the Great Nett Valley about five miles drive from Kolonia. These are twin falls, one above the other, and are especially spectacular after a heavy rain. (The same rain, however, sometimes causes washouts on the road leading to the falls.) It is a pleasant place to picnic with a number of thatched, lanai huts available for shelter.

Nanpil Dam Site

The wettest island in the Western Pacific has had continual water and power distribution problems over the past decade. To help alleviate the power problem, a hydroelectric plant is being constructed on the Nanpil River to supply 1,700,000 watts of electricity. There was a time in the 1930's when the Japanese would copy everything American. The tables have turned; the Nanpil project is a copy of a Japanese idea.

The upper Nanpil River basin has a measured rainfall of 340 inches annually. In the early 1930's, the Japanese built a dam twelve and a half feet high with a sixty-five foot spillway five feet below its crest across the Nanpil River. Water was carried 16,800 feet in pipes to a 300,000 gallon settling tank at Nan Pohn Mal where it was treated and piped to smaller tanks for distribution to the Kolonia area.

The jungle conceals much of the old site, but the 2,906 square foot dam and the 7,200 square foot power plant are still clearly visible. The 217 foot long dam is now split into two major sections laying on either side of the river. A mile and a half east of the dam at the end of the Nanpil River Road is the old hydroelectric plant built in 1936 where concrete structures and old pieces of machinery are rusting reminders of a more organized age.

In May, 1986, work began on the new $5.6 million hydroelectric plant. The project will contain a 4,600 foot long penstock and roadway, a powerhouse, and transmission lines. It is expected to be completed in about two years and will supply twenty percent of Pohnpei's power needs.

The old dam and hydroelectric plant are located a very pleasant three mile drive or walk off of the main road through Nett. The road hugs the Nanpil River most of the way to the dam site at 370 feet of elevation — with numerous cataracts and swimming holes along the way.

Henry Nanpei Statue

Henry Nanpei was the most influential Pohnpeian of his own time — or possibly anyone else's. His given name was not Henry, however, nor was his surname originally Nanpei. Born in 1862, the son of Nanku, Nahnken of Kitti, his original title was Nankirounpeinpok before he was baptized Henry. Nanpei en Kitti was his other traditional title, sixth in the royal line, that he shortened and adopted as his surname.

Devoted lay Protestant preacher, teacher, traditional leader, businessman, and master of local intrigues, Nanpei's sixty-five year life spanned the Early Contact Period, transcended the Spanish and German Periods, and ended during the Japanese Period in 1927. He took on three foreign administrations on their terms, and profited from each of them. He became a millionaire, Pohnpei's wealthiest citizen, and the largest landowner. At one time, twenty-five percent of all deeded land belonged to Nanpei. This included Ant Atoll, currently the only privately owned atoll in the F.S.M. Nanpei is remembered for his business acumen, but admired for his steadfast, unwavering Protestant faith. He was awarded Nanpei titles in U and Madolenihmw to add to his Kitti title for his church work.

Shortly after his death, Nanpei's son Oliver erected a statue as a memorial to the patriarch in Kitti with assistance of representatives of the Japanese Nanyo Boeki Kaisha Company. More than three thousand people, two-thirds of the population of Pohnpei at the time, attended the dedication. The larger-than-life statue of Nanpei shows him at his finest, wearing a Victorian frock coat with decorations, including a medal from the Kaiser of Germany awarded in 1905.

In his lifetime, Nanpei weathered all political and religious intrigues without faltering, wavering, or breaking. A falling mango tree, however, toppled the statue of Nanpei, damaging it in three places in early May, 1986. The bronze replica was repaired, and on Memorial Day, 1986, was returned to its rightful place in Kitti (away from mango trees) where it stands once again overlooking the decades.

Pwisehn Malek, Volcanic Rock

Pwisehn Malek is called Chickenshit Mountain, a literal translation from Pohnpeian. However, it is not a mountain, but a volcanic remnant with a very unusual shape that rises several hundred feet above the rolling countryside in Palikir, five and a half miles southwest of Kolonia. It is often climbed by hardy hikers who are rewarded with a remarkable westward view.

The name of the rock is derived from a Pohnpeian legend. It seems that a rooster, running around Pohnpei on an errand for the gods, had to relieve himself. His droppings are the Pwisehn Malek that we see today.

In late 1945, there were 7,900 military (mainly Japanese) in camps on Pohnpei. Now the military presence is a thirteen member U.S. Army Corps of Engineers Civic Action Team on six-month tours of duty from Hawaii. Their camp is located at immaculate Camp Kitti at the base of Pwisehn Malek.

Oomoto Foundation Plaques

Places of interest can be found in small packages on Pohnpei. A mile up the road leading to Liduhduhniap Falls is a clearing at a fork in the road. Two small black granite plaques reside there, one written in Japanese on a raised earth mound, and the other written in English at ground level. Both commemorate the fiftieth anniversary of the Oomoto Foundation, a Japanese association for the development of Pohnpei. On one momument are the words of Onisaburo Deguchi, co-founder of the Oomoto Foundation:

Memohuruni	Into the dim reaches
Kasumeru kumo no	Beyond cloud haze
Hate toku	I make my way
Susumi yuku nari	Toward Ponape

A longing for Pohnpei sometimes defies nationalities.

Principal Sources and Additional Reading

History

Anonymous, *Past Achievements and Future Possibilities* (*A Conference on Economic Development in Micronesia*, May 22-25, 1984), sponsored by the Micronesian Seminar, Majuro, Marshall Islands, July, 1984. (Available at the Micronesian Seminar, Moen, Truk.)

Ashby, Gene, "Japanese Investment in the Islands," *Pacific Magazine*, Vol. X (May/June, 1985).

Ayres, William S., "Micronesian Prehistory: Research on Ponape, Eastern Caroline Islands," (A paper presented to the Tenth International Congress of Anthropological and Ethnological Studies) Delhi and Poona, India, December, 1978.

Ballendorf, Dirk A., "Japanese Bastions in the Pacific," *Micronesian Reporter*, Vol. XX (First Quarter, 1972).

Blaz, Vincent T. and Samuel S.H. Lee, "Cross of Micronesia," *Naval War College Review*, (June, 1971).

Browning, Mary, "The Blue and Gray on Ponape," *Glimpses of Guam*, Vol. XVI (January, 1976).

Christian, F.W., *The Caroline Islands—Travel in the Sea of the Little Lands*, London, Frank Cass and Co. Ltd., 1967. (First published in 1899.)

Clune, Frank, *Captain Bully Hayes, Blackbirder and Bigamist*, Sydney, Angus and Robertson, 1970.

Clyde, Paul H., *Japan's Pacific Mandate*, Port Washington, N.Y., Kennikat Press, Inc., 1967.

Crowl, Philip A. and Edmund G. Love, *The U.S. Army in World War II. The War in the Pacific. Seizure of the Gilberts and Marshalls*, Washington, D.C., Superintendent of Documents, U.S. Printing Office, 1955.

Denfeld, Duane, "Colt," *Field Survey of Ponape: World War II Features*, Saipan, T.T.P.I. Office of Historical Preservation, 1979.

Ehrlich, Paul Mark, "The Clothes of Men (Ponape Island and the German Colonial Rule)," Diss., State University of New York at Stony Brook, 1978.

--------, "Henry Nanpei, Pre-eminently a Ponapean," in *More Pacific Island Portraits*, Derych Scarr (ed.), Canberra, Australian National University Press, 1978.

Fischer, John L., *The Eastern Carolines*, New Haven, Human Relations Area Files Press, 1970.

Force, Roland W., *Report to the Congress of Micronesia on Historical Preservation*, Saipan, T.T.P.I., 1977.

Gale, Roger W., *The Americanization of Micronesia*, Washington, D.C., University Press of America, 1979.

Gartzke, Kapitanleutnant (translated by Ivan Tilgenkamp), *The Rebellion on Ponape and Its Suppression by H.M.S. "Emden," "Nurnberg," and "Planet,"* Berlin, Marine Rundschau, 1911.

Grattan, Hartley C., *The Southwest Pacific since 1900*, Ann Arbor, University of Michigan Press, 1963.

Hambruch, Paul, *Ponape Ergebnisse der Sudsee Expedition 1908-1910*, G. Thilenius ed., Hamburg, Friederichsen, De Gruyter and Co., 1936.

Hanlon, David L., *From Mesenieng to Kolonia*, Saipan, T.T.P.I. Historic Preservation Office, 1980.

--------, "Upon a Stone Altar: A History of the Island of Ponape from the Beginnings of Foreign Contact to 1890," Diss., University of Hawaii, 1985.

Heine, Carl, *Micronesia at the Crossroads*, Honolulu, University Press of Hawaii, 1974.

Hempenstall, Peter J., *Pacific Islanders under German Rule*, Canberra, Australian National University Press, 1978.

Hezel, Francis X., *The First Taint of Civilization. A History of the Caroline and Marshall Islands in Pre-Colonial Days, 1521-1885*, Honolulu, University Press of Hawaii, 1983.

--------, *Foreign Ships in Micronesia, 1521-1885*, Saipan, T.T.P.I. Publications Office, 1979.

--------, and Charles Reafsnyder, *Micronesia through the Years*, Saipan, Education Department, T.T.P.I., 1972.

--------, "Spanish Capuchins in the Pacific," *Micronesian Reporter*, Vol. XIX (Second Quarter, 1971).

--------, and M.S. Berg, *Winds of Change, A Book of Readings on Micronesian History*, Saipan, T.T.P.I., 1979.

Lieber, Michael D., (ed.) *Exiles and Migrants in Oceania*, Honolulu, University Press of Hawaii, 1977.

McHenry, Donald F., *Micronesia: Trust Betrayed*, New York, Carnegie Endowment for International Peace, 1975.

McKinney, Robert Quentin, "Micronesia under German Rule, 1885-1914," Diss. Stanford University, 1947.

Mitchell, Roger E., "Kubary: The First Micronesian Reporter," *Micronesian Reporter*, Vol. XIX (Third Quarter, 1971).

Momm, Albert A., Captain, U.S. Navy, *Ponape: Japan's Island in the Eastern Carolines* (A report in the Pacific Collection, Community College of Micronesia dated 19 September, 1945.)

Morison, Samuel Eliot, *History of United States Naval Operations in W.W.II*, (Vol. VII, Aleutians, Gilberts and Marshalls, June 1942 - April, 1944), Boston, Little, Brown and Co., 1975.

Morrill, Sibley S. (ed.), *Ponape*, San Francisco, The Cadleon Press, 1970.

Moses, John A., and Paul M. Kennedy (eds.), *Germany in the Pacific and Far East, 1810 - 1914*, St. Lucia, Australia, University of Queensland Press, 1977.

Nanpei, Henry, *Letters from Henry Nanpei*, Honolulu, Hawaiian Missionary Children's Society Library, (n.d.).

Nufer, Harold F., *Micronesia under American Rule*, Hicksville, New York, Exposition Press, 1978.

O'Connell, James F., *A Residence of Eleven Years in New Holland and the Caroline Islands*, Saul H. Riesenberg (ed.), Canberra, Australian National University Press, 1972.

Oliver, Douglas L., *The Pacific Islands*, revised edition, Honolulu, University Press of Hawaii, 1979.

Teiwaki, Roniti, et. al., "Federated States of Micronesia, Unifying the Remnants," in *Politics in Micronesia*, Suva, Institute of Pacific Studies, University of the South Pacific, 1983.

Vincent, James M., and Carlos Viti, *Micronesia's Yesterday*, Saipan, T.T.P.I. Department of Education, 1973.

Ward, R. Gerard, (ed.), *American Activities in the Central Pacific, 1790 - 1870*, Ridgewood, New Jersey, The Gregg Press, 1967.

Wenkam, Robert, *The Breadfruit Revolution*, Honolulu, University Press of Hawaii, 1971.

Yanaihara, Tadao, *Pacific Islands under Japanese Mandate*, Westwood Conn., Greenwood Press, 1976.

Natural Features

Bryan, E.H. Jr., *Guide to Place Names in the Trust Territory of the Pacific Islands*, Honolulu, Pacific Scientific Information Center, Bernice P. Bishop Museum, 1971.

Castro, Francisco, "Ponape Land Tenure and Registration," in *Land Tenure and Rural Productivity in the Pacific Islands*, Ben Acquaye and Ron Crocombe, (eds.), Fiji, University of the South Pacific, 1984.

Christian, F.W., *The Caroline Islands—Travel in the Sea of the Little Lands*, London, Frank Cass and Co., Ltd., 1967.

Dahlquist, Paul Anders, "Kohdo Mwenge: The Food Complex in a Changing Ponapean Community," Diss., Ohio State University, 1972.

Denfeld, Duane "Colt," *Field Survey of Ponape: World War II Features*, Saipan, T.T.P.I. Office of Historical Preservation, December, 1979.

Fischer, John L., *The Eastern Carolines*, New Haven, Conn., Human Relations Area Files Press, 1970.

Glassman, Sidney F., *The Flora of Ponape*, Honolulu, Bernice P. Bishop Museum, 1952.

Laird, William E., *Soil Survey of Ponape Island, F.S.M.*, Washington, D.C., U.S. Department of Agriculture Soil Conservation Service, U.S. Government Printing Office, 1982.

Mott, William P. III, *Feasibility Analysis for the Commercial Production of Black Pepper, Ponape Island*, (Report submitted to the government of the T.T.P.I., January, 1979.)

Murphy, Raymond E., "The Economic Geography of a Micronesian Atoll," *Annals of the Association of American Geographers*, Vol. XL, (March, 1959).

Pohnpei Coastal Resources Atlas, (Prepared for the U.S. Army Corps of Engineers, Pacific Ocean Division), Honolulu, Manoa Mapworks, June, 1985.

Ponape District Education Department, *Islands of Ponape District*, PONTEC (Ponape Teacher Education Center), 1969.

Riesenberg, Saul H., *The Native Polity of Ponape*, Washington, D.C., Smithsonian Institution Press, 1968.

Trust Territory of the Pacific Islands, Office of Planning and Statistics, *Ponape Island Land Use Guide, A Comprehensive Study Based on Natural Elements*, Saipan, Office of Planning and Statistics, 1979.

--------, Public Information Division, *Briefing Masterials*, Saipan, T.T.P.I., 1974.

van der Brug, Otto, *Water Resources on Ponape, Caroline Islands*, Honolulu, U.S. Geological Survey, Water-Resources Investigations Report 83-4139, (March, 1984).

Wenkam, Robert, *The Breadfruit Revolution*, Honolulu, University Press of Hawaii, 1971.

Flora and Fauna

Baker, Rollin H., *The Avifauna of Micronesia, Its Origin, Evolution, and Distribution*, Lawrence, Kansas, University of Kansas, 1951.

Bascom, William R., *Ponape: A Pacific Economy in Transition*, Milwood, N.Y., Krause Reprint Company, 1976.

Bentzen, Conrad, *Land and Livelihood on Mokil: An Atoll in the Eastern Carolines*, Washington, D.C., Pacific Science Board, National Research Council, 1949.

Bryan, Edwin H., Jr., *Economic Insects of Micronesia*, Washington, D.C., National Research Council, 1949.

Castro, Francisco, "Ponape Land Tenure and Registration," in *Land Tenure and Rural Productivity in the Pacific Islands*, Ben Acquaye and Ron Crocombe, (eds.), Fiji, University of the South Pacific, 1984.

Cernohorsky, Walter O., *Marine Shells of the Pacific* (Vols. I and III), Sydney, Pacific Publications, 1972.

Dahlquist, Paul Anders, "Kohdo Mwenge: The Food Complex in a Changing Ponapean Community," Diss., Ohio State University, 1972.

Fischer, John L., *The Eastern Carolines*, New Haven, Human Relations Area Files Press, 1970.

Glassman, Sidney F., *The Flora of Ponape*, Honolulu, Bernice P. Bishop Museum, 1972.

Hiyane, James, "Ponape Rice Project Nears Completion," *Micronesian Reporter*, Vol. XXIII (Fourth Quarter, 1975).

Kira, Tetsuaki, *Shells of the Western Pacific in Color*, (Vols. I and II), Osaka, Hoikusha Publishing Co., Ltd., 1964.

Laird, William E., *Soil Survey of Ponape Island, F.S.M.*, U.S. Dept. of Agriculture Soil Conservation Service, U.S. Government Printing Office, 1982.

Mott, William P. III, *Feasibility Analysis for the Commercial Production of Black Pepper, Ponape Island* (A report to the government of T.T.P.I., January, 1979).

Murai, Mary, Florence Pen and Carey D. Miller, *Some Tropical South Pacific Island Foods*, Honolulu, University Press of Hawaii, 1958.

Murphy, Raymond E., "The Economic Geography of a Micronesian Atoll," *Annals of the Association of American Geographers*, Vol. XL (March, 1950).

Oliver, Douglas L., *The Pacific Islands*, revised edition, Honolulu, University Press of Hawaii, 1979.

Petersen, Glen Thomas, *Ponapean Agriculture and Economy; Politics of Commercialization in the Eastern Caroline Islands*, New York, Columbia University Press, 1976.

Pohnpei Coastal Resources Atlas (Prepared for the U.S. Army Corps of Engineers, Pacific Ocean Division), Honolulu, Manoa Mapworks, June, 1985.

Riesenberg, Saul H., *The Native Polity of Ponape*, Washington, D.C., Smithsonian Institution Press, 1968.

Segal, Harvey Gordon, *Birds of Micronesia*, Pohnpei, Eastern Caroline Islands, Good News Press, 1985.

Trust Territory of the Pacific Islands, Office of Planning and Statistics, *Ponape Island Land Use Guide, a Comprehensive Study Based on Natural Elements*, Saipan, T.T.P.I. Office of Planning and Statistics, 1979.

van der Brug, Otto, *Water Resources of Ponape, Caroline Islands*, Honolulu, U.S. Geological Survey, Water-Resources Investigations Report 83-4139, March, 1984.

Government and Education

Ashby, Gene, "Pohnpei's Resio Moses Looks Ahead," *Pacific Magazine*, Vol. X (March/April, 1985).

Bascom, William R., *Ponape: A Pacific Economy in Transition*, Millwood, New York, Kraus Reprint Co., 1976.

Colletta, Nat J., *American Schools for the Natives of Ponape, A Study of Education and Cultural Change in Micronesia*, Honolulu, University Press of Hawaii, 1980.

Cunningham, Frank, "PATS of Ponape," *Glimpses of Guam*, Vol. XV (January, 1974).

Federated States of Micronesia, *Constitution of the F.S.M.* (in English and Pohnpeian), Saipan, Micronesian Constitutional Convention, 1975.

--------, Plebiscite Commission, *Compact of Free Association and Related Agreements between the Federated States of Micronesia and the United States of America*, Kolonia, Ponape, Congress of the F.S.M., October 1, 1982.

Fischer, John L., *The Eastern Carolines*, New Haven, Human Relations Area Files Press, 1970.

--------, *The Role of the Traditional Chiefs on Ponape in the American Period*, Columbus, Ohio State University Press, 1974.

Gale, Roger W., *The Americanization of Micronesia*, Washington, D.C. University Press of America, 1979.

Hanlon, David and William Eperiam, "Federated States of Micronesia, Unifying the Remnants," in *Politics of Micronesia*, Roniti Teiwaki (ed.), Fiji, University of the South Pacific, 1983.

Momm, Albert A. Captain, U.S. Navy, *Ponape: Japan's Island in the Eastern Carolines* (A report in the Pacific Collection, Community College of Micronesia dated 19 September, 1945).

Nufer, Harold F., *Micronesia under American Rule*, Hicksville, New York, Exposition Press, 1978.

Pohnpei State, *Constitution*, Kolonia, Pohnpei, Pohnpei State Legislature, 1984.

Ponape District Code, Ponape District Legislature, Kolonia, Ponape, 1976.

Ponape Charter, P.L. 6-31, Ponape State Government, 1979.

Ponape Information Center, Community Development Office, *Ponape Almanac*, Kolonia, Ponape, Instructional Services Center, 1972.

McPhetres, Sam, "Four Stars over Ponape," *Micronesian Reporter*, Vol. XXVII (Second Quarter, 1979).

Richard, Dorothy E., *United States Naval Administration of the Trust Territory of the Pacific Islands (Vol. II, The Post-War Military Government Era, 1945-1947)*, Washington, D.C., Office of the Chief of Naval Operations, 1957.

Trust Territory of the Pacific Islands, *37th Annual Report*, (by the United States to the United Nations), Department of State Publication No. 9418 (September, 1984).

Culture

Alkire, William H., *An Introduction to the Peoples and Cultures of Micronesia*, Menlo Park, Calif., Cummings Publishing Company, 1977.

Ashby, Gene, *Never and Always*, Eugene, Oregon, Rainy Day Press, 1983.

Bernart, Luelen, *The Book of Luelen*, John L. Fischer, Saul H. Riesenberg and Marjorie G. Whiting, (eds.), Honolulu, University Press of Hawaii, 1977.

Carroll, Vern and Topias Soulik, *Nukuoro Lexicon*, Honolulu, University Press of Hawaii, 1973.

Christian, F.W., *The Caroline Islands — Travel in the Sea of the Little Lands*, London, Frank Cass and Company Ltd., 1967. (First published in 1899.)

Coale, George L., "A Study of Chieftainship, Missionary Contact and Culture Change on Ponape, 1852 - 1900," Master's Thesis, University of Southern California, 1951.

Force, Roland W., *Report to the Congress of Micronesia on Historical Preservation*, Saipan, T.T.P.I., 1977.

Grey, Eve, *Legends of Micronesia, Book I*, Micronesian reader series Honolulu, T.T.P.I., Department of Education, 1951.

Hambruch, Paul, *Ponape, Ergebnisse der Sudsee Expedition, 1908 - 1910*, G. Thilenius (ed.), Hamburg, Friederichsen, De Gruyter and Co. 1936.

Harrison, Sheldon P., and Salich Y. Albert, *Mokilese-English Dictionary*, University Press of Hawaii, 1977.

Hezel, Francis X., and Charles Reafsnyder, *Micronesia through the Years*, Saipan, T.T.P.I. Education Department, 1972.

--------, and M.L. Berg, *Micronesia, Winds of Change, A Book of Readings on Micronesian History*, Saipan, T.T.P.I., 1979.

Hughes, Daniel T., "Continuity of Indigenous Ponapean Social Structure and Stratification," in *Elites in Oceania*, Vol. LIII (September, 1972).

--------, *Democracy in a Traditional Society: An Analysis of Socio-Political Development on Ponape*, (A report supported by National Health Service Fellowship from the National Institute of Mental Health, 1968.)

Lieber, Michael D., and Kalio H. Dikepa, *Kapingamarangi Lexicon*, Honolulu, University Press of Hawaii, 1974.

Mason, Leonard, "The Ethnology of Micronesia," in *Peoples and Cultures of the Pacific*, Andrew Vayda, (ed.), New York, Natural History Press, 1968.

McGarry, William, *West from Katau*, Ponape, Department of Education, (n.d.).

Morrill, Sibley S., (ed.), *Ponape*, San Francisco, The Cadleon Press, 1970.

Oliver, Douglas L., *The Pacific Islands*, revised edition, Honolulu, University Press of Hawaii, 1979.

Petersen, Glenn Thomas, "External Politics, Internal Economics and Ponapean Social Reform," *American Ethnologist*, Vol. VI (February, 1979).

--------, *One Man Cannot Rule a Thousand, Fission in a Ponapean Chiefdom*, Ann Arbor, The University of Michigan Press, 1982.

Rehg, Kenneth L. and Damian G. Sohl, *Ponapean-English Dictionary*, Honolulu, University Press of Hawaii, 1979.

--------, with assistance of Damian G. Sohl, *Ponapean Reference Grammar*, Honolulu, University Press of Hawaii, 1981.

Riesenberg, Saul H. and J.L. Fischer, "Some Ponapean Proverbs," *Journal of American Folklore*, Vol. LXVIII (1955).

Vayda, Andrew P., (ed.), *Peoples and Cultures of the Pacific*, Garden City, New York, Natural History Press, 1968.

Vincent, James and Carlos Viti, *Micronesia's Yesterday*, Saipan, T.T.P.I. Department of Education, 1973.

Ward, Roger Lemuel, "Curing on Ponape: A Medical Ethnography," Diss., Tulane University, 1977.

Pohnpei Outlying Islands

Bentzen, Conrad, *Land and Livelihood on Mokil; an Atoll in the Eastern Carolines*, Washington, D.C., Pacific Science Board, National Research Council, 1949.

Bryan, E.H., Jr., *Guide to Place Names in the Trust Territory of the Pacific Islands*, Honolulu, Pacific Scientific Information Center, Bernice P. Bishop Museum, 1971.

Carroll, Vern and Topias Soulik, *Nukuoro Lexicon*, Honolulu, University Press of Hawaii, 1973.

Davidson, Janet M., *Archaeology on Nukuoro Atoll, A Polynesian Outlier in the Eastern Caroline Islands*, Bulletin of the Auckland Institute and Museum, #9, 1971.

Harrison, Sheldon P., with assistance from Salich Y. Albert, *Mokilese Reference Grammar*, Honolulu, University Press of Hawaii, 1976.

--------, and Salich Y. Albert, *Mokilese-English Dictionary*, Honolulu, University Press of Hawaii, 1977.

Hurd, Jane Newcomb, "A History and some Traditions of Pingelap, an Atoll in the Eastern Caroline Islands," Master's Thesis, University of Hawaii, 1977.

Lieber, Michael D., (ed.), *Exiles and Migrants in Oceania*, Honolulu, University Press of Hawaii, 1977.

--------, and Kalio H. Dikepa, *Kapingamarangi Lexicon*, Honolulu, University Press of Hawaii, 1974.

--------, *Porakiet: A Kapingamarangi Colony on Ponape*, Eugene, Oregon, Department of Anthropology, University of Oregon, 1968.

Morrell, Benjamin, *A Narrative of Four Voyages from the Year 1822 to 1831*, (Nukuoro), New York, Harper, 1832.

Ponape District, Commission on Economic and Social Development. *Ponape District: Outer Islands Indicative Economic Development Plan, 1977 - 1981*. (Published in 1976.)

Ponape District, Ponape Teacher Education Center (PONTEC), *Islands of Ponape District*. (Published by the PONTEC class, 1969.)

Poyer, Lin, "The Ngatik Massacre, Echoes of Tragedy," *Glimpses of Micronesia and the Western Pacific*, Vol. XXII (April, 1982).

Riesenberg, Saul H., "The Ngatik Massacre," *Micronesian Reporter*, Vol. XIV (September, 1966).

Trust Territory of the Pacific Islands, *34th Annual Report* (by the United States to the United Nations), Department of State Publication #9249, (May, 1982).

Wiens, Herold J., "The Geography of Kapingamarangi Atoll in the Eastern Carolines," in *Atoll Research Bulletin, The Pacific Science Board*, #48, 49, 50, (June 30, 1956).

Places of Interest

Ashby, Gene, "The Eye of the Wind, Ponape's Kolonia Town," *Pacific Daily News* (Islander section), (May 22, 1984).

--------, "Pohnpei's Reef of Heaven (Nan Madol ruins)," *Pacific*

Magazine, Vol. XI (March/April, 1986).

Athens, J. Stephen, *Archaeological Investigations at Nan Madol: Islet Maps and Surface Artifacts*, Agana, Guam, Pacific Studies Institute, 1980.

--------, "The Megalithic Ruins of Nan Madol," *Natural History*, Vol. 92 (December, 1983).

--------, "Nan Madol: Ponape's Spectacular Ruins," *Glimpses of Micronesia*, Vol. XX (Third Quarter, 1980).

Ayres, William S. and Allen E. Haun, *Ponape Archaeological Survey*, Eugene, Oregon, University of Oregon, 1978.

Cunningham, Frank, "PATS of Ponape," *Glimpses of Guam*, Vol. XV (January, 1974).

Denfeld, Duane "Colt," *Field Survey of Ponape: World War II Features*, Saipan, T.T.P.I. Office of Historical Preservation, 1979.

Ehrlich, Paul Mark, "Henry Nanpei, Pre-eminently a Ponapean," in *More Pacific Island Portraits*, Derych Scarr (ed.), Canberra, Australian University Press, 1978.

Fischer, J.L., "The Abandonment of Nan Madol, an Ancient Capital of Ponape," *Micronesia, Journal of the College of Guam*, Vol. I (June, 1964).

Gartzke, Kapitanleutnant (translated by Ivan Tilgenkamp), *The Rebellion on Ponape and Its Suppression by HMS "Emden," "Nurnberg" and "Planet,"* Berlin, Marine Rundschau, 1911.

Hanlon, David L., *From Mesenieng to Kolonia*, Saipan, T.T.P.I. Historic Preservation Office, 1980.

Michael, Roger E., "Kubary: The First Micronesian Reporter," *Micronesian Reporter*, Vol. XIX (September, 1971).

Moss, Frederick J., *A Visit to Ponape, Its Ruins and Its People*, London, Sampson Low Marston, Searle and Rivingston, 1899.

Nanpei, Henry, *Letters from Henry Nanpei, 1892 - 1899*, Honolulu, Hawaiian Missionary Children's Society Library, (n.d.).

Office of the Chief of Naval Operations, *Civil Affairs Handbook, East Caroline Islands*, OPNAV P22-5, (21 February, 1944).

Pohnpei State Tourist Commission, *Kaselehlia from Ponape, Travel Information*, 1985. (Available from Box 66, Pohnpei, F.S.M., 96941.)

Reed, Harvey, "Visions of Polynesia — Ponape's Porakiet Village," *Glimpses of Guam*, Vol. XVII (Fourth Quarter, 1977).

Ronck, Ronn, "Johann Kubary, Exploring the Backwaters of Oceania," *Pacific Magazine*, Vol. V (June, 1980).

Saxe, Arthur A., *The Nan Madol Area of Ponape: Researches into Bounding and Stabilizing an Ancient Administrative Center*, Saipan, T.T.P.I. Historic Preservation Office, 1980.

Stanley, David, *Micronesia Handbook*, Chico, California, Moon Publications, 1985.

Takahashi, Dick, "Silver Spokes on Pohnpei," *Pacific Daily News*, (Islander Section), March 15, 1986.

ILLUSTRATIONS, CHARTS, AND MAPS

Illustrations in the *Argosy* are taken from a number of sources. Copies of the postage stamps on p. 13, 48, 49 and 50 are used with permission of F.S.M. Postmaster General Leo A. Falcam. The S.S. *Thorfinn* on p. 11 was provided by Seward Holdings of Canada. Illustrations by C.C.M. students James Yorlong from Yap and Wilson Johannes from Palau appear on the following pages: breadfruit, p. 113; cassava, p. 117; coconut, p. 121; *mwaramwar*, p. 136; octopus, p. 199; giant, p. 205; and the Catholic bell tower, p. 264. Harvey Segal of C.C.M. provided the sketch of the Pohnpei lorikeet on p. 154. The following illustrations are from the picture files of the library of the Community College of Micronesia. From Paul Hambruch, *Ponape Ergebnisse der Sudsee Expedition, 1908-1910*; boathouse, p. 33; shell horn, p. 35; Mokilese canoe, p. 106; sakau root, p. 127; dip net, p. 157; *nahs*, p. 186; liquid container, p. 197; tattoo designs, p. 203; drum, p. 204; sakau stone, p. 207; canoe, p. 211; baby basket, p. 217; dance paddle, p. 218; stone masonry, title page and p. 251; and the Protestant church, p. 265. The illustrations of whaler, p. 39; Catholic missionary, p. 53; judo wrestlers, p. 73; crocodile, p. 144; turtle, p. 145; toad, p. 146; snail, p. 147; scorpion, p. 150; beetles, p. 151; and cowrie shells, p. 158 are taken from *Copyright-Free Illustrations of Mammals, Birds, Fish, Insects, etc.*, Dover Publications, New York City. The U.S. destroyer on p. 85 and the trochus shell on p. 159 are taken from *Micronesia, Winds of Change*, with permission of Fr. Francis X. Hezel, S.J.

The charts in the book were compiled by the author from various sources. The Pohnpeian language sound chart on p. xiii is from Dr. David Hanlon's excellent dissertation at the University of Hawaii, *Upon a Stone Altar, A History of the Island of Ponape from the Beginnings of Foreign Contact to 1890*. Most of the maps in the text were either drawn, redrawn, or revised by the author. The map of the ruins of Nan Madol on p. 289 is printed with permission of Moon Publications, Chico, California. The map of Langar Island on p. 277 and Nan Pohn Mal Airfield on p. 285 are from the Office of Historical Preservation, T.T.P.I.

Western Pacific Area

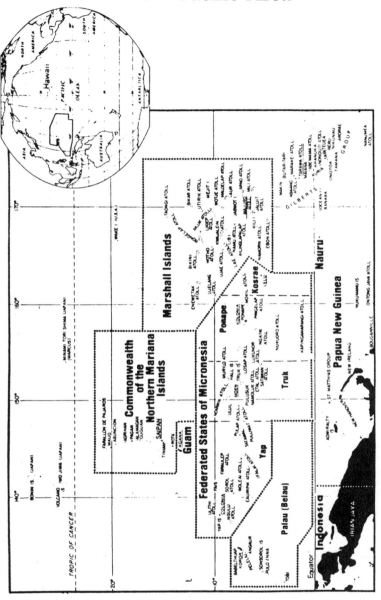

INDEX

A

Abigail, whaleship, 48
Ace Commercial Center, 270
Administration Pohnpei, 163
Admiral cone shell, 158
African cape buffalo, 14
Agriculture (also see Flora)
 Japanese, 75, 76
 local plants, 109-36
 station, Pohnpei, 263-64
 suitable areas (map, 111)
 U.S. Land Grant, 266
Air facilities,
 Langar seaplane base, (map, 227) 81-82, 276-77
 Nan Pohn Mal, (map, 285) 81, 83, 284
 Palikir, WWII, 83-84
 Pingelap, 11
 Takatik, Pohnpei Airfield, (map, 275) 274, 276
Air routes (map, 16)
Alabama, U.S. battleship, 83
Albatross, German warship, 54
Alfred, sailing ship, 51
Alliance, U.S. warship, 23, 56
Alphonse XIII, Fort, 55, 269
Aluminum mining, 77
Ambros Store, 257
American (see also United States
 Board of Commissioners for Foreign Missions, 47
 casualties, WWII, 79
 Civil War, 48
 flags, 1976, 1945, (ill. 23, 38)
 historical period, 85-92
Ant Atoll
 description, 223
 discovery, 38
 history, 223

legend, 224-25
 (map, 222)
 names, 223
 ownership, 224
 sea turtles, 145
Appomattox, 48
Archaeology, 34-35
Arctic Ocean, 48
Ascension Island, 44, 48, 252
Asia, 41, 153
Assembly of God Church, 9
Atoll, 105, 221-46
Attorney General, Dept. of, FSM, 166
Australia, 24, 42, 118
Australian National University, 71
Avocados, 122
Avola, sailing ship, 44
Awak village, (map, 101) 34-35, 182, 206
Atoll, 105, 221-46

B

Bachelot, Alex, Fr., *viii*, 47
Baha'i National, 9
Bamboo, 133
Banana Beetle, 152
Bananas, 121
Banks, 18, 172-73
Barnard, Moses, Capt., 38
Barracuda, 155, 210
Barrier reef (ill. 97) 96
Bascom, William R., 70, 139, 170, 187
Bars, 147
Beaufort Wind Scale, 104
Beche-de-mer, 41
Belgain, 77-78
Bell peppers, 123
Beetles (ill., 152) 151-52
Benningsen, von, Gov. 253
Berg, Viktor, Dist. Ad., 62-64
Bernart, Luelen, 21, 179
Betelnut, 129-30
Betham, G., Capt., 38,

238
Beverages, 125-29, 170
Birds, 152-54
Bishop Museum, 109, 148
Bligh, Capt., 112, 114
Board of Hawaiian Evangelical Associations, 47
Boeder, Gustav, Dist. Ad., 65-69, 269
Bonito (skipjack) tuna, (ill., 75) 155, 156
Book of Leulen, 21, 179
Boston Courier, 144-45
Boston, Mass., 43
Bougainvilla, 135
Bourne, Zenas E., Capt., 44
Boyles, Paul, 95
Brauckman, Secretary, 67
Brazil, 124
Breadfruit (ill., 113) 113-14, 263
British ensign (ill., 24)
Budget, annual, Pohnpei, 170

C

Calvary Baptist, 9, 176
Canaan (kenan) Mission, (ill., 265) 252
Canoe, (ill., 106, 211) 134, 238
Capuchin priests, 54, 63, 81, 174
Carabao, 141-42
Cardarso, Don Louis, Gov., 55-56, 174
Caroline Islands (also see Palau, Yap, Truk, Pohnpei, Kosrae)
 attack plan, WW II, 79-80
 discovery, 3, 22, 23, 38
 location, 3
 (maps, 169, 306)
 name, 22, 36
 papal determination for Spain, 25, 54
 purchase by Germany, 26, 62
Carving, 132, 259
Cassava, (ill., 117) 116

308

I

NOTES

NOTES

NOTES

NOTES

NOTES